The Political Possibility of Sound

The Political Possibility of Sound

Fragments of Listening

SALOMÉ VOEGELIN

BLOOMSBURY ACADEMIC
NEW YORK • LONDON • OXFORD • NEW DELHI • SYDNEY

BLOOMSBURY ACADEMIC
Bloomsbury Publishing Inc
1385 Broadway, New York, NY 10018, USA
50 Bedford Square, London, WC1B 3DP, UK
29 Earlsfort Terrace, Dublin 2, Ireland

BLOOMSBURY, BLOOMSBURY ACADEMIC and the Diana logo are trademarks of
Bloomsbury Publishing Plc

First published in the United States of America 2019
Reprinted 2019, 2020, 2021 (twice)

A catalog record for this book is available from the Library of Congress.

Library of Congress Cataloging-in-Publication Data
Names: Voegelin, Salomé, author.
Title: The political possibility of sound : fragments of listening / Salomé Voegelin.
Description: New York : Bloomsbury Academic, Bloomsbury Publishing Inc, 2019. |
Includes bibliographical references and index.
Identifiers: LCCN 2018038578 | ISBN 9781501312168 (pbk. : alk. paper) |
ISBN 9781501312151 (hardback : alk. paper)
Subjects: LCSH: Sound (Philosophy) | Sound in art.
Classification: LCC B105.S59 V64 2019 |
DDC 302.2/2–dc23 LC record available at https://lccn.loc.gov/201803857

ISBN: HB: 978-1-5013-1215-1
PB: 978-1-5013-1216-8
ePDF: 978-1-5013-1217-5
eBook: 978-1-5013-1218-2

Typeset by Newgen KnowledgeWorks Pvt. Ltd., Chennai, India
Printed and bound in Great Britain

To find out more about our authors and books visit www.bloomsbury.com
and sign up for our newsletters.

CONTENTS

Acknowledgements vi
Light song viii

Introduction: Writing fragments 1

The political possibility of sound 17

Hearing volumes: Architecture, light and words 45

Geographies of sound: Performing impossible territories 75

Morality of the invisible, ethics of the inaudible 103

Hearing subjectivities: Bodies, forms and formlessness 119

Sonic materialism: A philosophy of digging 151

Reading fragments of listening, hearing vertical lines of words 185

Putting on lipstick 215
Index 217

ACKNOWLEDGEMENTS

We write in communities, in networks of support and exchange, in a cosmopolitanism of the text and of thought that participates in what we say and makes it what it might mean. This book would not exist without the support of others, of family, friends and colleagues, people I know personally and some I only know through their words and works, all of whose ideas, interpretations and criticism have inspired and expanded how *The Political Possibility of Sound* might be written about.

I am particularly grateful to David Mollin for his love and encouragement and his ongoing critical engagement in my work. I am immensely thankful to Marcel Cobussen, Mark Peter Wright, Louise Marshall, Daniela Cascella, Catherine Clover and Angus Carlyle for their close reading of these essays and for their invaluable advice on their revision. I am appreciative of the supportive research environment at the Centre for Creative Research into Sound Arts Practice (CRiSAP) and of my colleagues at the London College Of Communication (LCC), UAL, Thomas Gardner, Cathy Lane, Lisa Hall, David Toop, Chris Petter, Milo Taylor, John Wynne, Ximena Alarcón, Ed Baxter, Rob Mullender and Peter Cusack, whose work and ideas inform and challenge my own. Many collaborations, discussions, invitations to talk and perform, participate in workshops and engage in debate have helped me develop this writing. I have been motivated and encouraged by debates and collaborations with Brandon Labelle, and have been inspired by working with Rebecca Bramall on Knowledge after Austerity and Brexit. My research into Listening across Disciplines with Anna Barney has brought a whole new network of people and points of view to my sonic thinking, and the ongoing co-curation of Points of Listening with Mark Peter Wright stands as a crucial reference point for the articulation of sonic possibilities.

I am grateful to Aurélie Mermod for inviting me to try some early ideas on the political and sound at the University of the Arts Zürich, to Adi Louria-Hayon for her invitation to speak about ethics at Tel Aviv University, to Kathleen Coessens for involving me in debates at the Orpheus Institute in Ghent and to Céline Hervet for the opportunity to perform between voice and politics at the Université de Picardie Jules Verne. I am very grateful for discussions with Holger Schulze, Jean-Paul Thibaud, Michael Bull, Serge Cardinal, Christoph Cox, Andrey Logutov, Iris Garrelfs and Abigail Hirsch, and valued the chance to work with Mary Ingraham and DB Boyko at

Alberta University, Edmonton, and the Westernfront in Vancouver. Thank you also to the students at the London College of Communication whose enquiry and learning infects my own. I am thankful particularly to my current PhD students Kevin Logan, Kate Carr, Louise Marshall, Victoria Karlsson, Sunil Chandy and Julie Groves, for reciprocal encouragement and a shared faith in the value of research and sound.

I owe gratitude to Charles Curtis, Jacqueline Kiyomi Gordon, Lawrence Abu Hamdan, Anna Raimondo and Jana Winderen, for their time and patience clarifying and discussing their work with me, and to all the other artists whose work moved my writing. Finally, I want to thank Ally Jane Grossan and Leah Babb-Rosenfeld at Bloomsbury for their trust and support, which made this book possible.

LIGHT SONG

stand underneath a light source
tilt your head up and stare into its glare
imagine its sound
tune into it and sustain its pitch as long as possible.

1 March 2017, 8:42 am, www.soundwords.tumblr.com.

Introduction: Writing fragments

In a lecture at the Pacific Northwestern College of Art (PNCA) on 2 November 2016, Cauleen Smith, an interdisciplinary artist from Chicago, 'whose work reflects upon the everyday possibilities of the imagination',[1] discussed the processes and materials of her practice not as installations, films or sculptures, but as arrangements of curiosity and improvised constructions. Her work brings together different images, tools and objects to create 'excavations and speculations that loosen our assumptions of what we know and encourage us to embrace the instability of knowledge rather than the certainty it broadly offers'.[2] She calls the resulting things 'speculative artefacts' or 'awkward objects', which include their own fragility and possibility for failure, and are not shaped through the necessity of their task and fitting into expectations of their outcome, but inspire re-engagement, or what I would call doubt and the practical suspension of habits.

Talking particularly about her long-standing admiration for Sun Ra, she traces her working methods and aims to his cosmology and tells us how she was fascinated by the fact that he became Sun Ra in Chicago, her own home town, implying a kindredness of spirit and cross-time collaborative possibility. Pursuing this admiration, she spent two summers in a row in his archive and tried to 'apprentice' herself to him, to learn and copy his processes and use his approaches to rethink how to make film and eventually how to make art. She discusses how she got inspired by the way he worked with others and the procedures of his practice, and explains, 'I am not making this because I know something, but I am making it because I don't know something and want to learn what is possible.'[3] In this spirit she brings together African figurines, landscapes and a Trinitron camera; creates a vortex of mirrors; or records a video to make a rainbow through a water bath. In all these instances, technology enables her to make 'infinity devices', things rather than objects that contain a source code that connects the past to the future to the present without chronology. Thus, her works are not linear but reach into a simultaneous time, as an infinite material rather than as a certain temporal unfolding. In this material time, they create an assemblage of things that she did not make but that she re-formulates through improvisation. This way of working brings a different sense of finitude to their form and a different demand of participation to their perception. Her improvisations between objects, media and technology open what is possible and produce unexpected connections. In this way she invites an exploration of the possibility of objects and technologies as well as of the subject and of perception, and brings things into a different light: to grasp a different capacity of and engage from a different perspective in what we thought we knew what it was and what it was there for.

Smith's work is playful and reminds us that there is more than what is manifest, actual and real; more than what we think something is, what its name suggests or its definition purports. It opens perception towards other possibilities and points to the realm of the surprising and to the unfamiliar purpose and meaning of things. Through her speculative artefacts and awkward objects, Smith provokes the idea that things, their uses and interactions, could be different and that they could set up a different imagination of the world and how we live in it. Thus she invites a different attitude towards objects, our expectation of their function and our interpretation of their application and worth, generating a different imagination of what things are and what they do, what criteria they fulfil or what possibilities they invent. Ultimately, her assemblages transform and challenge what we do and how we describe the world and ourselves, and suggest we could all, with Sun Ra, be 'Angels from Saturn'.[4]

To invite the possible into practice and into discourse signals an acknowledgement at once of an object and a subject's unseen dimension, the invisible edge of their definition and description, and of our limitation at grasping it. The possibilities of Smith's assemblages are invisible, inapparent perspectives and variants that show the unknown of the known and forge desire and anticipation for the unexpected. They do not just point to a potential, a term that suggests a transcendental relationship between the possible and the actual, a latent ideal that is always already there awaiting our discovery. Instead, it is our confrontation with the thing, or rather it is the thing confronting us, through the contingent formulation of what it is, that puts into doubt what we thought it was in a habitual and systematic reading, and provokes through art practice 'the creativity of thought' and a different imagination of the world.[5]

The possible is then, if it is a potential at all, not a transcendental but a contingent potential, not of the thing but of our encounter. It is its temporal realization dependent not only on the thing and what it holds before our encounter, but also on the context that frames the confrontation and enables the actions that are its possibilities produced in a creative and reciprocal perception. These possibilities are the actions of the light that produces the rainbow in a water bath, in a place without rain or sun, whose colourful arch invites me to reconsider my understanding of light, water, the gallery, myself, discourse and scientific knowledge. I do not see the work but contemplate its assemblage of things as a mechanism that builds a possible world.

Smith's work is a playground of the possible. Her assemblages are not trivial however, but sincere in their own circumspection of the norm. Her desire 'to learn what is possible'[6] does not involve the study of manuals and guidebooks and the learning to a standard of what something is or should do. Instead, it is a learning of the possibilities of the things that exist not because but in spite of the manuals and the guidebooks. Not as a simple subversion, an anti-guidebook, but as a critical extension of the material, cultural and technological possibilities that are attributed and taught in relation to a particular object or tool and that ensure a desired outcome or product. Conventional teaching and instruction hold always already within themselves the purpose of their object and tool, and thus also the limits of its use, value and context. Smith's treatment of tools and things goes beyond those narrow definitions inscribed in use-value, professionalism and a certain identity. It goes beyond those dimensions of an object that ground it within a rational and purposeful world view, and that anchor it in the discourse of the domestic or the professional respectively. Instead, her work reviews and brings into playful contestation the ideologies and conventions of what things mean: as tools and as designators of value and validity, and creates a view on what else an object as thing might be able to do; how else we might be able to perceive it, and what else, in other words, anything might mean and stand for.

In many ways her work can be experienced as an extension and contemporary reinterpretation in the gallery of the DIY ethos of Sun Ra as well as of much counter-cultural activism and artistic practice since the 1970s, embodied by punk aesthetic and carrying anti-consumerist ideologies: the turning on its head of cultural representation to provoke a questioning of its values and norms; and the avoidance of professional processes of production in favour of inexpert, contingent and improvised ways of doing things. This disruption of the status quo of representation and production was particularly relevant for the emergence of a feminist sound and compositional practice at the time. Not welcomed by, or unwilling to work in the male-dominated environments of music studios and academic departments, women needed to invent a different space and a different way to get their sounds made and heard. The lack of access to technology, to finance, public recognition and a sense that the territory of sonic or musical production was occupied by a dominant voice, necessitated a different strategy of working and enabled a new imagination of what could sound.

BECAUSE we know that life is much more than physical survival and are patently aware that the punk rock 'you can do anything' idea is crucial to the coming angry grrrl rock revolution which seeks to save the psychic and cultural lives of girls and women everywhere, according to their own terms, not ours.[7]

DIY is a practice of self-reliance that rejects the idea of a right way to make a sound or to perform, and abandons the esoteric knowledge of the discipline and the profession in favour of a more contingent making, where virtuosity is replaced with commitment and value becomes a matter for the community. Smith's disruption of the status quo is a disruption of the use-value and the normative imagination of the things she arranges together to make a work. She portrays and practices the lack of a right use of technology, and affords the audience a view on awkward things, to speculate and engage with rather than know their form and purpose, to practice things in a different way.

Her work, for various reasons, needs and seeks to cover a different ground, beyond the rule book, the right use of technology and the established expectation of the canon and virtuosity. It resists and challenges the conventions of what a thing can do, what art can do, what music can do and how it can mirror the world in the possibility of its sound. Therefore, the possible is a strategy and a point of action for those who do not share the high ground: understood as the voice of authority and the tone of the dominant in an economical, political, social and gender- as well as race- and class-based hierarchy. When the cultural and sociopolitical territory is occupied by a singular voice, which we perceive as the actual and singularly real, the possible gives cause for desire and a ground for hope that other voices might not just be incorporated or silenced, but could gain their own resonance, and that a whole other plane of influence, a completely different variant of the same territory can be established within which alternatives might strive not against the dominant and not as a parallel but ineffectual voice, but as a real alternative sounding loudly from within.

Essayer – to try

Listening out for alternatives, this collection of essays presents an attempt to reach, generate and articulate the possibility of the possible in relation to sound in the sphere of the political. Working through seven different themes within the same concern, that of politics and the indivisible dimension of the real, that of the transformative and transforming capacity of subjectivity and materiality and the ethics of their practice and the boundaries of the world, as well as that of the limits of language and representation, this book tries to grasp the radical promise of a sonic possibility and to articulate, beyond the expected, the power of the invisible. The focus on sound art, installations, compositions and performances allows for the conceptual and material articulation of another sphere that is not apart from the one we customarily refer to as the real one, which is not a parallel fiction, but is a real unseen that opens and gestures towards the idea of alternatives. Thus the deliberation of the political possibility of sound in the sphere of art does not avoid the politics of everyday life, but finds a new access to its practices and norms via the contingent experience of arts' possibility. It is not a privileging of art, but a privileging of practice, the creative practice of doing and of experiencing, outside purpose and function, that affords glimpses on what things do, and how things could be done. The purposeless configurations of awkward objects and the speculative intentions of creative production grant a different participation in how things are and how else they could be. And so if these essays privilege art then they do so in order to know about the world from a purposeless sound.

Sound art enables observations and discussions on a graspable variant that remains unseen but holds influence and ramifications for what is visible, and that remains inaudible but holds the power of speculation and the promise of the not yet heard. Sound, as material and as sonic sensibility, makes the possible thinkable in concrete terms and invites the impossible to reinvigorate an aesthetic and political consciousness and imagination. Therefore, listening is the main method of engagement throughout this book: listening to work and to the world to discuss their relationship on a continuum of actuality, possibility and impossibility.

This listening leads to a writing that aims to bring a sonic engagement into a text-based form without muting its communication: to write a sounding text, a textual phonography, that does not deny sound its ephemeral invisibility and mobile intensity – silencing the heard in theory – but works exactly on the unstable ground and the inexhaustibility of a sonic nature, not to claim comprehension but try curiosity towards the appreciation of awkward and speculative ideas that generate rather than represent thought. Smith's attempt to learn about what is possible through the play with technological tools and things, and my wish for a text-based form that is inclusive of sound's mobile formlessness and boundless materiality, resonates with the essayistic format. Essays are trials, they are moments of exploration, playful and incomplete. According to Theodor W. Adorno:

> Luck and play are essential to the essay. It does not begin with Adam and Eve but with what it wants to discuss; it says what is at issue and stops where it feels itself complete – not where nothing is left to say. Therefore it is classed among the oddities. Its concepts are neither deduced from any first principle nor do they come full circle and arrive at a final principle. Its interpretations are not philologically hardened and sober, rather – according to the predictable verdict of that vigilant calculating reason that hires itself out to stupidity as a guard against intelligence – it overinterprets.[8]

The desire to write a series of texts on the possibility of a groundless, non-hierarchical conception of an incomplete real in its own voice recalls Adorno's definition as well as his sentiments and motivation towards the essay. The notion of possibility, just like the essay, stands critical of calculated reason and hierarchy of thought. It rejects the need for first principle, which occupies the ground with its dominant authority and subdues an alternative imagination, and it rejects final principles as at odds with a discussion on the infinite, the formless and the incomplete. The opinion that, according to reason, the essay is not sober can only serve its reach and rhetoric to include ambiguity and make a game of words that can stretch beyond the ground of language and grammar, to invite the imagination of a more improvised and speculative world.

Both my previous books, *Listening to Noise and Silence* (2010) and *Sonic Possible Worlds* (2014), have looked to Adorno to inform their form in an essayistic tradition that abandons outcomes and the complete in order to pursue continual exploration. But each time the format of the book, as a finished work and scholarly expectation, has caught up with this aim and has at least outwardly given form to a more conventional shape. While the formless form of the essay, as concept and idea, remained central to the conception of both works, both publications ended up in long-form, answering all sorts of self-imposed demands on comprehensiveness in a horizontal narrative, whose drive enabled connections and overviews but at times impeded a closer look at odd details and the curiosity of smaller ideas.

This time I deliberately chose to approach the text as fragments and write essays not only as method but also in form. I hope this will enable a more detailed exploration of some of the key terms and issues that arose in the first two publications but that were hastened along in the horizontal drive of their narrative. By contrast, these seven essays are written vertically into the issues rather than moving them along. They stage autonomous explorations of ideas that do not have to find justification in the rest of the writing and owe no debt to its context or pretext, but open a view on fragments and slices that bring us to the playful tensions and unseen connections that decide a political possibility.

The essay film

In their introduction to *The Essay Film* (2016), Elizabeth A. Papzian and Caroline Eades trace the essay film back to its literary antecedents and declare that the essayistic is unique in its capacity to forge connections and set up tensions while exploring the space between fiction and non-fiction. They suggest that the dialogue of the literary essay is replaced by the movement of the film form, and state that, 'If the end point is the utopian, unattainable "film treatise", *Capital*, then the essay embodies the unrealisable attempt at the impossible endpoint, the fragments of an impossible totality.'[9] Continuing on this thought I want to suggest that the essay is not the unrealizable but does not want to be realized. It does not aim to find an end point, a final principle, but keeps on moving, creating tensions and dialogues that explore through an inexhaustible fragmenting of fragments what things and subjects actually are, and triggers through its playful disregard for the first principle the curiosity to think what else they could be. This desire to neglect the known and the preference towards the unknown and the incomplete is not a formal conceit, a stylistic fancy, but a serious response to the failings of a complete and reasonable world. The essay answers the possibility of the work and of the world with its own possibility of the text and of language. It tries the possibility of writing without the need to conform and achieve, or to make sense within the parameters of the dominant plane. Thus it is a practice of writing that wants to reach the unknown and that hopes to include the unseen of sound in its trial of words.

This understanding also coincides with Papzian and Eades promotion of another history for the essay film that claims its legacy in the lack of adequate equipment and training during the war and finds its manifestation in the representational crisis after the Second World War: 'A *film d'essai*, is not necessarily good. Made with improvised resources, it is often less perfect than films produced in regular circuits, but it always includes a principle of renewal and spiritual research that is worth encouraging and remembering.'[10] Their quoting of French film-maker Germaine Dulac, taken from her *Écrits sur le cinéma 1919–1937*, refers the cause of this representational crisis back to the technological and aesthetic predicament of the interwar period, and implicitly links it forward also to the DIY aesthetics of feminist sound making since the 1970s. Both express a condition of scarcity of resource and explain the consequent need for different processes and the articulation of another voice.

Following Dulac, the essay is the perfect format for a crisis. Its porous and contingent nature forgives a lack of formality and the absence of a good style, and the neglect of technological perfection or virtuosity releases the potential for the incomplete and the unrealizable. Additionally, it has the ability to respond to developments as they come towards it through its capacity for innovation and the looseness of its facticity. The essay is then the perfectly incomplete form to write about the possibility of the political at a time when austerity determines creative and intellectual production, when the imagination for a politics of transformation seems to have exhausted itself, and ecological questions need answers from unknown places. There, in the place of unknowing, we can draw on the essay format's capacity for 'renewal and spiritual research', its facility for innovation, and practice the possibility of a connected and collaborative world.

The essay as the format of the possible per se has the capability to make as yet unseen connections, try assumed truths and produce the creative tensions from which the hope and action of possibility can emerge. It has the potential to reveal and undermine authoritarian discourse and the ability to explore the possibilities and impossibilities of achieving through filmmaking (writing and sound making) a utopian world. Thus as work or as text the essay can probe the boundaries between fiction and non-fiction to bring the authority of the documentary to the imagination of the artwork and expand the notion and value of the real.

Description d'un combat (1960)

Eric Zakim's writing about Chris Marker's *Description d'un combat* (*Description of a Struggle*) makes this capacity for a political possibility of the essay film (sound, text) apparent. Zakim writes about Marker's 1960 work about Israel and its ultimate withdrawal from public screening in 1967, due to the Six-Day War.[11] He focuses his description and interpretation on the relationship between the images and their suspension in endless motility, unable or unwilling to communicate anything with certainty 'instead working to disrupt any fixed sense of this place'.[12] Zakim comments that the film does not produce a representation or final comment on the nation of Israel, but stands as speculative commentary witness to its own dissolution in an invented world: the dissolution of its material and content, symbolizing the deliberately weak authority of the essay not to make an authoritative claim but to be contingent, a material or text that stages its own imminent disappearance on the way to making something else possible: something that is not hindered by historical expectations and the desire for completion of a destined faith, but as the current invention of all that could be.

Zakim's text concludes on a description of the final frame of the film, a durational take on one scene that dissolves three images into each other: 'The final three objects – cygnet, signal, sign – dissolve into each other phonetically, like a mantric repetition of material sound that breaks down discourse, forging new identities through immanent relations to other things, other objects.'[13]

While we see these three signs dissolving into the possibilities of each other, we hear the voice over:

Look at her.

There she is.

Like Israel.

We've to understand her, remind her that injustice on this land weighs heavier than elsewhere, this land, the ransom of injustice.

The threats that surround her, to which she gave no cause.

Yes, look at her. A vision that defeats the eye, as words endlessly repeated.

Amongst all the wondrous things, most wondrous is her being there, like a cygnet, a signal, a sign.[14]

Kazim suggests that this closing shot dissolves the historical totalities that might engulf the work's meaning and enables the film to be something more than a cipher for something else: to be its own possibility of Israel. It produces, he suggests, what Marker means when he says 'a vision that defeats the eye', a vision that cannot be grasped by looking, by a visual discourse, whose historical visibility would correct and thus disable a present possibility. Instead, the notion of a vision that defeats the eye critiques and transcends the predetermination of the gaze, as the directive of a visual historical chronology, and focuses on the unseen, what is incomplete, dissolves and disappears, as the indeterminate, the mobile and unfixed. I understand this vision to produce the 'sight' of a sonic sensibility that sees the invisible relations and mobile circumstances of a political possibility, and that sees the land not as total sign or signal, tied to historical and ideological meanings and expectations, but as tendencies and capacities that create their own future.

This vision of a sonic sensibility and a 'material sound' presents a model for the creative rethinking and re-articulation of reality. It articulates the compossibility and inexhaustible complexity an invisible sight gives access to: to see not just what is, but how it is and how it might be. These essays on sound explore the capacity of such a vision that defeats the eye to engage in the condition of political reality as a possibility that does not repeat and reconfirm the status quo, but breaks down discourse and identity, and is invested instead in the imagination of the unseen that provides us with an access to other ways things could be: other ways things could relate, other ways we could make policy decisions, other ways we could engage in budgets, look at the details of women's rights, workers' rights, racial discrimination, national identity, global cohesion and so on.

To engage in the possibility of a political imagination beyond the status quo, and to lie the ground for the 'then what' of a political 'what if …?' this book consists of seven essays on themes that have come about in part explicitly and in part more implicitly in my previous writing. Here, I pick up on them and develop them through the imperfections and purposeful incompleteness of the essay form. These are fragments of listening turned into fragments of writing, which try their possibility in a vertical line drawn with random design around the political possibility of sound, and a number that is resolutely finite but makes room for the inexhaustibility of sound.

Seven essays

These seven essays as fragments can be read out of order and without the compulsion of the horizontal and the need to see the whole. Their number does not indicate a finitude to what might be said, but their place in a potentially infinite discussion, and their order outlines my own trajectory rather than the deliberate imposition of an order on its reader. And yet, sequentiality is persuasive. It forcefully suggests a linear narrative and progress, which might be there, inadvertently developing on these pages, but which is unintentional and unsolicited, since new ideas are more contingently and persuasively found in an arbitrary in-between of the texts, in their non-linear convergences and contradictions, and in their relationships to other essays and other texts elsewhere. Therefore the first essay does not have to be read at the beginning, and while it articulates the central claim pursued in this book, that there is a 'Political possibility of sound', from which it goes on to argue what its benefits might be, its deliberations might just as well be encountered after reading another. Nonetheless, in relation to the book as material object, it appears at the beginning. From this inevitable first position it identifies the political via Étienne Balibar, as what frames the practices and institutions of politics and thus what enables their objectives within the possibility of these practices and institutions and what delimits what remains impossible. The limitations of such a political possibility are investigated and put into question through a discussion of *Language Gulf in the Shouting Valley* (2013), a video essay by Lawrence Abu Hamdan, and Anna Raimondo's audiovisual installation *Mediterraneo* (2015). The deliberation of these two works, in search for a more plural possibility of the political via sound, is informed by the anthropologies of Petra Retham and Jane I. Guyer, the writing on International Relations by Roxanne Doty and Jack Holland, as well as the notion of a political and economic tone as an audible zeitgeist by Frances Dyson.

The second essay considers the architectural and ideological volume of political possibility. 'Hearing volumes: Architecture, light and words' articulates the notion of a sonic volume not as a measure of decibels but as the space of the environment's material and temporal expansion that creates an invisible interactuality of things in which we live as interbeings, as being in relation with everything else; inhabiting the in-between of sound from which the possible gets its plurality and plurality its legitimacy. This volume is imagined as a viscous and grasping expanse via Maurice Merleau-Ponty's idea of 'being-honeyed' discussed in relation to the work *Anywhen* (2016) by Philipe Parreno. In this way, the essay engages listening as the political possibility of a practical and collective capacity and empowerment. From there it debates the interactuality of sonic volumes in relation to the cosmopolitanism of David Held and Martha Nussbaum, and comes to contemplate human frailty and doubt within the cosmopolitan project via the writings of Catherine Lu. Thus it stages a deliberation on the contribution sound, a sonic sensibility and consciousness, can make to the political possibilities of a globalized world.

This globalized world finds an integrated study in the third essay, which writes about the 'Geographies of sound' as a geography of sonic possible worlds that performs rather than discovers impossible territories. I develop the idea of a performative discovery through participating in the installation *Inside You is Me, July/Surface Substance* (2017) by Jacqueline Kiyomi Gordon, and by listening to Susan Schuppli and Tom Tlalim's work *Uneasy Listening* (2015). From these two works a geography of all the 'stories-so-far', as proposed by Doreen Massey emerges, and the experience of the invisible volume as a sphere of performing and unperforming the representation of geography as discussed by Nigel Thrift becomes tangible. Both Massey's discussion of space as configuration of movements and narratives, and Thrift's promotion of performance to challenge the abstract knowledge of geography, aid the articulation of a geography of sound as a geography of the unknown that resists the hyper-invisibility of conventional reality in favour of the real unseen of sound.

Listening to these unknown lands, the sky, the ground and the underground are pulled into the political domain of geographical science, and the experience of the politics of a vertical geography articulated through Eyal Weizman's politics of verticality: his notion of the landscape as a three-dimensional matrix that can be used to divide an 'indivisible territory', is brought to experience. The military providence of this three-dimensional design urges a strategy that does not seek to represent, to map and to chart, but to perform the invisible terrain of sound to unperform its visual history. Thus I follow Erin Manning and Brian Massumi and run interference into the discipline. This interference takes the trajectory of a ship sailed at night, in defiance of disciplinary boundaries and with a mind to see a different shore in the dark.

The essay in the middle of the book does not produce a text, but a score, a set of instructions to listen, do and read the material and ideas that shape its research. Thus the fourth essay, 'Morality of the invisible, ethics of the inaudible', is an essay score. Its performative frame enables participation in the invisible mobility of sound to practice and try how sounding and listening to its unseen processes might contribute to the articulation of a contemporary morality, and how it might stretch towards an ethics of hearing and voicing the inaudible. It does not present a finishable text but a formless possibility of doing, as a re-doing and re-authoring, rather than knowing the ethical dimension of one's own actions and inactivities.

The fifth and sixth essays contribute via sound and a sonic thinking to the critical possibilities developed in contemporary discourses on subjectivity and identity, particularly in relation to trans- and feminist identities, and consider current debates on materiality and reality, specifically in relation to the notion of ancestrality and the mathematically real. They work towards the reconfiguration of history and identity, and of ontology and materiality, via the contingent performance of objects and subjects as things that inter-are. And so, 'Hearing subjectivities: Bodies, forms and formlessness' responds to and engages in the skinless and trans-objective identity of the sonic body through the performative practices of Evan Ifekoya and Pamela Z, whose works and processes are considered via Hito Steyerl's critique of the image, and whose autonomous agency and sovereign identity perform Hélène Cixous' rupture of the historical thread. The emancipatory force of their sonic identities has the potential to resound the violence of the lexicon, the limits of a Kantian taxonomy, and to disrupt the 'ultrasubjective' and 'ultraobjective' violence as articulated by Balibar, by unperforming definitions and calling instead the names of Saul Kripke's 'rigid designation'.

'Sonic materialism: A philosophy of digging', expands this heard and contingent subjectivity by expanding its audition into the sphere of things. Thus it joins a current debate on new materialism by developing via sound and listening the idea of materialism as a materialism of transformation that reconsiders an anthropocentric worldview without bestowing objects with mythical self-determination. Instead it involves an unperforming of the lexicon to hear echoes of responsibility in animate and inanimate things. In other words, this essay pursues, through a sonic sensibility, the agency of the invisible by its intensity, expanse and duration. It is written from listening to *Naldjorlak I* (2005), a work for cello composed in a collaboration between electroacoustic composer Éliane Radique and cellist Charles Curtis. Hearing in the work the resonance of their collaboration, of the instrument, the bow and the body, the space and the audience, this essay rethinks current ideas on speculative realism and new materialism via a fleshly in-between of things. Thus it engages in Quentin Meillassoux's critique of correlationism via Christoph Cox's search for a language that can grasp a sonic materiality, and develops its own contribution to the theorization of sound via Karen Barad, Rosi Braidotti and Luce Irigaray. Articulating a sonico-feminine new materialism that reads objectivity not as distance but as responsibility, and develops an embodied materiality that performs an 'agential realism' of the world through the 'diffraction' and 'intra-activities' of listening as a creative engagement in the between-of-things, where it re-meets Merleau-Ponty, his phenomenological correlations, not in opposition but as a modest collaborator.[15]

A seventh essay, 'Reading fragments of listening, hearing vertical lines of words', dives into the vertical depth of the text as sound, to hear it as a phonographic field. This phonographic reading is inspired by Leonora Carrington's book *The Hearing Trumpet* (1974), the invisible textures and rhythms of Jana Winderen's field recording composition *The Wanderer* (2015) and a performance of real, technological and ventriloquized voices by Andrea Pensado live at the Back Alley Theatre (2014). Listening to these works, this essay pursues with Adriana Cavarero a revocalization of the textual field and responds to the fragments of listening discussed in this introduction, with an invitation to read its fragments aloud, as sound sounding a vertical text. Thus this essay reconsiders the rhizomatic networks of Gilles Deleuze and Félix Guattari through an invisible vertical that finds no biological metaphor but lives in Merleau-Ponty's depth where I am too close to read but exist in dark simultaneity with letters as sound. In this regard, this last essay is a counterpart to this introduction. It follows its fragments into the deep and tries to encourage a reading according to the image of a material sound.

The text scores that bracket these essays, promote the performance of its first and last voice to be that of the reader, and offer neither an introduction nor a conclusion but instigate the performance of sounding and listening to the essays in between. They do not have to be read as the beginning or the end, but present an invitation into the practice of an awkward perspective and extend this invitation into the performance of a speculative artefact: to perform while reading, the 'vision that defeats the eye' but beckons the body into the as yet unthought and the unwritten.

Together these essays and scores provide simultaneous but different voices on awkward and impossible things. They are as fragments obstacle to symbols and signs, and present a resistance to historical meaning and the flow of a priori definition, and instead aim to enable the production of meaning as a sonic sense and a sonic vision: combining sensation and meaning, the thought and the beyond of thought, performance and reflection, without giving preference to either and without returning to a naïve apperception before thought. Instead they acknowledge the complexity of the ephemeral and appreciate its demand for engagement as a political possibility against easy opinions, populism, the singular and the unquestioned legitimacy of the visual: treading Sun Ra's 'pathways to unknown worlds' through collaboration and the resistance afforded by DIY; producing a joint listening and hearing of each other and of things without lexical definition, sounding from outer space.[16]

In each essay and between them there is room for contradiction, rephrased and reframed repetitions, conflictual perspectives and diverging lines of argument as well as spaces of reciprocal contestation. However, these do not make this project impossible or invaluable but are evidence exactly of the plurality of the actual and show the complexity at work in the imagination of the real. These essays are elements of each other rather than producing networked things, and thus while all the texts relate around the same issues of the political and the practice of sound, they remain fragments of listening that practice their sounding in different milieus, that draw on different references and consider different sources to stand autonomously in a joint endeavour.

Notes

1 Quoted from the invitation to an evening with the artist at University of California Santa Cruz (UCSC) on 2 November 2015, http://arts.ucsc.edu/news_events/evening-film-video-artist-cauleen-smith (accessed 15 December 2017).

2 Streamed live on 2 November 2016 by the MFA in Visual Studies Program and the Center for Contemporary Arts and Culture, welcoming Visiting Artist Cauleen Smith for a lecture on her work, https://www.youtube.com/watch?v=-1mwULFTXRk (12:54) (accessed 16 December 2017).

3 Ibid.

4 In 1972 Sun Ra, together with director John Coney and screen writer Joshua Smith, began working on *Space Is the Place,* an Afro-Futurist science fiction film, released in 1974, which narrates Sun Ra's time journey travelling from the future to 1940s America to fight racism with music from another planet. This movie, and his work with the intergalactic Arkestra, was influenced by a vision he apparently had in 1937 'of his visit to Saturn as an astrally-projected entity, where he met aliens that warned him of impending chaos on Earth and foretold that through his music, he "would speak, and the world would listen"' (Lukas Benjamin, 'Sun Ra: An Angel from Saturn', *Strange Sounds from Beyond*, January 2016, http://strangesoundsfrombeyond.com/magazineitem/an-angel-from-saturn/ [accessed 2 February 2018]).

5 This creativity of thought is inspired by Rosi Braidotti's reading of Michel Foucault's *The Order of Things,* his archaeology and excavation of the origins of human science, through which, according to Braidotti, 'Foucaults reinstates creativity at the core of philosophical thought' and which permits me to frame this endeavour as a creative and practical philosophy of sound and possibility (Rosi Braidotti, *Nomadic Subjects*, New York: Columbia University Press, 2011, p. 167).

6 Cauleen Smith from the live stream of her lecture at the MFA in Visual Studies Program and the Center for Contemporary Arts and Culture on 2 November 2016, https://www.youtube.com/watch?v=-1mwULFTXRk (12:54) (accessed 16 December 2017).

7 One of the points made in the Riot GRRRL Manifesto accessible online: http://onewarart.org/riot_grrrl_manifesto.htm (accessed 15 February 2018).

8 Theodor W. Adorno, 'The Essay as Form', in *The Adorno Reader*. Brian O'Connor (ed.), Oxford: Blackwell, 2000, p. 152.

9 Caroline Eades and Elizabeth A. Papzian (eds), *The Essay Film*, New York: Columbia University Press, 2016, p. 5. Here they are referring to Marx and Eistenstein's approach to the inevitable conflation between the process, the path to truth, in philosophy and film making respectively, and the truth thus generated itself.

10 Ibid., quoting Germaine Dulac from *Écrits sur le cinema 1919–1937 (Writings on the Cinema 1919–1937)*, ed. Prosper Hillairet, Paris: Éxperimental.

11 Chris Marker withdrew *Description d'un combat* (*Description of a Struggle*) from public display after the 1967 Six-Day War between Israel and its neighbouring states Egypt, Syria and Jordan. However, a restored and digital version of the film has since, in 2013, been screened at the Jerusalem Film festival.

I am including this information here as the war and the consequent withdrawal of the film from public viewing signify the only points of certainty and determination in the context of a work that plays with indeterminate juxtapositions and what Zakim calls the 'transitory semantics' of its material production. Both instances arrest the endless mobility of the film's signs and symbols, which enable the imagination of transformation and manifest a generative future and hope. Thus, they arrest the ambiguous possibility of the film and of the place in the certainty of bloodshed and boundary disputes.

12 Eric Kazim, 'Chris Marker's *Description of a Struggle* and the Limits of the Essay Film', in *The Essay Film*, New York: Columbia University Press, 2016, p. 146.

13 Ibid., p. 164.

14 Chris Marker, http://www.markertext.com/description_of_a_struggle.htm (accessed 8 November 2017).

15 Agential realism, intra-activity and diffraction are key terms in Karen Barad's theorization of materiality, describing a predicative realism, the action between things and subjects that reconfigure entanglements through difference, and the searching for difference rather than sameness and the recognizable outline. Karen Barad, 'Posthumanist Performativity: Toward an Understanding of How Matter Comes to Matter', *Signs: Journal of Women in Culture and Society*, vol. 28, no. 3 (2003): 801–31.

16 This notion of 'pathways to unknown worlds', trodden via resistance, collaboration and the imperfection of DIY, articulates the aim of this collection of essays, and refers to Sun Ra's musical and cultural journeys from Saturn, referenced in the title of a book on an exhibition of his work edited by John Corbett, Anthony Elms and Terri Kapsalis, entitled *Pathways to Unknown Worlds: Sun-Ra, El Saturn and Chicago's Afro-Futurist underground 1954–68*, Hyde Park Art Center (Chicago), WhiteWalls: Chicago, 2006.

References

Adorno, T. W., 'The Essay as Form', in *The Adorno Reader*, Brian O'Connor (ed.), Oxford: Blackwell, 2000, pp. 91–111.

Barad, Karen, 'Posthumanist Performativity: Toward an Understanding of How Matter Comes to Matter', *Signs: Journal of Women in Culture and Society*, vol. 28, no. 3 (2003): 801–31.

Benjamin, Lukas, 'Sun Ra: An Angel from Saturn', *Strange Sounds from Beyond*, January 2016, http://strangesoundsfrombeyond.com/magazineitem/an-angel-from-saturn/.

Braidotti, Rosi, *Nomadic Subjects, Embodiment and Sexual Difference in Contemporary Feminist Theory*, New York: Columbia University Press, 2011.

Corbett, John, Anthony Elms and Terri Kapsalis, *Pathways to Unknown Worlds: Sun-Ra, El Saturn and Chicago's Afro-Futurist Underground 1954–68*, Hyde Park Art Center (Chicago), exhibition catalogue, WhiteWalls: Chicago, 2006.

Eades, Caroline and Elizabeth A. Papazian (eds), 'Introduction, Dialogue Politics Utopia', in *The Essay Film, Dialogue Politics Utopia*, New York: Columbia University Press, 2016, pp. 1–11.

Kazim, Eric, 'Chris Marker's *Description of a Struggle* and the Limits of the Essay Film', in *The Essay Film, Dialogue Politics Utopia*, Caroline Eades and Elizabeth A. Papazian (eds), New York: Columbia University Press, 2016, pp. 145–66.

Marker, Chris, http://www.markertext.com/description_of_a_struggle.htm.

Riot Grrrl, Manifesto, http://onewarart.org/riot_grrrl_manifesto.htm.

Smith, Cauleen, Visiting lecture at Pacific Northwestern College of Art (PNCA), 2 November 2016, https://www.youtube.com/watch?v=-1mwULFTXRk.

The political possibility of sound

Possibility

This essay develops a notion of possibility that connects sound and an auditory imagination to the political understood via Étienne Balibar as the horizon of politics, as its condition of possibility and purpose.[1] Such a political frames the practices of politics and thus enables their objectives within its possibility and delimits what remains impossible. Balibar provides this definition in the context of a discussion on the political imagination of violence, its negation or sublation, understood as the circular force of politics. He suggests that the belief that violence can be eliminated is fundamental to our idea of politics and is expressed in its aim of order and control, its political institution. But that, at the same time, the attempt at controlling violence becomes a force that suppresses the possibility of politics in an infinite circularity between violence and anti-violence. He talks about the anti-nomic logic of the state 'that calls for the identification of opposites' good and bad, violent and non-violent, peace and war, that traps the possibility of politics within their incompatibility, from which even a revolutionary counter-politics does not escape, but which it only reaffirms, as 'merely its echo'.[2]

It is, however, not his focus on violence that is the aim of my discussion here. Instead I want to consider the possibility of the resistance or avoidance of its circularity and thus the unlimiting of its dialectical conditions and practices to reach a more plural and simultaneous possibility of politics via sound. Accordingly, it is the notion of a possibility of politics unthedered from the logic of negation or sublimation and employed in continuous territories and invisible zones that motivates my writing. I aim to position sound and listening as generative and innovative intensities in the space of the political in order to probe their potential for an exploration of politics and to try their capacity to imagine and effect its transformation into plurality without opposites. In this I do not limit politics to the condition of violence and anti-violence, which determines a dialectical frame and thus outlines a visual thinking – the corroborating of reality as an organization of 'this' or 'that' – but approach it as an autonomous order for creative production that also includes the unorganized and what has no clear definition or boundary. Therefore, the focus of my discussion is not Balibar's notion of violence, his terminology and argument, but the idea proposed in his writing on violence: that there is a possibility of politics evoked through the imagination of the political as a transforming and transformative condition, a noun that resembles an adjective and acts as a verb, that admits intent, and gives me permission and a context to imagine sound as generative of political possibility.

Relating to this initial identification and expanding its remit, I turn to discussions of possibility in anthropology and the scholarship of International Relations. Writing in 2013, Petra Retham suggests that the recent surge in focus on political possibility or the possibility of politics comes from the rejection of a 'politics of the antis' 'that is a politics that can only imagine itself in terms of antagonism and opposition':[3] anti-privatization, anti-neoliberalism, anti-globalization – positions that are complicit in Balibar's circularity of violence. Instead, the focus on possibility includes invention and creation as well as dimensions of ethics in the articulation of a politics that provides action and experiential change, and introduces the imagination of different possibilities and maybe even impossibilities that demand the discussion of normativity and transformation. This new engagement in possibility, in anthropology and the political sciences, employs terms such as becoming, generative and world-creating, a vocabulary and focus which resounds with my previous writing on sound and thus affords my earlier discussions a new contextualization and future possibility.[4]

In her text, Retham mentions Jane I. Guyer, who a few years earlier reflected on the status of possibility in anthropology by surveying the different uses of the term from its replacing of 'diversity' in the beginning of the twentieth century to a current definition: Presenting a change from the conception of possibility as variety and interchange, an aesthetics of possibility, to a present use of it as observations and ethics of transformation, as a generative possibility. This shift from perception of diversity to the production of plural possibility brings with it issues of self and participation: how far the anthropologist or practitioner is herself involved and invested in the transformation that the possible might hold; how much she is an object or a subject of ethnographic observation.

Both Retham and Guyer's focus is on anthropological diagnostics and analysis that allow for the investigation of possibility among affects, sentiments, the unpredictable, the imperfect and the incomplete, and aims to find 'alternatives within'.[5] Thus they identify for anthropology the task 'to examine individual and collective desires, the unpredictability of lives, and unexpected futures',[6] and urge the discipline towards an innovative analysis and form without hastening it forward, beyond the field and beyond a current actuality since, 'anthropology is the social science most familiar with a sense of unfamiliarity, so we should find signs of already knowing this problem within the disciplinary archive.'[7] In my articulation of the possible I pick up on the value of the incomplete, the imperfect and the unpredictable while also identifying with the need for historicity and the connection to a current circumstance and particularity, so that my notion of a political possibility of sound does not resemble a trivial fantasy, easily dismissed, but can move from the understanding of norms and normativity, their instigation as actual and real, into real possibilities that are transformative and radical.

Such radical possibilities do not go against perceived universals, as an anti-universalism, as they do not respond to a universalist view but engage in the complex particularity of things. They also do not depend on a future context to ensure their transformative potential. Rather, they are building future contexts presently through the acknowledgement of socio-historical norms, as the conditions and conditioning of actuality, which they transform by engaging in the particular circumstance of its acceptance and the possibility of a generative and plural view. In that sense, I see another inspiration and source for writing about possibility in the theories of Roxanne Doty, whose work on International Relations in the 1990s shifted the focus from 'why' a set of foreign policies appear possible as opposed to another, into a consideration of 'how' such a possibility is conditioned: what are the circumstances of this possibility? This, according to Jack Holland, opened International Relations (IR) up 'to consider the construction of ideas and identities that enabled a specific decision to be taken and a particular course of action to appear reasonable, logical and ultimately imperative or even inevitable'.[8] 'How possible' equates with 'how thinkable' and reveals a concurrent condition that accepts certain policies, military actions or governmental choices. It invites the consideration of the construction of a present actuality: to understand the political actors, the social and cultural terrain, the power structures and interpretative norms that make this possibility ultimately the only way to perceive, to act and to live, in the reality 'of the only thing possible'.[9]

Following this shift of IR towards the consideration of the condition of possibility, understood as the way a particular imagination and normative perception is produced and accepted, the 'how' has to be the initial focus of an auditory engagement. The task is to hear the how, to hear the condition of a singular actuality, in order to learn to listen out for alternative conditions that exist not apart from it, that are not its fictional parallel world, but that are real alternatives that sound a present polyphony, even when they are not listened to or heard.

At this point, Doty's focus on the precondition of reality as a singular constructed possibility of power that assumes the status of a given, a natural or naturalized order of things, resonates with Frances Dyson's focus on the monochord. In *The Tone of Our Times* (2014), Dyson writes about the construction of the Western tonal system as an attempt to avoid discord and the possibility of change, while making its harmony appear divine and angelic, and therefore immutable and beyond question. She explains the construction of the harmonic system as an expression of the desire to unitize the ephemeral multiplicity of sound, to make a system of discreet units known as tones that could represent and fulfil the Pythagorean ideal of a *Musica* that represents the natural proportion of the world.

> This required not only that irrational ratios be awkwardly suppressed, but that the possibility of incommensurable relations, incommensurability as such, was to be concealed at all costs, since knowledge of the incommensurable demonstrated the limit of the theory of the unities, showing that 'numbers cannot transcribe the measure of this world'.[10]

Dyson re-contextualizes the desire for the monochord and its methods of realization within a contemporary political and capitalist soundscape, and elaborates first on the concealment and suppression of the voice that utters other possibilities, and then offers access to this concealed voice through her elaboration of the echo as the reverberation of a different voice in the 'space of breathing'.[11] She suggests that the echo as repetition is the echo of angels, which reaffirms the existence of God and represents an acclamation of the heavenly administration of the world.[12] As she points out, the eternal repetition of the Sanctus confirms God but also obliterates the possibility for a silence that might make room for a different voice. This is silence as the breath that opens a gap between call and response, where a different voice can find articulation in the monotonous soundscape of power that has taken over the hierarchical structures from the divine. The lack of feedback between call and response at the place of the breath means the voice can return in a different shape. Not tied to what was said, its utterance always just a reaction, instead, it can challenge expectations and voice its own desire.

Her understanding of Western polyphony, a seeming multivocality being conducted to 'count-as-one' by the 'hierarchy of angels', articulates the objectification of the voice by the unresponsive echo of theory, statistics, forms and charts, and manifests a precedent for civil administration, which eventually becomes Doty's naturalized policymaker who owns the possibility of interpretation and action. Dyson's interpretation of a silencing echo as a modern-day form of acclamation, or what we might understand as popularism, allows her to critically engage in resonance beyond harmony, and to suggest the resistance of the corporeal to produce a dissonant and plural 'echo' that does not simply respond without a sound of its own but defies the monochord to contest ideas of a homogenous soundtrack of ecology and economy. However, she acknowledges that 'these possibilities are disabled in the absence of the time and the space of breathing', without whose silence there is no space for another, a plural response.[13]

In response and taking up on Dyson's suggestion of the echo of an autonomous voice that contrasts with the study of harmony and meaning and instead explores a plural sense, I want to propose an 'echography' of the inaudible: the practice of silent voices in the space of breathing that opens politics to the possibility of the political. Listening on sound walks, to the everyday, in conversation, in the gallery and the concert hall, or to an MP3 player, as well as making sound works, compositions and scores, or even just shout, talk and sing, are ways to pursue an 'echography' that resounds the how of power and actuality and makes their limits audible, attuning us to the tones that sound outside a harmonic singularity, so we might move away from the 'hierarchy of angels', to hear the devil at work in the monochord and start to pluralize its possibilities from the complex particularity of things.

Such an echography of material practice does not produce a visible geography, an organization of the invisible on a map, but explores the unseen reverb of reflection where plural causes become visible and their consequences thinkable, and where other voices can make themselves heard rather than theorized. This echography enables us to hear the dynamics of a political actuality and to imagine its sonic possibilities. In that it follows Dyson's suggestion of a 'resistive echo-ing' or 'echopraxia' of the 'people's microphone' that can leave the monotone echo chamber of media and politics.[14] But while agreeing with the affirmative of her echo practice, her resistive echo-ing implies a politics of the antis, the anti-stance of the 'people's microphone' and the centrifugality of its dissonance as a counter-politics remains trapped in the circularity of harmony and discord, violence and anti-violence, as the anti-nomic logic of power. I would like to imagine echography as a more agonistic and playful dispersion.[15] Thus while I am inspired by her notion of another echo that resonates in the gap of the breath, as a way to hear the political actuality and produce a political possibility, I aim for a sonic practice whose voice does not rise against harmonic tonality, the dominant self, but sounds itself, and whose clamour therefore, cannot be silenced in its opposition, but whose possibilities are inexhaustible: generative of an unfamiliar world that sounds actuality's hidden pluralities without reducing those into the notion of impossibility as 'the profoundly unrealistic' opposition to a rational world view.[16]

According to Guyer, 'Possibility is an ethical stance, demanding courage; it is an aesthetic of coexistence, demanding discernment; it is a vision of politics, demanding study and steadfastness.'[17] I propose that sound and listening can engage in this discernment of alternatives and can offer a practice that has the steadfastness to hear and generate 'the conditions that make possible or delimit possibilities' and that has the courage to ultimately unlimit the possibilities of actuality to include and make count, in perception and in the institution of politics, what appears impossible now.[18] This essay traces such courage and steadfastness through the work of Lawrence Abu Hamdan and Anna Raimondo to listen out for and give words to a political condition made apparent in sound. Thus it enquires via Jon Elster on the political possibility of artistic ambiguity and what simply is not there, and considers with David Graeber art's passage between reality and reason to get to the political possibility of sound that includes emotions and the fantastic as a legitimate resonance of a plural world.

Language Gulf in the Shouting Valley (2013)

This work is a 15-minute audio essay and audiovisual installation about the voice and the border by Lawrence Abu Hamdan, a British/Lebanese artist who works and lives in Beirut. I encounter it at the Pump House Gallery in London in a small square space that is painted in a flat black that expands into the screen, which too mostly remains black, granting us only the shortest glimpses of what must be the Golan Heights, barbed wire and people running. Visually I feel excluded, straining my eyes to see more when clearly more is not given. I remain outside, prevented from gaining an overview and barred from the goings on to which I obtain access only through prior reading on its history and politics, the press release, the brief moments when an image breaks through the blackout, and by way of a sound track of shouts, location sounds and two different voice-overs: that of Lisa Hajjar, a sociologist, who tells us about the role of the Druze soldiers working as interpreters in the Israeli Military Court system in the West Bank and Gaza, and that of a male voice-over artist who reads a script about the history of the Shouting Valley and the particular events that unfolded on 15 May 2011, when Palestinian protesters breached its frontier.

Hajjar's voice is an accented American English, that of the professional voice-over artist is subtitled Arabic. Apparently, recordings of the Druze soldiers working as interpreters in the Israeli Military Court system in the West Bank and Gaza are contrasted with recordings from the Druze community in the Shouting Valley. I cannot hear this juxtaposition, the nuance of difference within the same language is lost on me and reaffirms my outsider's position.

I have limited access to the world the work portrays, the represented remains largely inaccessible, and thus its world appears if not impossible then inscrutable and impervious to my comprehension. What I can access is the artwork and its possibilities as a video essay, which in its format combines the possibility of art, of aesthetic experience and transformation, with the possibility of documentation, of an ethnography that negotiates the object and the subject of recording and includes an ethical dimension.

Abu Hamdan's work shows 'fragments of an impossible totality' but also gives hope and 'includes a principle of renewal and spiritual research' which creates the condition for a different imagination and provides the support for an alternative view.[19] In its imperfect frame, a document of facts meets an artistic fiction narrated in the medium of the work that reframes them both beyond a singular and normative actuality, and opens them instead for more contingent and maybe even contradictory readings. The possibility of the artwork enables the possibility of the document and permits into the realm of truth also affects and sentiments, desire and the incomplete. The format enables the inclusion of the invisible and the inaudible within the authority of the actual, from where it can borrow a voice to make itself count as real while insisting on the precarity and mere possibility of its reality.

Hajjar talks about the translation process in court, about the status of the Druze in Israel, as a bilingual identity that occupies a precarious situation between Jew and Arab, conscribed to fight for the country against Arab nations and to work as translators in a court system that seeks to criminalize their identity. She tells us how the accused would not be given a translation of all that is said and discussed in court but only 'what he needs to know'. She calls him an object rather than a subject of the law, excluded from most that is discussed, entrusted only with the shortest glimpses that somebody else decides are pertinent to his case.

This information is told to me via what appears to be a phone conversation that starts with a dial tone a few minutes into the video and gives the soundtrack its quality of connection to an indoor space, when otherwise I remain outside, exposed to the wind and weather of the Golan Heights, a contested area that overlooks four countries: Syria, Lebanon, Jordan and Israel, and was seized from Syria in the 1967 Six-Day War, and annexed as Israeli territory in 1981.

The phone denotes a geographical distance but produces a sonic closeness and intimacy that evokes trust. By contrast, the image pretends a closeness and access that is impeded by the terrain's political status and its own blacking out, and makes me feel untrusted and remote. The blackouts highlight the image as a series of blindspots that do not reveal as much as conceal and suppress. At those moments, there is no ambiguity, things are just not there and the need for meaning closes in on me around the edges where it becomes generated from invisible sound and the practice of my listening. Reading these blacked-out frames in the blacked-out room of their projection, I am reminded of Jon Elster's notion of the limbo of politics, where what is politically possible – its actuality and authority, what is possible inside the limits of the institution of politics – and what is politically impossible – the issues and interests that reach beyond institutionally endorsed limits – meet, and the political is politicized: the border of the possible contested and its limits redrawn. In *Logic and Society* (1978), Elster suggests that the possibility or impossibility to transform a political circumstance from a situation where revolution is unthinkable and thus impossible, into one where it becomes recognized as a real possibility demonstrates that 'between what is unambiguously possible and what is unambiguously impossible there is a limbo where only *action* can decide'.[20] The blacked out frames present this limbo, where there is nothing, neither ambiguously nor unambiguously. This is a total absence, which undermines the singularity and norm of the images' actuality and opens alternatives within the contingent experience of the work.[21] These blindspots invite a politicizing of the visual border as divide or possibility for connection. From their darkness the soundtrack elucidates this indeterminate state and encourages the '*action*' of perception and production to 'decide' its possibility.

The Golan residents who fled the war are separated from their relatives by a 200m-wide valley, fence, coils of razor wire and minefield that divide the Syrian and Israeli sides. In the video, we hear the Druze community gather on both sides of the border and shout across to family and friends. With the shouts come glimpses of footage. It is as if the voices open the shutter on the camera to force through some light and give us a glance on a scene, which seems to be going on in the dark all along and holds a more unceasing reality than the image would have us think. The constant wind and distortion on the microphone, dogs barking and other location sounds keep the blacked out image life and make me appreciate that what I experience in short glimpses happens not just when I see it. Rather, the blackout symbolizes a more permanent and invisible condition of identity and belonging produced by a visible and solid division. The violence of the border is answered by invisible activity of resistance that meets in this valley not only when we are looking and not only when people shout, but the shouting is what gives me glimpses of its actuality and sounds a political possibility that can contest the status quo and transform its limits beyond a current institution of politics.

The soundtrack seems to activate a time-based pinhole camera that reacts not to exposure of light but to volume. The breath and shouts of running bodies, escalating into feedback, prise open the auditory imagination of a space that visually is conclusively drawn in wire fencing and border marks. The shouts gain a possibility beyond their communication with relatives. They attain the possibility to make visible the nature and limits of a present condition and to create the conceivability of a different one. They perform the activation of the lens and the activation of an as yet impossible imagination: What if there were no borders, no wire fencing, coils or land mines between the Druze? What if the Shouting Valley was a plateau to meet rather than a divide? The audiovisual essay cannot answer these questions, but it is asking them and through them conjures the 'then what' to its 'what if … ?' It prepares the ground for the current condition not to be beyond question, for it to be rethinkable, and for an alternative circumstance to be imagined. It invites the reconsideration of the political and cultural terrain and prepares a different consciousness than the one that instated and naturalized a space where wire fencing and land mines are the only way things can be. In this way, it opens glimpses at least on an alternative: another possible Golan Heights where Druze's working in the courts and shouting across the valley are not heard in opposition, and where neither voice has to be suppressed as irrational ratios and contained as the impossibility of incommensurable relations that might threaten the unity of one state. In sound, the space becomes a place where voices overlap and contradict each other to produce a true polyphony that follows no hierarchy and creates no unity but resonates the complex particularity of the situation.

On the day the footage was taken, on 15 May 2011, in celebration and memory of Nakba, the mass eviction of Palestinian Arabs from their homes in 1948, protesting Palestinians spontaneously broke through the wire fencing and ran across the valley to exercise their 'right of return'. The sound of their frenzied running and shouting opens the lens more frequently and makes more images appear on the screen and thus enhances my access to the visual document and supports my experience of its actuality. The rush culminates in calls of 'enough' 'enough' 'there are landmines' being shouted at the trespassers, arresting their possible world scenario through the reality of a politics that manifests as a weaponized border. Thus while the institution of politics is not changed by the charge, more indirectly and as its potentiality, the collective shouting, breathing and running crosses the borders of what is imaginable and complicates the normative condition of a visual divide. The amplification of unheard voices shows at least the limits of politics through the courage of political actions that defy a naturalized reality.

The soundtrack frequently breaks into feedback that ruptures the document, while its reverb dislocates the space of its composition. The shouts produce a force that crosses the borders of language and the notion of a work. They spill over aesthetic and linguistic barriers into non-translatability and make thinkable a different situation that has as yet no words and no material expression. The narrative of transgressing borders, the possibility of a voice that transcends the limits of the land, the frontier between Syria and Israel, creates a point of conflict, political and aesthetic, whose lines are practised and contested in sound.

In the gallery the work is too quiet, compromised by the other works around it that need to be heard too. Lawrence sends me the vimeo code and I can listen to it on my system. I overwhelm myself by the sound of shouting voices, cheering and full of fear at the same time. I crank it up until their emotion enables mine and affect stops to be an aesthetic device and becomes an experiential force. This is the possibility of sentiment, which has a place in anthropology as a sensory exploration, and which makes me a subject and an object of the audiovisual work, observed in my own reaction, and implicit in the creation of a shared humanity as a sonic possible world, through my voice, my breath and my running.

Possibility and difference

In *Sonic Possible Worlds* (2014), I develop the possibility of sound via literary criticism and its use of Possible World Theory. For literary theorists Ruth Ronen and Marie-Laure Ryan, the modal worlds of logic offer literary studies the opportunity to leave the textual properties and abandon hermeticist claims and inter-systemic evaluations in favour of the contemplation of writing in an interdisciplinary context, and permit alternative literary connections and references within a textual universe that is 'the sum of the worlds projected by the text'.[22] However, as Ronen states, 'fictional worlds are based on a logic of parallelism that guarantees their autonomy in relation to the actual world.'[23] Thus according to both Ronen and Ryan, while Possible World Theory provides literary criticism with a new exploratory potential and gives access to different connections and references, which enable the restaging of real agents and actions in a fictional domain, their fictional possibilities remain apart from an actual reality and its sphere of causality and consequence.

The worlds of logic are engaged in the consideration of counterfactuality and the ramification of possibility. Literary studies, by contrast, consider parallel worlds that have no impact on the real world. They produce what Umberto Eco calls 'Small Worlds' and what W. H. Auden refers to as 'Secondary Worlds'.[24] These worlds are created from elements of the primary world they relate to, but they always remain autonomous from the actual world and its ontology, its causes and consequences. They remain a proposition rather than an action, and while they can fictionally thematize and discuss real events, their interests and ideologies, they are unable to intervene in their construction.

Against this parallel world theory, I set via David K. Lewis a more radical sonic realism in which what I hear is an actual possibility for me, and while it remains but a possible possibility for you, it is nevertheless a real variant of this world. Thus modality is a matter of access and its restriction, to worlds that do not stand in opposition to an actual world but are its plural alternatives from which we negotiate a joint reality. Lewis's possible world theory articulates actuality in indexical terms: 'depending for their reference respectively on the place, the speaker, the intended audience, the speaker's acts of pointing, and the foregoing discourse.'[25] Applying Lewis's indexical possibility to sound engages hearing as an accessing of different variants of the actual, whose possibility is determined by my position, by my being in the world. In this 'phenomenological possibilism' the invisibility of sound elaborates Lewis's modal realism, 'which holds that our world is but one world among many' and that suggests that other worlds are '*un*actualised, possibility', by focusing on the qualifiers of possibility, the inhabitants that actualize a possible world.[26] Thus modality turns into quantification, clarifying that actuality is linked to modal operators who inhabit the possible world thus actualized, and whose power determines whether a possibility can make itself count in our perception of the actually real. Listening as inhabiting gives authority to the heard as a contingent variant, not as a literary fiction and parallel world but as a real possibility of this world. It offers a portal into difference and the differently real and allows us to hear alternative slices on an equal track, as a real sonic fiction. Its theorization grants it exposure and a vocabulary and allows us to contemplate in how far its possibility has impact and carries consequences, or remains 'unactualised', even while it is most definitely real for a particular inhabitant.

However, sound pluralizes not only the world but also the inhabiting index, conceiving of it not as a rigid grid of relative positions but as a plural mesh of invisible and contingent locationalities that are potentially infinite and through which we move in listening. This challenges the relativity and thus the marginalizability of sonic possible worlds, and emphasizes the practical intersubjectivity of listening as a fluid inhabiting of counterfactual situations through the reciprocity of the heard. As I suggest in *Sonic Possible Worlds*, 'Sonic possible worlds are private-life worlds that we negotiate: mine through yours and yours through mine, generating a contingent actual world in which we share but not always equally nor lastingly and that produces not a singular but a possible actuality – one slice of many slices of what the real could be.'[27] These inhabited possibilities also include non-human actors, their sounding and listening, to produce a plurality of worlds without the 'hierarchy of humans' that have taken over from the 'hierarchy of angels' since the move from a celestial and religious logic to the rationalism of a secular humanism and its administration.

Lewis believes that 'absolutely *every* way that a world could possibly be is the way that some world is.'[28] By connecting the actuality of his possibility to the indexical inhabiting of listening and declaring that every way the world could be is a way that the world is for somebody/something, I am assigning compossibility to the plurality of possible worlds as possible lifeworlds, which are all real perceptual slices of this world but that cannot make themselves count equally in the construction of actuality. This emphasizes the plural simultaneity of the real and grants the opportunity to politicize its access and restrictions: to consider the political conditioning that renders a variant possible and another impossible.

Those possibilities that exist in a textual sphere are at once enabled and contained parallel to a singular actuality, and thus they remain merely possible. Those that gain traction in the invisible and mobile sphere of sound, by contrast, have the power to make themselves heard, illuminating the how of a dominant actuality while providing the tools to sound and thus actualize alternatives from within. The possibility of sound, composed or incidental, linguistic or technological, does not present a parallel fiction, a possibility held within the universe of the text, the aesthetic construct of the work; it does not make a proposition about the world from which it remains autonomous, but generates a world that is an actual possible world with ramification beyond the confines of the material or medium of its construction. Sound makes thinkable the possibilities of this world, not as metaphor and parable or in relation to a textual universe, but as a portal into real possibility, and shows us the world through its variants: the slices of a timespace geology that holds the cavernous simultaneity of all the possible possibilities of this world.[29]

The possibilities thus accessed are not only sonic. The soundscape and sound work as sonic possible worlds do not propose an essentialism and separatism apart from a visual world. To the contrary, sound in its invisible mobility and depth, provides access into the possibility of a visual world, where its singular actuality is illuminated and fragmented into the mobile and plural processes of its production, which gives us the insights and tools to resound time and space with different echoes that resonate in their blindspots and blackouts.

In this sense, the calls echoing from either side of the Shouting Valley are at once a device for a political imagination of its naturalized condition and generative of an affective possibility for its transformation. They are productive rather than representative and generate a world that is an actual possibility even if it remains blacked out, concealed, hidden or ignored. Their sound gives a voice to the political possibility of the Golan Heights by providing glimpses of its circumstance as a divide, while also providing a portal into the imagination of the territory and its institution as an open landscape, not limited by barbed wire and not set against this frontier either, but as an alternative within: as a continuum and simultaneity of land, culture and language.

This thought is provoked by the blacked out screen and the occasional glimpse triggered by the shouts. But the principle of access retains beyond this particular aesthetic device as an access not to sameness and recognition, an ignoring of difference, but as an access to the unfamiliar and incomplete possibility of another life, whose actuality I negotiate, carefully and temporarily in relation to my own incomplete possibility. The sonic denies the divide representation and instead drags it into its own imaginary as an action and desire rather than a proposition. It shows us an invisible zone and ephemeral identities, and renders intelligible the hope for alternative realities. Elster suggests that 'the notion of political possibility is also dependent upon the intentional and intelligent production of desired states.'[30] In response to this, I identify the shouts across the valley as the desire for a political state that includes the possibility of those who are shouting here because they are not heard elsewhere, and I hear the action of shouting as making intelligible the production of this possibility. In this regard, the world behind the black screen of Abu Hamdan's video essay presents not a parallel world, isolated from this world and without impact or ramification, but produces alternative realities that are as true and authentic as the world we pragmatically refer to as real, but whose possibilities are concealed or suppressed: they have less power to make themselves count and thus the production of their intention, the telos of their politics, remains *un*actualised but not without cause or consequence.[31]

On this point of suppression, we re-meet Balibar's violence and its circularity with anti-violence, and recognize it as the condition of a politics that determines Doty's 'how' of power and actuality, truncating its echo into the shape of the only thing possible. 'If the means and forms of sublating it [violence] appear not contingently but essentially as the means and form of pursuing it – if there exists, consequently, an intrinsic perversity of the political – then politics becomes desperate and a cause for despair.'[32] If in other words the political is legitimated through the pursuit of violence, then we have a politics that has no resonance or breath, no blackouts or blindspots, places of limbo from which to reimagine the condition of its actuality in an invested and inhabited possibility, but are left with the perversity of a truncated and singular response.

The political possibility of sound sidesteps this perversity and its desperation with a different voice. It does not answer violence with anti-violence but with a shout that calls from the unseen different possibilities into being that activate desire and create the actions of a plural imagination. This sonic imaginary does not limit its possibility to opposition, but generates an alternative that is neither parallel, and thus without ramification and impact, nor circular, and thus incapable to leave its causality. Instead it invites a listening to the breath as a continuous resonance of otherness in a shared space. This is the breath of Dyson and it is the breath of the Palestinian's running across the Golan Heights, illuminating blindspots to see not the divide but understand and imagine its connections. In this sense, the breath is not a signifier but a space of action; the site of a plural echo: the echoes of the shouts that break through the blacked out screen.

At this site, we encounter a basic tenet of the political practice of sound in relation to an instituted politics and fiction: the political of a textual fiction is genre specific, regarding the economies and institutions of the literary, its canon and discourse. It is able to represent and propose an alternative but not to enact it. Sonic fictions, by contrast, are political actions that generate a politics of possibility and transformation that outlines, with invisible lines and from a mobile depth, the condition of its narrative without sublimating the how, but illuminating its singularity and breaking its dominant echo. Listening is thus a political practice that hears and generates alternatives. It is not an essentialist practice however. Its possibilities go beyond that of its own materiality and sensibility, as well as beyond the dynamics of the telos of its politics, into the possibility of a plural and multisensory world, revealing its norms and giving agency to its transformation: in sight, hearing, touch and smell.

The politics of this sonic engagement is the politics of the invisible. It is not collapsed into the totality of the image, and neither does it fulfil preexisting normative codes, but responds to the demand of the dark, when we have lost our anchorage in things and rules, and are forced to suspend our habits and values, to listen in order to perceive the complex plurality of the real as simultaneous possibilities that include also impossibilities: that which has no part in a singular actuality, and it makes us reconsider also the part we play ourselves.

Mediterraneo (2015)

Anna Raimondo's audiovisual work *Mediterraneo* engages me in the imagination of another political divide, that of the sea between North Africa, the Middle East and Europe, whose border exist not as barbed wire fencing but as a watery depth, and whose distance cannot be breached by shouts but only through the risk of one's life, in small boats, floats and rubber dinghy's, organized by traffickers and the imagination of despair. The vessels attest to the anguish and hope that this stretch of sea symbolizes. Its watery terrain cannot be inhabited but only transited in a precarious fashion by a people who cannot even shout.

On a bleached out white background we see a glass slowly, drip by drip filling with a blue liquid that as the poet Paul Claudel would say has a certain blue of the sea that is so blue that only blood would be more red. And as the sound of dripping water slowly fills the glass, Raimondo's voice catches her breath, accelerates, slows down and stutters, speeds up again, and repeats over and over again 'Mediterraneo' until her voice is drowned in the water she has conjured with her own words. Until then, on the unsteady rhythm of her voice, we are pulled through the emotions of fear, excitement, hope and death that define the Mediterranean as the liquid terrain that is the ephemeral space between Africa, the Middle East and Europe today.

Raimondo is an Italian artist who works between Morrocco and Belgium. Her life is invested in the passage between the continents, while her practice articulates a possible imagination of the water that divides or connects them. Her voice, repeating over and over again the word 'Mediterraneo' takes us to the centre of the liquid expanse that is not simply *between* Africa, the Middle East and Europe, a connecting and separating passage only, but *is* the material and metaphor of their relationship as a deep and treacherous actuality produced from the political narrative that is currently considered and practiced as the only one possible.

In her voice, the water is not limited to this one actual possibility. Instead, her words' rhythmic calling of the sea triggers between the unambiguous actuality of a naturalized 'how' – our implicit acceptance of the political actions, the social and economic conditions and power structures that make this actuality ultimately the only one possible – and the absence of an alternative worldview, the curiosity to know 'why'. Listening to her repetitive chant of a solitary word makes us question the legitimacy of this one political reality, and lets us ask why it seems to be the only one possible, and it brings us to consider also how we are bound up with its normative actuality, how we agree with it and facilitate its singularity.

Raimondo's audiovisual composition brings us to the unheard position in the politics of migration and war, that of the Mediterranean sea, which is the silent witness to the violence of a current actuality and reveals its cost. The water takes on an observer's position while calling from within again and again a despair only heard in the depth of the sea.

This is an insight that emerges over the time it takes for the glass to run over and that evokes ambiguity and doubt and enables the 'what if ... ?' of another possibility: What if another power was at play? What if the continents connected on land? What if we all looked and spoke the same? Questions that motivate the imagination at least for other actions and alternative realities that are not 'profoundly unrealistic' oppositions to a rational worldview, and are not simply its parallel fictions, but that engage reason and legitimacy in a different way, beyond the desire for the monochord and the measure of the dominant in a multivocality that has no hierarchy but brings with it different consequences and ramifications.

Referring to Giorgio Agamben's pre-enlightenment reading of the term imagination, David Graeber defines imagination as 'the zone of passage between reality and reason. Perceptions from the material world had to pass through the imagination, becoming emotionally charged in the process and mixing with all sorts of phantasms, before the rational mind could grasp their significance'.[33] He states that it is only after Descartes that imagination comes to denote irreality, fantasy, the parallel worlds of the imaginary that have no impact or ramification for the real world. This more porous medieval view of imagination as a force implicated in the constitution of the real that is portrayed not as a fact but as a 'passage' holds a useful model for the notion of a political possibility of sound.

Sound's reality is not bound up in the absolutes of rationality and neither is it a trivial fiction. It is the reality of the invisible and the ephemeral, a reality that defines the actuality of the world as process, as a 'zone of passage', that engages relational and contingent truths, which are the possibilities found among affects, sentiments, the unpredictable, the imperfect and the incomplete. Sound generates a possible reality that does not represent a singular actuality but renders the real a mobile and unseen complexity. It makes the how of the dominant appreciable and sounds the minor, the suppressed, the hidden and the ignored. In that sense, Graeber's definition of imagination is useful to apportion sound the capacity to be more than a thought, to be a thought engendered through process and participation that has the power 'to have real effects on the material world'.[34]

Once we stop thinking of the imagination as largely about the production of free-floating fantasy worlds, but rather as bound up in the processes by which we make and maintain reality, then it makes perfect sense to see it as a material force in the world.[35]

The passage between the Mediterranean is a real passage, with life and death consequences. But its reality is not born from rationality, from rational thought and reason, but from the imagination on the one hand of a political desire to wage and win a war, and on the other of despair and the hope not to lose one's life. The two positions meet not in the realm of reason but in the realm of imagination, which produces their co-dependence in political necessity and the perverse lack of another vista. Sidestepping this singular actuality and the perverse circularity of its violence, Raimondo's voice can be heard as a ritual call that vibrates both shores on an even tone and does not proffer a moralizing framework, a judgment or rational conclusion, but offers us the passage as a passing through to contemplate and reimagine what possibilities this ephemeral expanse could open.

In sound, the Mediterranean is the crossing not the crossed. Its actuality is a process, a passing that reframes otherness and distance through the practice of desire, fear and hope rather than as a measure of geography and identity. It is not the infrastructure of connecting and separating, a bridge between continents that enables us to cross while at the same time maintaining the distance that exists in the first place; determining either side through the actuality of what it is not. Rather it is a volume, whose passing in words or as subjectivities, those of the artist and those of the refuges and traffickers or military personnel and weapons does not define a boundary, a cartographic line, but enables the actual possibilities of multiple points of views sharing in the same timespace. The crossing does not generate the real actuality of this continent and the apparent impossibility of that, but creates the possibility of the water's own expanse and how that time and space defines things together. On the treacherous waters, index points meet in the weave of the sea, enabling a simultaneity and continuum of different possibilities, which are all 'bound up in the processes by which we make and maintain reality'.[36] Listening and sounding create a crossing of the sea's volume that does not measure and name but engages in its watery depth to understand the defining lines by coinciding with them, and that unlimits those lines through the possibility of its own echo.

Raimondo's work brings us into the urgency of the situation through the focus on the sea as the common texture of the adjoining continents, rather than through the confrontations of their different shores. The repetitive mantra of her voice entreats me into the water in order to, from within the fluid materiality, understand physically the complexity of its fabric, form and agency: of what it weaves together formlessly rather than what it is as a certain form, and in order to suspend what I think I know of it and pluralize what it might be as the invisible organization of different things: salt, water, waves, holidays, routes of escape, yachts, aquatic life, sand, handmade dinghies, bodies, dreams and desperation. Listening, I am persuaded to understand these things in their consequential and intersubjective relationships: what they sound together as sonic things and what thus they make me hear of their ecosystem of invisible processes. This does not mean that some do not have more authority than others. These invisible processes do not hide but reveal inequities. The sonic bind makes apparent the interdependencies of power, organization, self-organization and control, and provides an opportunity to revisit economical and political values that depend on the divides and distances that are established in the theoretical language of a humanist philosophy and that are perpetuated in the economy of the visual.

The image pretends the possibility of distance and dissociation, to be apart as mute objects and subjects, and to be defined by this distance, which cuts the link to any cause and masks the relationship to any consequence. Thus, a mute ocean enables my withdrawal from the sociopolitical and ecological circumstance of its waves and permits me to deny responsibility in its unfolding. Distance creates the distortions of what Maurice Merleau-Ponty terms 'dis-illusions': the semblance of another real, which if we look from afar retains its authority and reality that dissolves, however, once we step closer, affirming the actual reality that was there all along.[37] By contrast, sound affords no distance and enables no view from afar. Instead, the simultaneity of an inhabited listening creates the dis-illusions of plural possibilities, perception's true variants, which are the different slices of this world that cannot be resolved into one singular and actually real: foreign policy, military intervention, war, fighting, right and wrong, but that practice the inexhaustible ambivalence between measure and experience: what something is as material form and name, and what it appears to be in perception, so we might understand and respond with engaged and practical doubt to what seems incommensurable from ashore.

Raimondo composes a different image from the ambiguity of the how and the drowning of its singular echo. The hypnotic rhythm of her voice and the steady dripping of blue water generate the political possibility of the Mediterranean. Slowly submerging, with her words, into the deep blue sea, I abandon my reading of its terrain within the rationale and reason of existing maps and the actuality of its politics, and come to hear its texture woven of unresolved material and positions. I do not follow its outline but produce a dark and mobile geography of the Mediterranean as a formless shape, whose possibilities and impossibilities undulate to create a fluid place that defies measurement but calls forth an attitude of listening-out to understand where things are at and to take responsibility within that invisible factuality. Since, within this dark and mobile geography we hear, as William E. Connolly suggests we should, 'the human subject as a formation and erase it as a ground'.[38] In the watery depth of *Mediterraneo* humanity appears as formless form that has lost the access to its grounding in the traditions of knowledge and the established canon's of thought and its hierarchies of reason; in political certainties and journalistic judiciousness, as well as in relation to historical and geographical identities and philosophical language. Instead the rhythmic drip, drip, drip, and the reiteration of its name call for another ground, a groundless ground of invisible processes that create, contingently and through constant negotiation, the possibilities of actuality.

Listening and sounding we enter the privilege of darkness and enjoy the loss of anchorage in rationality and so can reach the unfamiliar to reconnect and make accountable what we call actual. Thus sonic reality emerges not from maps and words but from the fluidity of blue liquid and the drowning of the voice. And as the fluidity gives access to a groundless world, a world without a priori reason and rationality, the drowning words do not fade but re-emerge in the plurality of the audible.

'The Lover of Blue Writing above the Sea!' (excerpt)

It is not true that the shortest path between two points is the
     Straight line!
That is what I learnt when I was with you!
Dialogue? Is the longest part between the heart and the lips,
between my voiced waves and your silent waves.
Intuition alone led me to you ...
It screamed one night without sound
that candles had gone out, that we were finished.
Parting poured poison in our coffee ...
Once, I gave you my heart, naked like a white sheet of paper.
I wrote on it the plot for my murder ... and my death certificate!
You did not forgive me, for leaving my death with you
and going with the gulls to the sea ..

... Here I am, running alone in the rain, without a man or a nation –
thousands of windows gaze at me with aggressive, burning eyes ...
Like any rebellious black ewe
I weave the threads of my freedom far from the paths of the flock ...
I try in vain to create a third fate
for a woman coming from the third world.
'Do you want to know the secret of my power?
No one has ever really loved me ...'

Here I am, falling
but I insist on leaving traces of my steps, traces of my pens
on the darkness of the abyss ... and the whiteness of the page!

Ghada Al-Samman[39]

Imagination and responsibility: Conclusion

Having lost our grounding and reason in the deep blue sea, an alternative reality needs to be found in the obscure mobility of sound that sings not as dissonant anti-violence, as a dialectical position easily sublimated into a normative condition, but through the simultaneity of many voices that echo in the gap between call and response. In this blacked out space at the place of the breath, silence reverberates with the unheard human and non-human slices of this world, and sounds a political possibility that includes their formless form. The loss of the angelic hierarchy of tonality and the rejection of its humanist replacement, the monotonous soundscape of power, symptomized in the monochord of rational thought and manifest in neo-liberal capitalism, requires that sense and meaning are produced through participation and a practice of listening and sounding that generates reality and its legitimacy as a complex plurality, whose politics is not conditioned by a dominant and truncated echo but takes account of the minor and the complex and diverging resonances of everything that sounds without rejecting it as dissonant or ignoring it as inaudible.

The possibility of a politics of sound is the possibility of a politics of the incomplete, the unfamiliar, the unrecognizable and the unheard; that which we have no words for and that which is incommensurable in relation to current norms, but which presses through a naturalized reality, and impresses on us the need and courage to listen-out for alternatives within. Ultimately, among the practices of this politics of the minor must be an echography of the inaudible that gives access to its concealed sounds and allows other voices to be heard in the gap between what sounds and what is heard. However, it is not a matter of theorizing these voices, of objectifying them, rendering them mute, collapsed into the image of a representational language, but of hearing their sounds generate a different world that is accessible by a steadfast desire to embrace the unfamiliar, and the actions of a political will that does not mean to shut them down.

Connolly's call to acknowledge the ideological construction of humanity and humanism and to erase it as the ground for thought and knowledge, cited above, is quoted from an essay that discusses within the context of New Materialism the fragility of things and deliberates the consequent notion of an ethics of care. Here it might be read as a call to hear the fragile within the circumstance of the possible, and to construct reality in a contingent practice of listening that hears with a care for the unexpected and the unheard. He continues:

> as we confirm the human subject as a formation and erase it as a ground, as we detect more vitality and periodic capacity for surprise in a variety of nonhuman forcefields, we also seek to contest a set of classical conceptions of command or derived morality within an *ethic of cultivation* grounded in the contingency of care for this world.[40]

This care does not articulate an idealized ethics, a transcendental notion of right and wrong, the obeying of one set of sociocultural standards or biblical commandments and judicial law, but resembles what I have termed an 'ethics of participation': the need to engage, to participate in composing the reality of the world from its possibilities and from the contingent actualities heard on the weave of indexical positions. On this plural weave, all the things and circumstances that are possible are actual possibilities for somebody, and reality is not a singular actuality but infinite alternatives that as simultaneous variants create the complex particularity of the world. This ethics engages the how of a particular circumstance in the question of its naturalization as the only thing possible. It performs the critical consideration of what it enables and what it silences, what it gives access to and what it restricts, and pursues alternatives that unlimit the possibilities of the status quo through the creative imagination of what else might be possible.

Connolly's *ethic of cultivation* necessitates my creative imagination, which generates the opportunity for the multivocality of the world to count-as-plurality, and demands responsibility and care for the notion of reality and truth that it produces. Responsibility prescribes me to understand my own position in the world as only one possibility among many, and it is the humility of this position that drives my participation in its ethical production and defines the value of any engagement and the worth of any sense thus produced. The end of a singular actuality and reality, as religious belief or rational truth, is not the beginning of 'alternative facts', lies and untruths, however, but is the beginning of truth as an engagement with the world that does not shy away from the incommensurable but measures and challenges its own nominal reality on what is not heard.

'When one is asked to be "realistic" then, the reality one is being asked to recognize is not one of natural, material facts; neither is it really some supposed ugly truth about human nature.'[41] Rather, it is ideological, sociopolitical norms and expectations backed by historical precedent and enforced by at least the potential for violence that one is being asked to recognize and respect: a violence at any rate that acts against the possibility of one's autonomous imagination. Accordingly, the status quo presented as the only one possible becomes a political imperative that disavows alternatives as threats: to the state, to national security, to peace, to the economy, to identity and so forth, which legitimizes their suppression by any means. 'In international relations, a political "realist" is considered one that accepts that states will use whatever capacities they have at their disposal, including force of arms, to pursue their national interests.'[42] In relation to this, a fertile auditory imagination poses a threat to the national interest due to its capacity to reveal the condition and vested interests of ideologies and sociopolitical norms, the how of a current circumstance, and its ability to transform its enabling conditions by sounding diverging resonances and breathing life into alternative possibilities.

The contention throughout this essay has been that the ephemeral mobility and generative nature of sound can open the narrow confines of politics to different political possibilities. The unseen is uncertain, unreliable and incomplete, and thus it invites a quasi-medieval view of the relationship between reality and reason, where reality is not a visible status but an invisible zone within which perception passes through imagination and emotions and is touched by the possibility of phantasms, which deliver it not into trivial fictions, but into the power of creative desire and hope.

The actions of sonic possibility, charged with emotions and imagination, enable the re-imagination of a political practice and its material truth: determining how else politics could be instituted and how else the truth of a community, the shared practice of living, might be effected. They do not sound untruths or post-truths, however, but complex and plural truths not based on a calculated objectivity of natural laws only, but produced in the negotiation of their facticity: their condition rather than their statement. Listening's responsibility for the imagination of reality and factuality does not follow a simple rationalism and singular authority, but critiques, from the dark depth of sound, the nominal of a rationalist monochord without descending into the proliferation of invested phantasms. Sonic fictions, sound's political possibilities, are not political lies or popular falsehoods: the populist echo of a counter politics. Instead they are imagination as a generative and responsible engagement in a current condition that probes its normative sheen and creates from doubt and with humility the unexpected of its materiality and sense, to produce a different truth that is inclusive also of what might seem unthinkable, profoundly unrealistic, a surprise even. A truth, in other words, that goes beyond the scope of a rational political imagination, but which is exactly from where the biggest issues facing us today: global warming, mass migration, war, health and care, will find their answers.

Sound's mobile and ephemeral constitution enables and motivates this echographic practice of inclusion: including the formless, the invisible and the barely audible, the unfamiliar and the affective in the generation of knowledge and the knowable. Knowledge is a fundamental engine of political change and transformation. Sonic knowledge, the knowledge of the invisible and what remains unheard, opens politics, political actions, decisions and institutions to the plural slices of this world. Listening as a care for the fragile within the condition of actuality produces knowledge as a responsibility towards the plurality of its possibility, questioning the singularity of its authorship and authority and thus its partisan investment and legitimacy. Knowledge is refracted in the invisible light of sound: more voices come to be heard as barer of information, insight and facts. However, its plural rays do not find easy consensus, and they also do not simply contradict or deny existing ideas but enter into an agonistic game of doubt and speculation, which enriches and augments the possibility of knowledge through alternatives from the plurality of what could be known.

Consequently, reality becomes a matter of fragments fragmenting into sounds not tones, which are heard contingently on the indexical weave and remind us through their possibility of the seemingly impossible, read not as the dissonant, the anti-tone, but experienced as the inaudible and the barely heard. Thus it demands a listening-out for the minor, so we might hear and excavate from the slices of reality the less heard ones to produce different narratives.

Engaged with in this way, sound illuminates the limits of the norm, the how possible, and effects a different resonance that can grasp and communicate the possibility of the impossible. Its groundless ambiguity and at times sheer absence demonstrates the limitation of the rationality of Western thought and opens us to an imagination that takes from the invisibility of sound the capacity to hear the irrational not as a profoundly unrealistic worldview, but as a fragment, as a legitimate slice of what the world is and might be. A sonic sensibility produces an awareness for blindspots and demands participation. It affords capacities to act and become an actor; to invent the circumstance of one's own audition and listen out too for those voices that remain impossible. Listening and sounding with a care for the possible we can appreciate the variants of this world and 'partake(s) of the powers that could transform the world into something better'.[43]

Works with sound, music and the soundscape of the everyday, subjects and objects, dominant and fragile things, can be the platform on which this awareness finds articulation, and where we can practice a political echography of the unheard and the unexpected. In this sense, my listening to Abu Hamdan's *Language Gulf in the Shouting Valley* and Raimondo's *Mediterraneo* pursues an anthropology of reinvention that, rather than categorizing and pulling what cannot be seen into the familiar of existing language, explores the unfamiliar, the incomplete, the ambiguous and what is not even there, in order to experience the limits of its condition and hear the creative force of its possibility open what appears unreasonable and break through the circularity of suppressed imaginations.

Thus to articulate and analyse political possibility through sound not only gives us insights into the dynamics of the actually possible, helping us understand how a present circumstance is accepted as 'reasonable, logical and ultimately imperative or even inevitable', the only thing possible.[44] It 'may also start to open a space for its contestation or at the very least foster an appreciation of why such contestation is often so very difficult.'[45] However, and in tune with Guyer's sense of anthropology stated in the beginning, as a science familiar with the unfamiliar and thus already equipped to deal with its problem, the political possibility of sound in art and everyday life is not simply a forward movement in a temporal sense, striving towards a future horizon, building an avant-garde of listeners, but is an alternative exploration of the present as a geological formation, a timespace place, whose diversity is its possibility now.

My sense of the present moment is that the realities of the world may make us confront the Caroline Islanders' views of the horizon as moving towards us, rather than vice versa, and that navigation techniques may pivot again accordingly. I doubt that we will ever give up 'possibility' in its hopeful sense, as the matrix of ground from which one can sense originality.[46]

Notes

1 In the introduction to *Violence and Civility,* Étienne Balibar discusses the institution of politics by referring it to the possibility of the political: 'on the horizon of politics, as a condition of possibility and a telos of all its practices, is *the political* [*du politique*]' (Étienne Balibar, *Violence and Civility, On the Limits of Political Philosophy*, New York: Columbia University Press, 2015, p. 2).

2 Balibar, *Violence and Civility*, p. 5. While Balibar does not use a hyphen to emphasize the separation of the anti and violence, or indeed between non and violence and the anti nomic, but writes them as one word, I will adhere to a hyphenated spelling to illustrate the oppositional terminology that ultimately allows for a circular, dialectic dynamic to take hold.

3 Petra Retham, 'Imagining Political Possibility in an Age of Late Liberalism and Cynical Reason', *Reviews in Anthropology*, vol. 42, no. 2 (2013): 228.

4 World-creating is a term that at once refers back to my discussion of the predicative in *Sonic Possible Worlds* and at the same time invites via Hannah Arendt a political reading of building worlds. It refers to the semantic construction of worlds within modal realism elaborated via literary theory: in her book Marie-Laure Ryan mentions James McCawley's notion of 'world-creating predicates', which are verbs such as to dream, to intend and to believe, that create possible worlds as mental constructions, where the 'propositions embedded under the predicate yield the facts of the related world', and produce its imagination (Marie Laure Ryan, *Possible Worlds, Artificial Intelligence and Narrative Theory*, Bloomington and

Indianapolis: Indiana University Press, 1991, pp. 19 and 22). It also brings this propositional and imaginary world into the realm of a future politics via Arendt's notion of 'world-building' as a co-creating of life that demands 'a plurality of men':

> There is an element of the world-building capacity of man in the human faculty of making and keeping promises. Just as promises and agreements deal with the future and provide stability in the ocean of future uncertainty where the unpredictable may break in from all sides, so the constituting, founding, and world-building capacities of man concern always not so much ourselves and our own time on earth as our 'successors', and 'posterities'.

> (Hannah Arendt, *On Revolution*, London: Penguin Books, 1990, p. 175.)

5 Jane I. Guyer, 'On "Possibility", a Response to "How is Anthropology Going?"' *Anthropological Theory*, vol. 9, no. 4 (2009): 355–70, p. 36.

6 Retham, 'Imagining Political Possibility in an Age of Late Liberalism and Cynical Reason', p. 231.

7 Guyer, 'On "Possibility"', p. 357.

8 Jack Holland, 'Foreign Policy and Political Possibility', *European Journal of International Relations*, vol. 19, no. 1 (2011): 51. In this essay, Holland pursues the question of 'how thinkable' into the legitimation of the Iraq War. He observes the normative and singular political rationale of going to war, the how, through a comparison of the acceptances of this how in the United States and Britain respectively, and comments on the building of a cultural resonance, which results in a lack of acceptance for alternative possibilities. Consequently, in the end, only one course of action seemed possible, which is then emboldened by rhetorical force and dominance.

9 'Realism is the absorption of all reality and all truth in the category of the only thing possible.' Jacques Rancière, *Disagreement, Politics and Philosophy*, London: University of Minnesota Press, 1999, p. 132.

10 Frances Dyson, *The Tone of Our Times, Sound, Sense, Economy and Ecology*, Cambridge, MA, London: MIT Press, 2014, p. 23.

11 Ibid., p. 105.

12 Ibid., p. 31.

13 Ibid., p. 105.

14 Ibid., p. 152.

15 Ibid.

16 David Graeber, *Direct Action and Ethnography*, Edinburgh and Oakland, CA: AK Press, 2009, p. 510.

17 Guyer, 'On "Possibility"', p. 363.

18 Rethman, 'Imagining Political Possibility in an Age of Late Liberalism and Cynical Reason', p. 238.

19 Germain Dulac quoted in Caroline Eades and Elizabeth A. Papazian (eds), *The Essay Film, Dialogue Politics Utopia*, New York: Columbia University Press, 2016, p. 5.

20 In this passage from Jon Elster's book *Logic and Society, Contradictions and Possible Worlds,* he calls this situation pre-revolutionary, 'implying some kind of latent or partly crystallized unrest, that only needs the right word at the right time in order to emerge in recognizable form' (Jon Elster, *Logic and Society, Contradictions and Possible Worlds*, Chichester, NY, Brisbane: John Wiley & Sons, 1978, p. 51). I read this latency not as immanence, not as a transcendental moment, but as part of the ongoing political condition within ephemeral territories and invisible zones.

21 This interest in blindspots and the blackening out of images is a theme discussed in more detail in my essay, jointly written with David Mollin, for the catalogue of the exhibition *Nietzsche, Cyclists and Mushrooms, Language in Contemporary Art*, Kunst Raum Riehen, CH, 2015.

22 Marie-Laure Ryan, *Possible Worlds, Artificial Intelligence and Narrative Theory*, Bloomington and Indianapolis: Indiana University Press, 1991, p. 24.

23 Ruth Ronen, *Possible Worlds in Literary Theory*, Cambridge, New York and Melbourne: Cambridge University Press, 1994, p. 8.

24 Umberto Eco and W. H. Auden outline their sense of literary and artistic possible worlds in their respective texts published in *The Limits of Interpretation* (1994) and *Secondary Worlds* (1984).

25 David K. Lewis, 'Anselm and Actuality', *Noûs*, vol. 4, no. 2 (May 1970): 175–88, p. 185.

26 David K. Lewis, *On the Plurality of Worlds*, Oxford: Blackwell, 2001, pp. 2 and 5.

27 Salomé Voegelin, *Sonic Possible Worlds: Hearing the Continuum of Sound*, New York: Bloomsbury, 2014, p. 33.

28 Lewis, *On the Plurality of Worlds*, p. 2.

29 The term 'timespace' has been developed in relation to sound in my previous publications, most notably in *Listening to Noise and Silence* (New York: Continuum, 2010, p. 124). It presents the non-dialectical co-constitution of space and time. In this particular instance, its association with geology, as simultaneous geological timespace slices, addresses the preconceptions of a time as forward-moving in a human-centred time sense, and instead considers time as a geological timespace, measured in the duration of the earth's events, as stratigraphy or deep time.

30 Elster, *Logic and Society, Contradictions and Possible Worlds*, p. 50.

31 'What actually is the case, as we say, is what goes on here. That is one possible way for a world to be. Other worlds are other, that is *un*actualised, possibilities' (Lewis, *On the Plurality of Worlds*, p. 5).

32 Balibar, *Violence and Civility*, p. 2.

33 Graeber, *Direct Action and Ethnography*, p. 521.

34 Ibid., p. 521.

35 Ibid., p. 523.

36 Ibid.

37 Merleau-Ponty's dis-illusions are the illusions of a first impression. What we think we see, which, as we step closer reveals itself as to what it really is. However, he does not consider these initial perceptions as unreal or wrong, and appreciates that they play a part in what it is we think we see finally. He thus acknowledges that perceptions are mutable and probable rather than real: 'But what is not opinion, what each perception, even if false, verifies, is the belongingness of each experience to the same world, their equal power to manifest it as possibilities of the same world' (*The Visible and the Invisible*, Evanston: Northwestern University Press, 1968, p. 41).

38 William E. Connolly, 'The "New Materialism" and the Fragility of Things', *Millennium Journal of International Studies* (2013): 399–412, p. 400.

39 Ghada Al-Samman, 'The Lover of Blue Writing above the Sea!' (excerpt), in *The Poetry of Arab Women, A Contemporary Anthology*, trans. Saad Ahmed and Miriam Cooke, ed. Nathalie Handal, pp. 274–6. Northampton, MA: Interlink Books, 2015, reprinted with permission.

40 Connolly, 'The "New Materialism" and the Fragility of Things', pp. 39–40.

41 Graeber, *Direct Action and Ethnography*, p. 510.

42 Ibid.

43 David Graeber, *Possibilities, Essays on Hierarchy, Rebellion and Desire*, Edinburgh and Oakland, CA: AK Press, 2007, p. 2.

44 Holland, 'Foreign Policy and Political Possibility', p. 51.

45 Ibid., p. 64.

46 Guyer, 'On "Possibility"', p. 367.

References

Al-Samman, Ghada, 'The Lover of the Blue Sea!', in *The Poetry of Arab Women, A Contemporary Anthology*, trans. Saad Ahmed and Miriam Cooke, ed. Nathalie Handal, 274–6, Northampton, MA: Interlink Books, 2015.

Arendt, Hannah, *The Life of the Mind*, San Diego: Harcourt, 1978.

Arendt, Hannah, *On Revolution*, London: Penguin Books, 1990.

Auden, W. H., *Secondary Worlds*, London: Faber and Faber, 1984.

Balibar, Étienne, *Violence and Civility, On the Limits of Political Philosophy*, trans. G. M. Goshgarian, New York: Columbia University Press, 2015.

Connolly, William E., 'The "New Materialism" and the Fragility of Things', *Millennium Journal of International Studies*, vol. 41, no. 3 (2013): 399–412.

Doty, Roxanne, 'Foreign Policy as Social Construction: A Post-Positivist Analysis of U.S. Counterinsurgency Policy in the Philippines', *International Studies Quarterly*, vol. 37, no. 3 (September 1993): 297.

Doty, Roxanne, *The Law into their Own Hands, Immigration and the Politics of Exceptionalism*, Tucsan, Arizona: The University of Arizona Press, 2009.

Dyson, Frances, *The Tone of Our Times, Sound, Sense, Economy and Ecology*, Cambridge, MA, London: MIT Press, 2014.

Eades, Caroline and Elizabeth A. Papazian (eds), *The Essay Film, Dialogue Politics Utopia*, New York: Columbia University Press, 2016.

Eco, Umberto, 'Small Worlds', in *The Limits of Interpretation*, 64–82, Bloomington and Indianapolis: First Midland Book Edition, 1994.

Elster, Jon, *Logic and Society, Contradictions and Possible Worlds*, Chichester, NY, Brisbane: John Wiley, 1978.

Graeber, David, *Direct Action and Ethnography*, Edinburgh and Oakland, CA: AK Press, 2009.

Graeber, David, *Possibilities, Essays on Hierarchy, Rebellion and Desire*, Edinburgh and Oakland, CA: AK Press, 2007.

Guyer, Jane I., 'On "Possibility", a Response to "How is Anthropology Going?"' *Anthropological Theory*, vol. 9, no. 4 (2009): 355–70.

Holland, Jack, 'Foreign Policy and Political Possibility', *European Journal of International Relations*, vol. 19, no. 1 (2011): 49–68.

Lewis, David Kellogg, 'Anselm and Actuality', *Noûs*, vol. 4, no. 2 (May 1970): 175–88.

Lewis, David Kellogg, *On the Plurality of Worlds*, Oxford: Blackwell, 2001.

Merleau-Ponty, Maurice, *The Visible and the Invisible*, Evanston: Northwestern University Press, 1968.

Mollin, David and Salomé Voegelin, 'During the Night, Crops Will still Grow', in *Nietzsche, Cyclists and Mushrooms, Language in Contemporary Art*, exhibition catalogue, Heidi Brunnschweiler (ed.), Basel: Kunstraum Riehen, 2015.

Rancière, Jacques, *Disagreement, Politics and Philosophy*, London: University of Minnesota Press, 1999.

Retham, Petra, 'Imagining Political Possibility in an Age of Late Liberalism and Cynical Reason', *Reviews in Anthropology*, vol. 42, no. 2 (2013): 227–42.

Ronen, Ruth, *Possible Worlds in Literary Theory*, Cambridge, New York and Melbourne: Cambridge University Press, 1994.

Ryan, Marie-Laure, *Possible Worlds, Artificial Intelligence and Narrative Theory*, Bloomington and Indianapolis: Indiana University Press, 1991.

Voegelin, Salomé, *Listening to Noise and Silence: Towards a Philosophy of Sound Art*, New York: Continuum, 2010.

Voegelin, Salomé, *Sonic Possible Worlds: Hearing the Continuum of Sound*, New York: Bloomsbury, 2014.

Work

Abu Hamdan, Lawrence, *Language Gulf in the Shouting Valley* (2013), audiovisual installation, Pump House gallery, London, 12 October–11 December 2016.

Raimondo, Anna, *Mediterraneo* (2015), audiovisual installation, Curators' Series #8. All of Us Have a Sense of Rhythm, curated by Christine Eyene, DRAF (David Roberts Art Foundation), London, 5 June–1 August 2015.

Hearing volumes: Architecture, light and words

Architecture

So you enter into a space. It's big, people keep on saying it's large.[1]

In 2012 I did two soundwalks, one at Tate Britain and one at Tate Modern, with a group of postgraduate students from the London College of Communication, UAL. They walked each exhibition space guided by instructions that they had to follow in pairs. These were written as simple text scores telling the students where to go, what to listen out for, how long to listen, what sounds to make and so on. These instructions encouraged the students' engagement with the location through its sound, but took away their freedom to listen to anything and in any way they wanted. Consequently, they created a focus beyond habits or expectation and challenged what it was possible to hear.

Enter the museum

walk up and down the ramp inside the museum for 3 minutes, listening to your footsteps and that of other visitors.

go to the escalators (main gallery) stand still and listen to the space while moving to the top level.

walk through the gallery to a window facing the Thames, look out and listen.

go back on the escalators, stand still, listen to the space while moving down back to ground level.

walk back up the ramp inside then continue outside.[2]

The reason I did these walks with the students was for us to experience the exhibition space as an acoustic environment and to hear it with new ears; to find a way to understand and ultimately articulate how the sound of the gallery changes the works shown therein; and how our own movements and the action of other people within the space influence the way we perceive the work and the architectural context of its staging. Walking through the galleries, following the listening and sound-making instructions we noticed how every space and every room transformed into a sonic shape of invisible relationships, mobile simultaneities and audible contradictions. Our walking-sounding-listening became a form of co-habitation of ephemeral rooms that do not remain rooms but become 'volumes', triggering an understanding of the exhibition space not as a construction of walls, floors and ceilings, windows and doors, but as a dimensionality that has a capacity: the capacity of the work and the capacity of our experience of it.

This volume is not a measure of decibels but the space of the environment's material and temporal expansion. It is an invisible architectural volume that while causally related to its visual construction, materiality and context, nevertheless produces a different engagement and brings about a different agency. The notion of volume arrived at via sound provides us with the terminology and the imagination for the experience of the gallery as a mobile and viscous expanse that enables and holds the work and the viewer without visible boundaries in a generative and reciprocal embrace. This embrace recalls Maurice Merleau-Ponty's 'being-honeyed', his notion of phenomenological intersubjectivity described through the metaphor of honey's sticky grasp and applies it in relation to the grasping density of sound. In this conflation it produces the imagination of sound as a slow-moving liquid that 'comes apart as soon as it has been given a particular shape, and what is more, it reverses the roles, by grasping the hands of whoever would take hold of it.'[3] Merleau-Ponty's honey articulates the inevitable and reciprocal hold of sound's volume, and enables my consideration of how we exist therein. What it means, as Jean-Luc Nancy asks, 'to exist according to listening?'[4] And what, as I would like to query further, it means to exist *together* according to listening?

The conceptualization of the gallery as volume renders the space formless but expansive, invisible but felt. It gives it a viscosity within which we move and breathe together as in an unavoidably connecting but plural sphere, suggesting an intersubjectivity and interactivities that enable the imagination of being in an environment as a being together with other things, and creating the sense of what can be 'seen' as an experience of 'inter-vention': as a perceptual agency between things.

Pursuing the notion of the gallery as volume is not an essentialist stance, however. It is not the articulation of sound against vision, and it brings us not to a pure sonic awareness but into a multisensory sphere, where as a 'viewer' I become increasingly aware of how my reading and understanding of a piece is not only constructed from the work, its artistic context or its discursive or actual vicinity and association to other works, but is produced also by the contingent circumstance of its experience conceived as the invisible and formless capacity that gives the work its expanse and us the crucible of a shared viewing. In sound, the gallery becomes an intensity rather than an architectural structure. The acoustic environment is a viscid connecting of materials, lights, sounds, works and people in co-production. The space produced is contingent and temporary but persuasive through the affective energy of its volume. Sound compels, it obliges. It puts into contract and conversation everybody's and everything's contribution to a current composition of a space. Thus it brings into view and experience the interconnectedness and reciprocity of a generative listening: the agency of experience as 'inter-vention' is an 'inter-invention' of what there is and of what we are with it.

In *Listening to Noise and Silence* (2010), I discuss listening as the invention of sound and describe auditory perception as a generative process that does not recognize or receive but creates the heard from what is there and even from what remains unheard. The volume as crucible, as test and capacity of a shared experience enables me to reconsider the subject's responsibility and singularity in this process, and allows me to clarify the invention of listening as an inter-invention: a generation of the world not from an anthropocentric position but from the co-relational between-of-things and from the between-of-subjects-as-things. Thus what could have been read as self-centred fantasy, the generation of an auditory world for me, gives access to the complexity of a contingent circumstance, whose contingency is a contingency with others, people and things, to whom it connects not through the self-certainty of authorship, but via the sensitivity of co-relation and a fragile activity between what might sound and what it might mean.

Sound as a concept invites us into the materiality of things, not to deny the visual but to augment how we might see; and it transgresses the boundaries between the object, the thing looked at, and the space and context of its appreciation, introducing a sense of simultaneity instead of pre-existence, and promoting the reading and experiencing of things as agitational, interventionist, multisensory and capacious.

We do not inhabit a finished building but cohabit its production to which we belong in the order of the material, the things that it is made from. Architecture as sonic volume brings objects and subjects together and brings to consciousness the agency and relevance of all things, challenging an anthropocentric hierarchy and bias and the possibility of a disconnected self. Instead, a non-anthropocentric reality becomes clarified as 'interactuality': actuality produced contingently through the practice of the in-between rather than the separation of things. Accordingly, 'to exist according to listening' comes to suggest 'interbeing': a term borrowed from Thich Nhat Hanh, whose concept derives from the practice of Buddhist meditation and takes the word 'to be' as to 'inter-be' to acknowledge that everything relates to everything else, and that there is no independent self but that every 'I' and everything is made of non-'I', non-thing elements.[5] While not adhering to the Buddhist context of his philosophy, I will be using the notion of interbeing in relation to sound and listening to develop the idea of intersubjectivity within the broader context of interactuality, and to stress the perceptual focus on the in-between.

Interbeing enables the consideration of being according to listening as a being together and a being of each other. It acknowledges that the invisible embrace of sound highlights the co-being and interbeing of things and makes thinkable, at least, a plural participation in the production of a situation or circumstance, and it reminds us also of our responsibility in the interpretation and valuation of that circumstance: our ethical position and positioning as communicating agents in an interrelated sphere.[6]

This essay deliberates, via sound and listening, on our ethical participation at the co-relational between-of-things. And engages the political possibility of a practical and collective capacity and empowerment by discussing sonic volumes, interactuality and interbeing in relation to *Anywhen*, a work by Philippe Parreno. From there it finds a connection to the cosmopolitanism of Martha Nussbaum and David Held, and the contemplation of human frailty and doubt within the cosmopolitan project, explored via the writings of Catherine Lu and Merleau-Ponty. The aim is to deliberate on the contribution sound, a sonic sensibility and consciousness, can make to the political possibilities of a globalized world.

Light

Anywhen (2016)

Phillipe Parreno's *Anywhen,* produced in the context of the Hyundai Commission for the Turbine Hall at Tate Modern in 2016, is not an installation in the sense of a work set up and played in an architectural space. Instead it is lights, sounds, words and things exploiting the capacity of the Turbine Hall to produce an invisible volume of their interrelation, contradiction and reciprocation. The work expands beyond what can be installed and what we would be able to capture in an installation shot. It is not arranged in space, it has no boundaried spatiality, and it also has and takes no time. Or rather, it has all the time and all the space as it produces them both in the in-between and the overlaps of their dimensions. What happens in the Gallery relates to and is a consequence of what happens outside, around the place and in other locations. As an *Anywhen*, the Turbine Hall is not a limit or a form, but provides the opportunity of connecting things and processes to produce the site as a capacity that reaches beyond the measurability of its space and the finitude of its time into the imagination of its possibility as volume.

As I walk down the broad ramp of the Turbine Hall, my first encounter is with a large grey carpet, feeling soft and unexpected underfoot, and a gaggle of children wrestling with an outsized silver balloon fish, fighting for its release. Freedom finally achieved it ascends into the rafters, floating by a row of square lamps going on and off in different patterns that answer the square shapes of the Tate's own windows and the light-box like structures that protrude its wall on one side of the hall. On the lights' rhythm I am drawn into the building, beyond the concourse that straddles the work, to a vast projection screen, where an aquatic landscape with underwater creatures even bigger than the balloon fish that met me earlier, expand the world on the carpet into a shared pool of light. In this light, the viewers – sitting, standing, walking and lying on the soft surface – are embraced as co-inhabitants of the volume of the work. Their movements are integrated into the large fishbowl that apparently is a normal-sized fish tank located in Parreno's studio, but that here is blown-up and out of proportion, turned from its everyday existence of a domestic aquarium into the production of an aquatic world.

The uncanny shape of big fish, the beauty and strangeness of their overblown size on screen, their slow movement circumscribed by the mass of water, corresponds with and amplifies the out-of-placeness of the carpet and the languid passage of their balloon cousins into the netting just below the beams of the Turbine Hall ceiling. Air filled and moving upwards they reflect on their silvery scales the intensity of flat lights, which start to enter into a rhythm that connects to the movement of the white screens that enable the projection of the oversized fish and impact on the sense of density and expanse experienced by those sitting on the carpet, which stretches all the way to the back of the Turbine Hall with its church-like tall and narrow windows, and provides the ground for a different imagination and inhabiting of this place as conceptual capacity and invisible volume rather than as architectural space. The carpet's softness invites children to turn wheels, groups of people to sit or lie down, chatting, dreaming, eyes closed, eyes open, viewers talking, lovers necking, looking at and being part of the work that is not a work but a connecting of things that expands the dimensions of the actual Turbine Hall and creates from between them the experience of another possibility that has the capacity to reconfigure the real and the legitimacy to question our responsibility within its definition.

From my position on the carpeted floor, lying on my back, I see three oblong screens that hang horizontally and trapeze like under the high roof. They descend at times to press on the volume of the hall and transform an upwards view. Seven shorter squarer screens, one at the front and three each side, hang vertically from the same construction and move, in equally unpredictable frequency, to play with the lateral expanse and to build an open room for the video projected at intervals. The movement of suspended screens within this aquatic world, rather than producing the certainty of walls and partitions, however, performs the temporary displacement of invisible matter while revealing the indivisibility of its volume. The mobile screens impact on my sense of capacity and viscitude, on how much air there is to breathe, on how much space to move. The suspended walls are sensible rather than visible, their movements are felt rather than seen, not through their wallness, but through their displacement of invisible air. There is something deliberately absurd about this attempt at dividing an invisible volume with floating screens. It is as absurd as what is projected on the front screen's surface: a video of the ventriloquist Nina Conti with her dummy standing mute within a recording of her own as well as her ventriloquized voice, performing the absurdity of recording out of synch, a disconnected voice that for its curiosity relies on connection and synchronicity.

The deliberate unconnecting, oversizing, carpeting and lighting transform what the architecture, the space and the projection are and snap them out of nominal proportions to become what they could be also. Taking things out of scale and out of purpose the work makes us experience the norms and habits of measure and its representation. Shifting and resizing encourages a questioning of what things are in their cause and consequence, and provokes a new imagination of what they could be: how to measure and how to call them. So we might reconsider what can belong together and where we might belong in relation to it all: whether I am a fish too, speechless, mute swimming; or a ventriloquist, mouthing what comes from elsewhere; or a balloon rising into the rafters to get stuck in a net.

The different elements – carpets, fish, voices, light and screens – are drawn together in the soundtrack that makes their interbeing apparent and accessible beyond visual associations. The ever-changing composition of musical and everyday sounds, rhythms and white noise produces the volume of Parreno's aquatic world as a tangible sphere that expands beyond what can be seen. It opens the invisible and indivisible dimension of the space to the experience of its expanse and draws out the interactions and interagencies of all there is to ring their interactuality: their actual possibility generated through the practice of the in-between, the overlaps, the coincidences and conflicts, which largely remain invisible but felt, and which make the place a volume that uses the capacity of the Turbine Hall to make its own shape.

Above me hang six rows of sixteen loudspeakers, evenly spaced on thin black leads. Despite this neat arrangement, I cannot source the soundtrack to this system as it is diffuse and everywhere, liberated from the structure that enables it by the expansive capacity of its own sound, while the system of its production, the ninety-six suspended speakers, are heard by the creaking and squeaking of the mechanism that moves them up and down. We are told Parreno has miked-up the building and the area between Tate Modern and the river, and that the sounds we hear are at least partially those from over there. But now they sound the over here as a place of proximity and reciprocation rather than as a visual location and distance. Wherever they are from, the sounds find no source or reality but create their own. They connect the carpet to listening, the fish to my slowed down movement and the ventriloquized body to my own voice, and trigger from these connections our agency and behaviour: children dancing and playing, adults lying on their backs expanding time, people sitting in meditative out-time, chatting, dreaming; walking slowly on the unusual surface and in a strange light.

In home improvement terms, it is the carpet that pulls the room together. But here, the carpet is but the cypher that invites the leisure and pause needed to hear the soundtrack that agitates and gives energy to the production of the space as volume, as invisible crucible that holds and activates the in-between. Listening, the visual impression of the large fish tank meets the sonic sense of a honeyed existence and persuades us into a watery world whose density resembles that of a sticky liquid with the capacity to grasp us into its midst. The honey water binds us into the viscous volume that slows our movements and words, amplifying their path rather than their destination; derailing us away from aims and signification into the process of meaning and meaninglessness.

It is the density of sound's 'aquatic' volume that makes the exhibition space thinkable as connections, influences and reciprocities. With every move, each thing and subject agitates the viscous thickness that 'holds' it all and that shows the being of our interactions as unseen undulations; as ripples of immateriality through which we exist temporarily and contingently not as 'this' or 'that' but as the agitation of the between-of-things. The volume creates interactuality. It generates the reality of the real not from the certainty of things apart, their signification and name, but from their coincidence and encounter; outlining being as being together and from each other rather than apart and as separate pieces; and producing closeness and a tangible in-between.

At the very back of the Turbine Hall is a glass-fronted little room that we cannot enter but only peer in to. Here are computers and bottles, measuring devices, tubes and jars. The room operates as a mysterious bioreactor installed by the scientists Jean-Baptiste Boulé and Nicolas Desprat. There are apparently sensors on the roof of the Tate that relay to this laboratory the outside measures of wind speed, humidity, temperature and other atmospheric data, which in an unfathomable way connect to a pitcher of yeast that reacts to changes in this information and influences the actions of the work. This microorganism seemingly activates what happens in the gallery space: every change of light, movement of screens and speakers, images played and compositional decisions is apparently controlled by 'micro-organisms that control you.'[7] This however appears like a red herring, or a metaphor and invitation into a post-human world rather than a truth. It is not an untruth however, but a possibility that holds the promise of a post-human fantasy. It invites the imagination of the room as a sensitive automaton: a sensibility machine that as apparatus, as dispositive, is, according to Parreno, 'a half organic, half mechanic and half digital kind of machine.'[8]

The laboratory, its intricate connections and mystical operations appear like another element rather than the cause of the work. It carries a possibility and thought, just like the carpet, the screens and the fish do, rather than being the causality and engine that controls them. This does not diminish its contribution to the actuality of the work's possibility, however. In fact, its fantasy of control permits us to desist a decoding of the logic of the movements of screens and lights or of the changes in the soundtrack as an artistic intention, and instead compels us to experience forcefully and without a rationale their interrelation and conversation as actions that do not represent but co-compose the volume of *Anywhen*.

The interactuality of the work as an anywhen of a generative, inter-inventive capacity, makes the space of the Turbine Hall possible, as a 'global' space: a space that does not demarcate a site, but that is composed of processes and relationships that expand beyond a certain territory, a map or a floor plan, into a watery cosmos made from honey and sound. At the same time, the narrative of a yeast-like cause permits us to consider the authorship and dominance of this global interactuality beyond an anthropocentric intentionality and guides us to appreciate that its causes and consequences are experiential and without a purpose beyond their own contingent connecting and making of an open and inter-inventing place. This non-anthropocentric cosmos of reciprocal connecting provides an expanded imagination of the Turbine Hall, itself a building and site that explores the possible rather than the actual use of a Power Station. The work restages, through invisible relationships, the warped proportions of architecture and ideologies and creates interrelations between screens and walls, the stable and the mobile, dark footage and flashing lamps, fish, balloon fish and videoed fish, to come to the possibility of their interactuality.

This possibility includes the interactuality of my own subjectivity: who I am as an 'I' made of other 'I's and of other things. I am among others on the carpet, in an interactuality caused apparently by yeast but made sensible most strongly by light, sounds and carpet fibres. I am acutely aware not only of the work but also of others experiencing the work with me. The carpet permits and enhances the engagement in the shared viscosity that the sound makes accessible as an invisible cosmos and that the notion of a honeyed 'waterworld' makes articulable as a possible thought.

The invisible intensity of sound creates the clammy and slowed down reciprocity that honey established and water recalls. Listening we gain access and the ability to grasp the complex connections and processes that the automaton machine creates without having to distil and separate its actions and materialities but from their co-production exactly. This co-production involves the shared and reciprocal production of ourselves. The sound and the carpet hold us in a space where we co-inhabit and co-produce the work and the architecture as an indivisible volume. In this undividable dimension, the audience is not consisting of independent selves but as interbeings bound into the processes of its built and existing according to listening as selves and things made of non-selves and non things. Thus, strange and familiar elements produce each other in the rhythm of lights, the growing of yeast and our breathing in and out together in the density of water as within a social sphere that is contingent, mobile and inexhaustible.

Words

The New Sound Meditation (1989)

Listen

During any one breath

Make a sound

Breathe

Listen outwardly for a sound

Breathe

Make exactly the sound that someone else has made

Breathe

Listen inwardly

Breathe

Make a new sound that no one else has made

Breathe

Continue this cycle until there are no more new sounds.

Pauline Oliveros®[9]

Sonic cosmopolitanism

'Not only are we "unavoidably side by side" (as Kant put it), but the degrees of mutual interconnectedness and vulnerability are steadily growing.'[10] The interbeing and co-habitation that a sonic volume brings to the fore and invites us into, chime with the contemporary discourse on cosmopolitanism: the political, institutional and ethical focus on global inter-connectedness, where the notion of 'a small world' does not refer to its fictional status, but to 'the idea that events, peoples, climates, economic systems and cultural life-worlds in one part of the world have bearing, meaning, and impact on places and people in other parts of the world'.[11] Cosmopolitan thinking is invested in these interconnections as a source for the conceptualization of common structures, universal values and practices, to find potential solutions to global problems such as migration, war, climate change, exploitation of labour, and so on. It talks of interconnected and overlapping communities to try and theories a world not divided into nation states, as oppositional forces, but lived-in as in a collaborative sphere, a cosmos that can sustain humanity and the sharing of our planet.

The imagination of the world as cosmos is not new. Martha Nussbaum traces a contemporary cosmopolitanism back to as early as the Stoics, who according to her followed Diogenes the Cynic in his assertion that rather than a citizen of the polis, of the city-state, he was a 'citizen of the world'. Developing his stance the Stoics' philosophy articulates the world as universal sphere of justice and rights, and suggests that humans reside in two communities: that of birth and our physical belonging, and that of 'the community of human argument and aspiration'.[12] In this view, the place of birth becomes an accident, a sheer coincidence of fate, which is, however, not dismissed as irrelevant, but whose incidentality demonstrates the potential of its substitution and thus reminds us of the greater field of humanity as a place we belong to through a 'moral duty' towards each other.

Political, economic and ecological forces of globalization give this historical cosmopolitanism a current context and relevance. With global market forces determining local economic and political decisions, with the closeness of a smaller world impressing the responsibility of local actions into a global sphere and bringing global actions to local consequences, the idea of a retreat into the comfort of a self-determined sovereignty seems ever less of an option. Instead the need for a connected and connecting imagination of identity and sociopolitical agency becomes apparent. Consequently, contemporary cosmopolitanism foregrounds a concern with every human being and promotes the will and provides the context to work from the incident of birth into a contingent world that is shaped by the fluidity of markets, wars, climate change and migration, whose global influence and reality cannot be reversed but needs to be responded to through the re-imagination of what we have in common and a re-invention of how we could act together in a shared and global world. Such a project overcomes the dichotomy between free transborder movement of goods and finance, climate and war, and the restrictions on movements of bodies and the fixed limits of identity and social belonging, and imagines the social and political possibilities of connecting and being together in an equivalent project of global empowerment.

For David Held the enemies of the nation-state are not other states, a dialectic and rationality, which encouraged the constitution of the nation-state from a consciousness of territory and conflict, but 'failed-states' and 'non-state actors' who cannot be fought off with traditional methods of state-on-state warfare but demand a collective and less territorial but global effort of intervention.[13] Equally the financial and ecological threats facing us today have cross state causes and consequences that cannot be dealt with by one state alone or in limited 'trading blocks' and inter-state affiliations. Motivated by this reality, Held proposes a cosmopolitan approach based on the autonomy of each person as a moral agent who exists within local affiliations and is willing and able to contribute in a collective political enterprise.[14] Cosmopolitanism thus sketched out is a political and a moral project that answers the social, economic, ecological and ethical problems of a divided world by considering its indivisibility, and that replaces the comfort and passive nature of national identity with a demand to participate, to be involved in the reality of both communities: that of one's birth, what we are as separate identities, and that of 'human argument and aspiration', of what we want to be together. In the following it becomes apparent that the two communities are entirely interlinked, they inter-are, since the identity of birth is itself not a natural state but a naturalized identity deformed and dominated by the conceptions of how we are together, which in turn and inevitably is determined by the powers at play in forming this naturalized identity of birth in the context of what Held terms the general 'asymmetry of the world':[15] the unequal distribution of life-chances in respect to access to education, healthcare, food and housing, and so on, which he terms 'entitlement capacities' that enable or disable the possibilities of political participation and present a requirement and form the basis of an equal interconnectedness.[16]

In relation to this it is interesting to note that one criticism of cosmopolitanism is the elitism of its historical origin. The fact that the humanist brotherhood aspired to by the Stoics is a very exclusive club: a cosmos of upper class, educated and free males, which in many ways resembles a contemporary global elite. Hence the argument could be made that the cosmos thus envisaged as a sociopolitical possibility has always been an actuality for those who share in a common humanity of their own devising comprised of money, property, influence and the control of women, children and lesser males, and whose morality might not be virtuous but is legitimized and protected by a judiciary fashioned in their own image. However, rather than dismiss the cosmopolitan project on this basis, it is exactly because of the unhindered 'cosmopolitanism' of the rich, of finance and of multinational corporations, that a reconsideration of its concept beyond their limited number and on a more sensorial footing gains in relevance today. If the powers that control our national identity have the fluidity of global finance and multinational trading that lack local accountability, morality and engagement, and if its consequences are the exploitation of labour, an inability to address climate change, forced migration, poverty and Held's asymmetrical world, our fixed patriotic positions do not seem to serve us too well in opposing them and turning 'nautonomy': the lack of equal participation, into the 'autonomy' of shared political empowerment and agency as 'the basis of non-coercive collective agreement and governance'.[17]

Within a fluid global context, entrenched positions can only ever help to pitch the regulations that aim to provide ecological safeguards, economic balances and rules of law within one nation-state against those of another, while leaving those operating beyond their shores and field of influence free to exploit and use their differences. This is why I accept Diogenes's invitation 'to be an exile from the comfort of patriotism and its easy sentiments, to see our own ways of life from the point of view of justice and the good'.[18] In order to, in other words, give ourselves a conceptual and actual position in the global sphere, which does not deny the significance of birth and belonging but is not entrenched in the expectations of a national identity; that shows us ourselves as entwined with the world and gives us a view on the conventions, habits and norms that inform our actions, so we can reframe them through inter-actions that can reach into the globality that controls the local and make another noise. This stance acknowledges the inevitability of my locality but appreciates the global influence of its construction. It answers the asymmetries between states and individuals by offering a new critical vocabulary and consciousness which takes into account and is aware of the danger of an idealist cosmopolitanism that presumes equal participation on an uneven playing field, and it eschews a realist cosmopolitanism that makes its viability dependent on institutional possibilities. Thus the cosmopolitan project I aim to promote through sound does not ignore the identity of birth, which might be incidental but has concrete consequences. Instead it understands those very consequences as the reason to urge participation in a global field to show its asymmetries and inequalities and make its terrain more evenly accessible to all. Additionally it does not focus on the institutional realities of a cosmopolitan democracy, but aims to make thinkable a materialist and aesthetic cosmopolitanism that articulates a contingent and boundless practice and consciousness rather than outcomes and particular methods.

To this end I argue that a sonic sensibility encourages the position of a 'local cosmopolitanism', a cosmopolitanism from the ground up as it were, that connects the world from my individual position, where ever that might be, without recourse to a certain identity or intention of a colonial charge but as an outward reach to seek contingent sense and value in the between-of-things. This local cosmopolitanism finds articulation and a practice in listening and sounding as a process of negotiating and inventing the in-between, the invisible connecting that is not 'this' or 'that', as things defined against each other, a matter of differences and similarities but is the moment of coincidence and of inter-invention: where what the world, the thing and the subject are is generated in their interaction that produces the possibility of their interactuality as a contingent reality with little recourse to habits and certainties, built instead from the generative capacity of the world and our capacity to participate in its production: from our locality on the invisible index of sound. In this way, listening and sounding bring to cosmopolitanism their insistence on the locale, the private life-world as a contingent place of habitation and engagement, and promote a phenomenological interbeing in the world as the negotiation of these life-worlds. In this sense listening and sounding suspend what things are separately and a priori, and focus on what they are together at the moment of their sonic encounter. This sonic practice at the interbeing of things provides doubt and uncertainty in the identity and recognition of their autonomous definition and that of the listener: allowing me to question myself and my own sounding-listening: finding in the heard the between-of-things, and gaining what Catherine Lu terms the 'recognition of their inherent complexity and permanent state of inner doubt and contestation rather than harmony'.[19]

Just as in Parreno's work strange and familiar elements produce each other in a mobile and invisible bind, so too the cosmopolitan imagination enables the co-production of the familiar and the unknown through their complex inter-agency, at once conflictual, playful and consensual. The indivisibility of a sonic volume presents a model for a cosmopolitan imagination. Listening to *Anywhen* allows us to imagine our co-habitation of a mobile and connected world. The carpet, fish, voices, light and screens are drawn together in the soundtrack that makes their interbeing apparent and accessible beyond visual associations and separate identifications in the invisible stretch of a sonic-between. In this conception they are not separate elements of an installation but building blocks of the cosmos of the work that as a form remains in doubt and as a content carries the contestation of its material. The elementality of each building block, its 'local' identity and source, is thereby not erased. To the contrary, the local is revealed and realized not as a transcendental referent, but in its contingent complexity through the contact and exchange with another. In this encounter, the fish do not have to remain fish according to a pregiven conception, the carpet does not have to limit itself to its defined self and purpose, the voices seize to ventriloquize and become their own sound, and the yeast becomes a parable and tool for the possibility of their interaction and the imagination of a 'collective enterprise'.

The work according to listening brings into focus its interactuality and enables the imagination of the interactuality of the world. It brings our existence as interbeings, our self as selves with others and with other things, to the practice of an 'aesthetic of interconnectedness' and makes its possibility accessible to a social and political imagination. Thus it contributes the participatory and generative ethics of listening to the condition of a cosmopolitan politics as a political possibility of sound.

Sound, as sonic material and sensibility, produces the political possibility of co-habitation and interactuality that makes thinkable the interconnectedness of the world as an invisible and mobile in-between, and makes audible '*the asymmetrical production and distribution of life-chances which limit and erode the possibilities of political participation*'.[20] Thus it offers the capacity for their re-imagination in a shared cosmos.

Hearing the in-between we become aware of the asymmetries of the world: what voices are heard, what accents dominate its landscape, what interests are represented in its soundscape and what in turn remains inaudible, unable to make itself count, silenced, muted even and ignored. In this sense, the silence of the inaudible is not a material but a political privation, which at least as concept is accessible. The inaudible creates no in-between but throws back at us our own echo, whose empty reverb should alert us to the fact that something remains unheard and should trigger a more earnest and curious listening out for an absent sound.

The virtuosity of listening is then not its skill, hearing the right thing, but its willingness to listen beyond the expected to hear what we might not know could sound. It is an ethics of participation that connects the actuality of sound and the impossibility of the unsound and appreciates their equal possibility in the multilayered sphere of the in-between.

Engaging with the invisible in-between, sonic cosmopolitanism responds to the asymmetries that hinder a true collective enterprise and disable its imagination, and makes appreciable the force and the possibility of a shared cosmos. In this sense, 'sonic cosmopolitanism' is a political and ethical project that brings the power of listening to the conditions of politics via the non-sense[21] of the sensorial encounter. Its sensate sense accesses the invisible dynamics of a global force and influence in the between-of-things and makes imaginable the audition of other connections: connecting the global not through finance, dominance and control, but from the contingent locale of listening and the continuous practice of expanding one's ears.

The worn cotton sheets of our little beds had the blurred texture of silk crêpe and when we lay against them in the evening we'd rub, rhythmically, one foot against the soothing folds of fabric waiting for sleep. That way we slowly wore through the thinning cloth. Our feet would get tangled in the fretted gap.

We walked through soft arcade. We became an architect.

The knitted cap on the wrinkled skull of the mewling kids is the first boundary. At the other tip the bootie dribbles. There are curious histories of shrouds. That is not all. Memory's architecture is neither palatial nor theatrical but soft ...

... Soft architecture will reverse the wrongheaded story of structural deepness. That institution is all doors but no entrances.[22]

Conclusion: Listening education

One of Nussbaum's key concerns in relation to cosmopolitanism is education. She remarks on the irrationality of teaching only from a singular point of view, which in her opinion, confirms 'the unexamined feeling that one's own preferences and ways are neutral and natural' and thus endorses rather than questions the geography of the world drawn in lines of national boundaries and cultural divisions that validate visually and permanently accidental and contingent turns of history and apportion them 'weight and unshakeable validity'.[23] Her emphasis on a civic education that takes account of and shows the interconnections rather than the separations of nations and cultures, promotes learning about the other from their point of view, their geography and history, as well as their culture so 'we may be capable of respecting their traditions and commitments'.[24]

While agreeing with Nussbaum's preference for a globalized teaching of geography and a cultural studies that breaches national boundaries, I feel myself rejecting her model as it retains the idea of a certain knowledge to be learnt, and preserves the stability of the identity of the pupil and its subject, which by necessity and unavoidably remains *his* subject. In its stead or additionally, I propose a teaching that does not rely on the shared foundations of a historico-geographical world, but delves into the shared contingency of its existence according to listening, where the secret that is at stake might be an understanding of the world as an invisible network of contingent and mobile connections that defy geographical mapping and historical canonization altogether and instead follow lines of doubt and uncertainty into the temporal negotiation of its indivisibility and our fragile selves.

Listening has an exploratory capacity that does not seek to know *about* the world but approaches learning as a practice, as a physical and continuous effort to understand momentarily and always again how to live in the between-of-things. Its aim is not to know definitively, but to engage through doubt in a temporary and sensorial knowing. A listening education makes a call for a contingent literacy of the in-between, to read the invisible patterns and tensions between things, to hear their connecting and gain the ability to understand, act and articulate the world as an indivisible and mobile sphere. However, listening we do not *read*. Its literacy is not that of a visual language, but of a diffuse and invisible materiality performed contingently and demanding reciprocation, and thus the comparison fails to convey the particularity of its process and can only hint at its location.

The ability to perceive the world created in the invisible patterns, tensions and dynamics between things, and to 'read' their connecting, presents a great advantage in a globalized world whose real dominant is finance and whose real threat is climate change, neither of which is held by borders and lines on a map, but moves freely while creating the lines of our fixed abodes. Contemporary forces of globalization are rarely locatable within the consciousness of a conventional visuality. To grasp their power and influence and effect our perception not as a reception but as an interaction and agency, a different access is needed. This is an access into the force of connecting that drives a global production, and affords us the view of its mechanisms and consequences, which makes an inter-invention at least thinkable. A sonic education as an aerobics of the exploratory capacity of the invisible, and as a literacy of the in-between aspires this access and generates social knowledge as a knowledge of interbeing, whose collectivity presents a political practice for a globalized world.

I do not focus on the fish, or the carpet or the lights, but perceive, in a conceptual and actual listening, their interactions, which create the space of the Turbine Hall as a volume, as an indivisible and expansive sphere, that as capacity enables my perception as an inter-invention of all I see in its aquatic light without offering recourse to a referent or an a priori sense. Soundwalks, listening exercises, sonic meditations, and so on, eschew the source, the border and the line, and hear the process and the encounter instead. They practice not a different knowledge but a different path to knowledge, where, as in Parreno's work, the 'honeyed' water grasps us into the volume *and slows our movements and words, amplifying their path rather than their destination; derailing us away from aims and signification into the process of meaning; and bringing awareness to our interbeing, our way of being as being together and from each other rather than apart and different.*

Engaging in the world through movements of connecting and taking apart of things that are not separate elements but building blocks of a common sphere – screens and speakers, lights and balloons, yeast and carpets – building between them the cosmos of the work, I practice its processes and interdependencies and come to understand the work through these movements rather than its things. However doubtful and uncertain the knowledge thus produced, this engagement places me in a better position to think and act in a global world. It enables me to articulate and respond to the influences and consequences of its forces on my locale from my own mobile positioning. In this regard, listening is a radical educational element in the realization of cosmopolitanism's political possibility. It avoids not only the a priori and the bias of seemingly neutral or natural knowledge, but also its replacement with another's fixed definition and presents a practical way into the world as an indivisible volume instead.

This exploration of the world as volume is always also an exploration of my own expanse, my own habits and prejudices, power and influence or marginality, exposed in the shape of the absent and reframed as invisible interbeing. Listening as a locational practice, even of recorded sound, will always carry with it my own fragile and doubtful reality, from which it negotiates a collective knowing of the invisible and mobile between of the heard. In this sense, the teaching of listening as a cosmopolitan sensibility and practice does not instruct and train a listening to the other as separate other, to learn about *their* geography and history, which remain *our* concepts of knowledge, but promotes a social knowing from our inhabiting of a common terrain that is complex and uneven, so we might hear in a common expanse the uncertain and fragile interactuality of the real and the asymmetry of our relationship with it.

Lu remarks on the unsurprising fact that the earliest cosmopolitans were medical writers who did not focus on the dominance of humans in a global network but commented on 'the physical and mental frailties of the human body and mind'. With reference to Shakespeare's dramatic identification of the human essence as dust, she suggests that 'the unity of humankind consists in this common human condition: a wretched, feeble and pitiable existence, marked by uncertainty, insecurity and eventually death'.[25] I see in this frailty and doubt not cause for despair but the beginning of an ethical participation in the volume of the world, which appreciates the limitations of the listener's locale and at the same time invests this knowledge not to retreat into its location but to practice its connection to the world. In this context, the 'I' is not itself only but is only itself. From the consciousness of this intractable limitation, I seek connections to the possibility of others and other things on the uneven plateau of a precarious and finite existence without meaning to find them, but to engage nevertheless in the process of searching as an ethical process of communality.

It is from this insight and acknowledgement of our own uncertain existence as an existence in the world that I can bring the phenomenological doubt of Merleau-Ponty to the cosmopolitan project so we might understand the negotiations of the cosmos as the practice of intersubjective doubt developed into a notion of 'interbeing doubt', where the reciprocity of perception extends beyond human agency into the agency of colour, shape, forms and things, and where the between is acknowledged to lay beyond vision in the sphere of their invisible connection that generates them in their possibility: 'Between the alleged colors and visibles, we would find anew the tissue that lines them, sustains them, nourishes them, and which for its part is not a thing, but a possibility, a latency and a *flesh* of things.'[26] Merleau-Ponty finds this 'new tissue' and 'flesh of things' through the suspension of the relationship between knowledge and its object, which he suggests 'contains neither the whole nor even the essential of our commerce with the world'.[27] Instead he urges us to place the expected and undisputed link between knowledge and the known in a more muted relationship with the world, to reconsider our faith in their natural connection and to question their dominant and singular position in relation to reason and truth. I understand him to propose the bringing into play of other possible absences, other in-betweens, which force an a priori knowledge to relinquish its status as the only possible truth, and allow other connections, other interbeings to bring about a different imagination. This effort is what he calls within the idea of the *ouverture au monde,* a practical and applied openness to the world through the reconsideration of the relationship between knowing and its object, which enables the 'finding anew' as the exploratory capacity of the in-between.[28] This openness suspends the known as a naturalized and naturalizing practice of the a priori and challenges the illusion of absolute, geographical, historical, and so on, knowledge in favour of an interrogation of reflection by experience, based on a centrifugal and thus a quasi-cosmopolitan being in the world. In this way, we are invited to question not only the content but also the categories and conditions of knowledge and the processes that interpret and translate it into a social truth.

While Merleau-Ponty rejects the idea of an *intermonde,* the intermundane space, 'where our gazes cross and our perceptions overlap', he does so because he rejects it as an a priori existence and possibility, not however as the possibility of an exploratory and intersubjective practice of perception performed through the suspension of normative knowledge relations and the doubt in perceptual faith.[29] The elaborated world he wants to take us to, through the intertwining of our lives with each other and with things, can contribute distrust in the a priori and doubt in perceptual faith to the cosmopolitan project, which in turn can open the world to connect beyond borders in a global sphere without already knowing it and without neglecting the locality of the private life-world from which every present knowledge comes to be built. Thus I take from his philosophy the doubt and the suspension of truth and read them within a sonic *ouverture au monde,* which promises to hear the connection between all things so we might experience and bring into the realm of knowledge the tissue that lines and nourishes all.

> My access to a universal mind via reflection, far from finally discovering what I always was, is motivated by the intertwining of my life with the other lives, of my body with the visible things, by the intersection of my perceptual field with that of the others, by the blending in of my duration with the other durations.[30]

I sit on the grey carpet, listening. I am part of the work and perceiving it. I experience it from my private life-world that is unavoidably connected with the life-worlds of others sitting, playing, necking and dozing on a greyness that seems like the concrete floor beneath but gives its built a different sense, putting into doubt my first impression and giving me a different view, but holding within this carpet still the relationship to the floor beneath on which as a fragile surface our life-worlds meet in interbeing.

Listening brings a phenomenological approach to cosmopolitanism, whereby its method of reduction, the suspension of habits of perception and the promotion of doubt in a naturalized reading of the world, taking the perceived out of context and reference, does not stand in contradiction to a cosmopolitan aim of outwards connecting. To the contrary, the reconsideration of the thing as a sonic thing through an epoché, the bracketing off of what it means a priori and as referenced source, enables the cosmopolitan drive towards a new connecting, overlapping and sharing of meaning and terrain. Once the fish does not sound as fish but as concrete material, the focus of my audition is not on its a priori fishness but on its temporal connecting, what it is with others rather than as fish. This is not to deny specificity, particular needs and claims, or to override the voice of the other, the unknown, the silenced and the unheard, but to acknowledge the politics of specificity: the narrative and the objectives through which something attained its particular role and definition, which carries the cause and consequence of a current need and claim.[31] Consequently, it is through the re-imagination of the 'how' of description and delineation and from the indivisible and concrete sphere of sound that other narratives and definitions become thinkable and gain a voice.

To hear the fish as a concrete sound I hear them as an equal part in a shared and viscous space where they can be what they are contingently and make their own claim in the world. The bracketing off of the fish from its source ensures that in our encounter we do not discover 'what it and what I were all along', but what we inter are in our encounter, so we might hear our autonomy, nautonomy, asymmetry or even our silence and inaudibility in the particular circumstance of our meeting and become able to access and articulate the dynamic rather than the outline of this specificity.

This articulation is importantly not a speaking on behalf of the other. It is not a ventriloquism that focuses on synchronicity and the curiosity of having a dummy speak. Rather, it is about the amplification of the unheard, the invisible and the incoherent, not through the referent that calls it, but from the concrete sound of its own voice. A sonic cosmopolitanism is not a speaking for but a hearing of. It practices a listening out not for the signifiers and the references of the other, whose meaning will inevitably be read within the criteria of the self but focuses on our meeting in the viscous expanse of sound where we are indivisibly together and negotiate what that makes us both contingently.

The alienation that we experience when we see Nina Conti, not moving her lips, nor those of her puppet, and yet the sound of their voices filling the space of the Turbine Hall, resembles the alienation that occurs 'when one's self-definition clashes with the way one is defined or categorized within the larger society'.[32] Her act and her voice are commandeered by the audiovisual recording that speaks for her and for the dummy. Their sounds are ventriloquized by the construct of the video. The fact that they are a ventriloquist act ironically emphasis the hijacking of their voices. Sitting in front of their oversized projection on screen I contemplate their gaze as they listen to their own voices that come back at them, defined and deformed by the playback system of the auditorium that is not that of the theatre they are in, but that of the Turbine Hall I am in. The voice off-screen confronts the viewer as listener with the absurdity of the displacement implicit in a priori definition: the camera, as ideological apparatus, speaking in their stead. Thus the dubbed representation of the ventriloquist act of stage craft, heard within Parreno's work as volume, makes available for contemplation the defining processes of a nominal reality and identity and provides the condition for a different imagination that includes the possible and even the as yet impossible voice. Within the concrete expanse of *Anywhen* I practice listening as a sensory-motor *ouverture au monde*, which finds contingent meanings in connecting and hears the voice that is not heard rather than speaking for it.

This is a listening practice that hears the in-between and does not only listen to what is audible but lends its ear also to the inaudible, which often does not lack in decibels, in sonic intensity, but in the ability to be heard and counted among what makes a valid sound. This as yet inaudible is accessed by an education that expands hearing beyond what seems audible, what is legitimate and conforms to expectation, and that hears in silence not the lack of sound but the echo of the unheard. It appreciates the need to participate and connect if I want to make my local identity count and invest my 'individual agency into collective political enterprises',[33] and it pursues doubt in preconceptions and a priori definitions to hear not only the dominant but 'the whole of our commerce with the world'.[34]

This outlines a phenomenological cosmopolitanism founded on the interbeing of life-worlds where the local, the personally significant, is not abandoned as a source for authentication but becomes the engine for living with others, and where the sensate sense of the in-between provides the basis for considering the real as the shared capacity for doubt, unreason and non-sense. It does not practice what we know to be true but what is possible to be real, and generates from that the volume of a present actuality.

Accordingly, a listening education, as I am proposing it here, teaches a focus on sensate sense. It is not rational or realist but possibilist and phenomenological: it creates unities of doubt that are practiced contingently in the interbeing of our lives and of things and expand the reality of our world into the possibility of its indivisible volume. This unity of doubt stands in contrast to Immanuel Kant's unity of rationality, which drives the Greek notion of cosmopolitanism into an Enlightenment age.[35] Kant's philosophy is according to Nussbaum, 'a profound defense of cosmopolitan values', and brings a reformist, optimistic and truly universalist pronouncement to a modern discussion of the common.[36] However, Kant's cosmopolitanism is not based on a unity of practical materiality and sense but on a shared rationality that finds it universality in the laws of nature from where he pursues the ideal 'of a kingdom of free rational beings'.[37] Consequently, while he writes about a common participation in law, hinting at a participatory drive, which makes his philosophy interesting in relation to a sonic cosmopolitanism, the reliance on the laws of nature compromise the contingency of this participation. The notion of the laws of nature that guide his cosmopolitanism are developed through the extension and critique of the laws of god, which recasts humanism as a monotheism that does not see the neutralization of its own stance, but takes it as a given and that does not take account of the ideology and exclusivity of its singular point of view, but pretends, by appealing to a humanist brotherhood, that the universality and accessibility of its position is mutual and equal.

> Kant stresses that the community of all human being in reason entails a common participation in law (*ius*), and, by our very rational existence, a common participation in a virtual polity, a cosmopolis that has an implicit structure of claims and obligations regardless of whether or not there is an actual political organization in place to promote and vindicate these.[38]

Thus while I recognize the radical reformist drive towards a modern cosmopolitanism as the basis for lasting peace in global togetherness, I reject its basis in a shared rationality since it feeds the illusion of universal thought, of borders, lines, divisions and separations while pretending we share in their negotiation equally.

This difference between a doubtful cosmos and the unity of reason to me is epitomized in the contrast between Seneca's claim, quoted in Nussbaum, to 'measure the boundaries of our nation by the sun', and Nussbaum's rephrasing that 'the air does not obey national borders'.[39] The first presents a scopic ideology that sees clear outlines and ownership and seeks to expand them into its own universals, while the latter practices the transgressive material of the ephemeral that cannot be measured but is felt on the feeble surface of one's own formless form that is local but connects into the possibility of a shared cosmos.

Kant develops the mainly moral ideas of the Stoics via the notion of a shared rationality.[40] By contrast, I understand phenomenology to be able to contribute to a practical interpretation and performance of cosmopolitanism via the sensate sense of the invisible, the ephemeral the fleeting and even the unheard. The possibility of a sonic cosmpolitanism is thus not a contradiction of universality but provides a generative critique and expansion of its principles and their ideological investment and naturalizing tendencies in reason. Listening pursues the universal and the shared not as a foundation but as a contingency of fragile and uncertain subjects and things that do not move with the agency of a single body but the agitation and inter-invention of an anxious plurality stirring within a connected and interdependent sphere. This allows for a political imagination beyond nationalism and the sovereign nation-state and without a priori identification of shared reason, or the colonialization, oppression and domination within a shared goal. Accordingly, a sonic cosmopolitanism does not practice a multiculturalism that is the adaption of plurality into one, hearing one voice, but the meeting of plural voices in an invisible, fleeting and uneven volume. Thus a sonico-phenomenological cosmopolitanism founded on the interbeing of private life-worlds practices the doubt of the in-between and explores an alternative conception of the world from the patterns, tensions and dynamics between things, and 'reads' their invisible connecting rather than the visual outline of objects.

What I promote then is not thinking beyond boundaries but without boundaries through the practice of being together in the volume of the 'air' of sound. Listening can provide one method for this practice, to attain and retain a focus of the processes of interconnection, to put into doubt the naturalized how of things, and to use this doubt as the engine for an affective volume within which we explore our intersubjectivity as an interbeing that via Nhat Hanh develops the 'moral duty' of cosmopolitanism into a 'participatory ethics', and that extends the experiential reciprocity of listening to all human beings to incorporate a duty towards and reciprocity with all things. The suggestion is that ethics as a participatory and contingent production in sound contributes to the critique and re-definition of the moral duty of a historical cosmopolitanism. Instead of referring rationality to natural laws and produce a 'kingdom of (moral) ends', the aquatic world of sound's cosmopolitanism generates a world citizenship in a shared and ephemeral volume without reason or a moral ground. Thus it critiques historical cosmopolitanism's foundationalist stance and dialectical drive, and serves to highlight the cause of its asymmetries while providing the condition to rethink them through ethics as action that includes what might seem irrational such as fish swimming in air and yeast deciding my playlist.

This is an anti-foundationalist practice that finds meaning as signifying, a process that cannot be completed in a finalistic sense but remains on trial. The focus is not on results, but on the sustained attitude of doubt and the desire for connecting as making sense. Therefore, the aim of a sonic cosmopolitanism, in as far as it has an aim at all, is not to suggest how each country, region or culture should become cosmopolitan. This is not a project of democratic politics and realization, nor is it about dominance and hegemony, an imposition of political institutions or governmental rules. Rather it is an aesthetic and material project of connecting, co-habiting and interbeing that arises from particular and local forms. It practices its co-relating with others and illuminates what we are together rather than how to remain apart. Sound makes visible, tangible and articulable the cosmopolitan idea, not as a firm democratic strategy and not as a utopian ideal, or in opposition to the idealism of the nation-state, but as an 'attitude of mind': as an appreciation of the world in its voluminous complexity and interdependency.[41] Not to suggest what the world should become, but to understand that it already is cosmopolitan; to comprehend its cosmos and to practice, to live and act, interact and agitate within this connected sphere.

A sonic cosmopolitanism in this sense is neither realist nor idealist, it does not presume an utopian global community and it has no concrete political, institutional or social strategies or outcomes. Instead it is an aesthetic and material consciousness that makes accessible the world as volume, as a sphere of interbeing, which, as concept and sensibility, contributes to the political imagination of shared resources and possibility, without defining its values or aims. In this sense cosmopolitanism is a sonic enterprise through which the material realizes and holds political intent and invites a participation in its possibility.

PS: Soundwalking

One of the conclusions reached through the soundwalks was that every curator should do soundwalks in the space or on the site or the non-sites they are curating at, in order for them not to curate places and things, artefacts, objects and relationships, but volumes: the invisible and ephemeral expanse that realizes the capacity of the work, its possibility and our possibility to experience it through our interbeing. To this conclusion I would like to add that the gallery visitor too needs to practice listening and sounding in the exhibition space, in order to hear in its diffuse volume the permeating and expansive indivisibility of the work extend into the expansive indivisibility of a world that defies the possibility of separation, collecting, naming and seeing of things, in favour of experience as creating the generative capacity of a shared sphere from the co-relational between-of-things.

Notes

1 Philippe Parreno in Tate Modern video interview, http://www.tate.org.uk/whats-on/tate-modern/exhibition/hyundai-commission/philippe-parreno-anywhen (accessed 24 April 2017).

2 This is an excerpt of one of the soundwalk scores, produced for the MA Sound Arts Students, London College of Communication in 2012. This project can be read about in more detail in the essay 'Soundwalking the Museum: A

Sonic Journey through the Visual Display', in *The Multisensory Museum, Cross-Disciplinary Perspectives on Touch, Sound, Smell, Memory, and Space*, Nina Levent and Alvaro Pascual-Leone (eds), Plymouth, UK: Rowman and Littlefield, 2014, pp. 119–30.

3 In *Listening to Noise and Silence* I discuss Maurice Merleau-Ponty's association of the complex unity of perception with the act of being honeyed to articulate the reciprocity of being in sound:

> Honey is a slow-moving liquid; while it undoubtedly has a certain consistency and allows itself to be grasped, it soon creeps slyly from the fingers and returns to where it started from. It comes apart as soon as it has been given a particular shape, and what is more, it reverses the roles, by grasping the hands of whoever would take hold of it.

> (Maurice Merleau-Ponty, *The World of Perception*, London and New York: Routledge, 2008, p. 41.)

4 Jean-Luc Nancy, *Listening*, New York: Fordham University Press, 2007, p. 5.

5 'Everything coexists with this sheet of paper. That is why I think the word inter-be should be in the dictionary. To be is to inter-be. You cannot just *be* by yourself alone. You have to inter-be with every other thing. This sheet of paper is because everything else is' (Thich Nhat Hanh, *The Pocket Thich Nhat Hanh*, ed. Melvin McLeod, Boston and London: Shambhala Pocket Classics, 2012, p. 57).

6 My focus on 'ethics', rather than on 'morality', and the reference to both these two terms throughout this essay signals not their presumed equivalence but is a deliberate stance, outlining the participatory and contingent ethics of a sonic cosmopolitanism, against a morality of natural laws and as moral duty that is outlined in a historical cosmopolitanism.

7 Parreno, Tate Modern video interview.

8 Ibid.

9 Pauline Oliveros, *Deep Listening a Composer's Sound Practice*, Lincoln, NE: iUniverse, 2005, p. 44. Published with permission of The Pauline Oliveros Trust paulineoliveros.us.

10 David Held, *Cosmopolitanism, Ideals and Realities*, Cambridge, UK: Polity, 2010, p. 39.

11 Garrett Wallace Brown and David Held, *The Cosmopolitanism Reader*, Cambridge, UK: Polity, 2010, p. 1.

12 Martha Nussbaum, 'Patriotism and Cosmopolitanism', in *The Cosmopolitan Reader*, Garrett Wallace Brown and David Held (eds), Cambridge, UK: Polity, 2010, p. 157.

13 In Georg Wilhelm Friedrich Hegel's *Philosophy of History*, the engine of history is identified as the dialectical conflict between Freedom and Necessity. In its drive, individual communities, or later nation states, develop their independence and freedom through a circular violence of conflict, subjugation, conquered territory and further conflict. The individual too is subjugated to the state, which is 'the Divine Idea as it exists on Earth' (G. W. F. Hegel,

Philosophy of History, New York: Dover Publishing, 2004, p. 39). This implies an overcoming, sublation of individual will and inner necessity to achieve freedom as the coincidence of state with moral principle. Individual will, that of subjects, and that of other communities or nation states, are to be reconciled into the morality of the state. Thus history becomes a contest between nations.

Hegel's philosophy draws a progressive historical consciousness from boyhood to adolescence to manhood observed from the ancient Greeks to Modernity. This decidedly masculine progression implies an idealism that as intuition and drive determines historical development towards a transcendental Ideal Objectivity, the sublation of weaker factions, on a rationale of violence and expansion, which always depends on defeating and subjugating another.

In order not to continue this dialectical progression, the cosmopolitan project has to step outside this dialectic circularity. It cannot be seen as its logical next step, a further advancement in a dialectical chain towards ideality. Instead, it has to establish a common ground outside of history, with a new terminology, imagination and a nonheritable heritage to avoid comparison to empire, rule and territory as subjugating Universalisms, and promote the consciousness of a shared cosmos: to pool resources, produce a collaborative frame to deal with conflict, scarcity, global warming, epidemics and so on.

14 Held, *Cosmopolitanism, Ideals and Realities*, p. 15.

15 According to Held equal participation understood as ideal 'autonomy', measured in the equal distribution of life-chances, connected to access to education, health care, water and so on, can be considered in relation to its opposite 'nautonmy', *'the asymmetrical production and distribution of life-chances which limit and erode the possibilities of political participation'* (David Held, *Democracy and the Global Order, From the Modern State to Cosmopolitan Governance*, Cambridge, UK: Polity, 1995, p. 171).

16 'Entitlement capacities' are rights that create space for action while not curtailing and infringing on the liberty and rights of others (Held, *Democracy and the Global Order,* p. 154).

17 David Held, 'Principles of Cosmopolitan Order', in *The Cosmopolitan Reader*, Garrett Wallace Brown and David Held (eds), Cambridge, UK: Polity, 2010, p. 231.

18 Nussbaum, 'Patriotism and Cosmopolitanism', p. 157.

19 Catherine Lu continues this passage by considering the consequences of 'the desire to reduce this conflict, and to solidify loyalty to one cause or group', the desire to lose doubt and find harmony, as an attempt to reduce the multiplicity. She understands this desire to have historically and in our time resulted in the 'forced uprooting of entire groups and the whittling down of complex individual personalities into thin shadows' ('The One and Many

Faces of Cosmopolitanism', *Journal of Political Philosophy*, vol. 8, no. 2 [2000]: 257–8). In relation to this reduction of conflict via homogeneity and enforced universals, she evokes the shadows of fascism and the ethnic cleansing of Jews, Albanians, Serbs, Tutsis, Hutus and so on. In response, she promotes a cosmopolitanism that is complex and that recognizes at once a shared suffering, humanity as one, as well as the distinctly individual nature of this suffering. Suggesting that cosmopolitanism is not a matter of harmonization but of recognizing complex difference, she suggests that the cosmopolitan perspective promotes the ability to recognize in the human condition our irreducible difference.

20 Held, *Democracy and the Global Order*, p. 171.

21 In a collection of his essays brought together in the book *Sense and Non-Sense* (1964), Merleau-Ponty articulates 'non-sense' not in reference to rational sense, as its nonsensical opposite, but as a sense that comes out of 'sensation'.

22 Lisa Robertson, 'Soft Architecture: A Manifesto', in *Occasional Work and Seven Walks from the Office of Soft Architecture*, Ontario, Canada: Coach House Books, 2011, pp. 18 and 21.

23 Nussbaum, 'Patriotism and Cosmopolitanism', p. 159.

24 Ibid., p. 160.

25 Lu, 'The One and Many Faces of Cosmopolitanism', p. 254.

26 Maurice Merleau-Ponty, *The Visible and the Invisible*, Evanston, IL: Northwestern University Press, 1968, pp. 132–3.

27 Ibid., p. 35.

28 'We will miss that relationship – which we shall here call the openness upon the world (ouverture au monde) – the moment that the reflective effort tries to capture it, and we will then be able to catch sight of the reasons that prevent it from succeeding, and of the way trough which we would reach it' (Merleau-Ponty, *The Visible and the Invisible*, pp. 35–6).

29 Ibid., p. 48.

30 Ibid., p. 49.

31 Held, *Democracy and the Global Order*, p. 171.

32 David Graeber, *Direct Action and Ethnography*, Edinburgh and Oakland, CA: AK Press, 2009, p. 524.

33 Held, *Cosmopolitanism, Ideals and Realities*, p. 15.

34 Merleau-Ponty, *The Visible and the Invisible*, p. 35.

35 Nussbaum suggests that the Greek idea of the world citizen is the source for Kant's 'kingdom of ends', which interprets 'kingdom' as 'the systematic union of several rational beings through common laws' and outlines the definition of its 'ends', as the abstraction of difference and private concerns or actions in the service of a common moral necessity. Together they construct a 'kingdom of ends' as a kingdom of rational beings functioning under the rationality

of shared objective laws 'because what these laws have as their purpose is precisely the reference of these being to one another, as ends and means' (Immanuel Kant, *Groundwork of the Metaphysics of Morals*, trans. Mary Gregor and Jens Timmermann, Cambridge, UK: Cambridge University Press, 2012, p. 45).

36 Martha Nussbaum, 'Kant and Cosmopolitanism', in *The Cosmopolitan Reader*, Garrett Wallace Brown and David Held (eds), Cambridge, UK: Polity, 2010, p. 28.

37 Ibid., p. 33.

38 Nussbaum, 'Kant and Stoic Cosmopolitanism', *Journal of Political Philosophy*, vol. 5, no. 1 (1997): 12.
Kant's brotherhood, in reason, assumes a shared rationality and morality, which is given rather than generated and whose legitimation in laws of nature, which take over from the laws of God, prevents a discussion on its authorship and bias, and thus prevents a consideration of the foundation and conditions of its practical institution. It assumes an unquestioned fit between laws of nature and human morality: 'every rational being, as an end in itself, must be able to view itself as at the same time universally legislating with regard to any law whatsoever to which it may be subject, because it is just this fittingness of its maxims for universal legislation that marks it out as an end in itself' (Kant, *Groundwork of the Metaphysics of Morals*, trans. Mary Gregor and Jens Timmermann, Cambridge, UK: Cambridge University Press, 2012 [1785], p. 49).

39 Nussbaum, 'Patriotism and Cosmopolitanism', pp. 157 and 160.

40 In her text 'Kant and Stoic Cosmopolitanism', Nussbaum argues how Kant, although mentioning the Stoics only in a brief and general way, develops his cosmopolitanism from their notion of 'world citizenship', adopted from the Cynics, and developed as a moral concern connected to a shared rationality, rather than a matter of particular identity and belonging. 'According to the Stoics, the basis for human community is the worth of reason in each and every human being' (p. 7). She identifies their influence on Kant's cosmopolitanism not in an outline of institutional or practical goals but in the moral and rational core of their ideas.

41 H. C. Baldry quoted by Lu, 'The One and Many Faces of Cosmopolitanism', p. 245.

References

Brown, Garrett Wallace and David Held (eds), *The Cosmopolitan Reader*, Cambridge, UK: Polity, 2010.

Goldblatt, David, Review of 'At the Limits of Political Possibility: The Cosmopolitan Democratic Project', *New Left Review*, vol. 1, no. 225 (September–October 1997): 140–50.

Graeber, David, *Direct Action and Ethnography*, Edinburgh and Oakland, CA: AK Press, 2009.

Hegel, Georg Willhelm Friedrich, *Philosophy of History*, trans. J. B. Sibree, New York: Dover Publishing, 2004 (orig. lectures given 1822–1830).

Held, David, *Cosmopolitanism, Ideals and Realities*, Cambridge, UK: Polity, 2010.

Held, David, *Democracy and the Global Order, From the Modern State to Cosmopolitan Governance*, Cambridge, UK: Polity, 1995.

Held, David, 'Principles of Cosmopolitan Order', in *The Cosmopolitan Reader*, Garrett Wallace Brown and David Held (eds), Cambridge, UK: Polity, 2010, pp. 229–47.

Kant, Immanuel, *Critique of Pure Reason*, trans. Friedrich Max Müller and Marcus Weigelt, London: Penguin Classics, 2007 [1781].

Kant, Immanuel, *Groundwork of the Metaphysics of Morals*, trans. Mary Gregor and Jens Timmermann, Cambridge, UK: Cambridge University Press, 2012, [1785].

Lu, Catherine, 'The One and Many Faces of Cosmopolitanism', *Journal of Political Philosophy*, vol. 8, no. 2 (2000): 244–67.

Merleau-Ponty, Maurice, *Sense and Non-Sense*, trans. Hubert L. Dreyfus and Patricia Allen Dreyfus, Evanston, IL: Northwestern University Press, 1964.

Merleau-Ponty, Maurice, *The Visible and the Invisible*, Evanston, IL: Northwestern University Press, 1968.

Merleau-Ponty, Maurice, *The World of Perception*, trans. Oliver Davis, London and New York: Routledge, 2008.

Nancy, Jean-Luc, *Listening*, trans. Charlotte Mandell, New York: Fordham University Press, 2007.

Nhat Hanh, Thich, *The Pocket Thich Nhat Hanh*, ed. Melvin McLeod, Boston and London: Shambhala Pocket Classics, 2012.

Nussbaum, Martha, 'Kant and Stoic Cosmopolitanism', *Journal of Political Philosophy*, vol. 5, no. 1 (1997): 1–25.

Nussbaum, Martha, 'Kant and Cosmopolitanism', in *The Cosmopolitan Reader*, Garrett Wallace Brown and David Held (eds), Cambridge, UK: Polity, 2010, pp. 27–44.

Nussbaum, Martha, 'Patriotism and Cosmopolitanism', in *The Cosmopolitan Reader*, Garrett Wallace Brown and David Held (eds), Cambridge, UK: Polity, 2010, pp. 155–62.

Oliveros, Pauline, *Deep Listening a Composer's Sound Practice*, Lincoln, NE: iUniverse, 2005.

Parreno, Philippe, Tate Modern video interview, http://www.tate.org.uk/whats-on/tate-modern/exhibition/hyundai-commission/philippe-parreno-anywhen.

Robertson, Lisa, 'Soft Architecture: A Manifesto', in *Occasional Work and Seven Walks from the Office of Soft Architecture*, Ontario, Canada: Coach House Books, 2011, pp. 11–22.

Voegelin, Salomé, *Listening to Noise and Silence: Towards a Philosophy of Sound Art*, New York: Bloomsbury, 2010.

Voegelin, Salomé, 'Soundwalking the Museum: A Sonic Journey through the Visual Display', in *The Multisensory Museum, Cross-Disciplinary Perspectives on*

Touch, Sound, Smell, Memory, and Space, Nina Levent and Alvaro Pascual-Leone (eds), Plymouth, UK: Rowman and Littlefield, 2014, pp. 119–30.

Work

Parreno, Philippe, *Anywhen*, Hyundai Commission at Tate Modern, London, October 2016–2 April 2017.

Geographies of sound: Performing impossible territories

*This poem was written by a sailor and i am on the
ocean while writing this*
Steve Roggenbuck[1]

A geography of sound has no maps; it produces no cartography. It is the geography of encounters, misses, happenstance and events: invisible trajectories and configurations between people and things, unfolding in the dimension of the actual while formlessly forming the dimensions of its possibility, and secretly performing the impossible territories of a poet on the night-time sea – on the ocean in the dark, she hears the rhythms and textures that are the material and content of an invisible terrain that leaves no trace and holds no certainty beyond its experience on the body as a material among things. These textures and rhythms can't be measured and drawn on a flat surface to make maps or a score. They can't be rendered visible but hold a knowledge of the world that lies in its invisible contingency: in its capacity as a timespace place not to refer back to the dialectic – the opposition between time and space, whose purpose and ideology furnish the visible and produce its bias for division, control and definition – but to perform its indivisibility in the voluminous movement of a watery earth. Thus we have to enter into its undulations, to feel our bodies perform the geography of waves, the volume of water and the fragile connections between all that moves in its dark expanse.

This is the geography also of Arturas Bumsteinas's piece *Night on the Sailship* (2013), a composition that is based on the recordings of theatre noise machines and refers to the fact that 'in the old days of theatre the technical crew had to be trained as sailors in order to operate the complicated rigging mechanisms of the coulisse machinery.'[2] The stagehand-cum-sailor is a 'technician of space'.[3] Her seafaring imagination has an effect on the place created. She navigates through the night where a place can emerge that is not bound to the shore as line and boundary, as recognizable symbol and sign of territory and land. Instead a dark geography unfolds that mobilizes space, generates environments and reveals their depth.

Bumsteinas's piece invites us into a movement of things that seem to share a rhythm and a place but pull and push on its configuration and shape. Its sounds remain without a firm ground or a steady line, as fragments and events coinciding and passing each other by, expanding and contracting an invisible territory made from their performance, the materiality of things and the practice of listening. They wrestle with the uneven and mobile terrain that they create themselves, and rather than trying to find a ground beyond themselves in which their sounds play out, their groundless ground is their coincidence and simultaneity as the contingent place they create. Thus they evoke the imagination of a geography of ephemeral and unseen lands produced on board a blind ship at sea. This unseen view meets Steve Roggenbuck's poetry, quoted earlier, in the movements of its practice: at once the location and duration of what it is, rather than anywhere else. This is a generative and also fragile geography. It is a geography that enables a different imagination and insight into how and where things are and move, providing a different focus and demanding a different vocabulary of how to speak of the physical organization of this world.

This demand is important not just aesthetically but also politically, since, spatial imaginaries, as Doreen Massey reminds us, are powerful and have the capacity to influence political consciousness and agency: 'the way we imagine space has effects'.[4] It has an effect on our geographical subjectivity, our sense of where we belong and what belonging might mean; on the way we understand our distances and proximities; the manner in which we experience frontiers and openness, and the way in which we perceive our trajectory and being to have or fail to have an impact on the construction of place. For Massey the vision of global space, the cartography of its territory and movement, 'is not so much a description of how the world is, as an image in which the world is being made'.[5] Geography is not a neutral notation of territory, space and void, but a conquering of its possibilities that is enabled and framed by the impossibilities of its own technology of representation.

For Michel Foucault space is geographical as well as strategic. Conventional geography is born from a military thinking, from the desire to command and administrate space.[6] Consequently it is important to consider the authorship and ideology of its representation, to investigate its sociopolitical interests and to understand its perspectives and aims, and come to appreciate the normativity of its absolute vision of the world as the *hyper-invisibility* of visual language left unquestioned, before we are won over entirely by the certainty of its singular point of view and become unable to enter the geographical rhythms of a ship moving in the dark blue sea.[7]

To resist the persuasive singularity of geography, this essay seeks to engage in geography via sound, a sonic sensibility and listening, without making any claims about the scientific methods or technologies of the discipline. Instead, the notion of geography as an integrated study of the world is taken as a philosophical and conceptual activity that enables the reconsideration of geographical knowledge understood via Foucault as the pouvoir and savoir of spatiality: the expression of 'knowledge' of space at once as 'capacity to' and 'expertise of' that furnishes one reality with the power to be real.

> Dès lors qu'on peut analyser le savoir en termes de région, de domaine, d'implantation, de déplacement, de transfert, on peut saisir le processus par lequel le savoir fonctionne comme un pouvoir et en reconduit les effets.[8]

This conflation of *savoir* and *pouvoir* in the constitution of space renders geography political and provides an incentive to reimagine the conditions of living in and perceiving the world as a sphere of possibility. I will investigate this sphere of possibility as a sphere of sound engaged in relation to the thought processes, perspectives and foci that geography pursues rather than the land that it (un)covers. In this way, geography as an applied philosophy of space and time, social actions and material configurations lends a framework and context to the investigation of the ephemeral territories of a sonic world beyond the purpose of its discipline and without the power of a singular knowledge determining its reality. Thus geography does not remain the study of the world we consider to be actual, its territorial, social, economic, and so forth, reality but comes to practice the exploration of possible worlds: naming and defining alternative measures, shapes and forms; discussing their interrelation, simultaneity and truth untethered from the political duality of expertise (savoir) and capacity (pouvoir) that determines the influence of actual knowledge.

Therefore this essay pursues a geography of sound rather than a sonic geography. Its listening does not tune into the actual, but hears its variants. It does not seek to hear the sonic as part of the discipline, contributing an auditory layer to its scientific work, but aims to establish the geographical imagination of a different world, ostensibly practicing the geography of sonic possible worlds: a geography of the worlds we hear in the textures and rhythms, movements and stillness that produce the invisible slices of the actual world, but which are not reduceable to its measure or the duality of its knowledge, and instead drive towards a different imagination of an intangible and unconquerable terrain of mobile things.

These sonic worlds are not parallel worlds, fictional untruths or illusions, but are the variants of our actual reality that need a geography to practice and articulate their invisible territories, immaterial things and unseen activities; to give them legitimacy and make them count as knowledge and as power of the real. The aim is not to incorporate them into the measure of a visual world, nor to simply add listening and sound to the subject of geography. Rather the aim is to reimagine the reality of the discipline and the reality of the world from the possibility of sonic lands by practising their invisible variants.

This move away from sonic geography into a geography of sound does not avoid the real, but circumnavigates its biases, measures and histories. It is also not a retreat into an essentialized world, or a denial of its multi-sensoriality, and it does not propose a dialectical world view, reinvigorating via sound and image the dichotomy between time and space. Rather, it is an acknowledgement of the persuasiveness and implicit ideology of a visual point of view – the seduction of its apparent completeness and the power of its reality – and expresses the desire to add another knowledge: a possible knowledge that does not insist on its singularity but proposes to perform contingently the invisible slices of the world from which the world draws the political possibilities for a future design that can contradict and rethink the images that have been made for it.

Ultimately, maybe the geography of sonic possible worlds can add its insights, strategies and ideas to geographical practices and their interpretation. To help establish what Philip Boland, Jonathan Prior, Michael Gallagher, Anja Kanngieser and David Matless, among others, call a sonic geography, but which always remains on dry land, on maps and within the measurable. Thus it might not, and it might instead show that a geography of sound proposes a wholly different knowledge of the world that might conflict with the very aims of the discipline.

To conjure this possible geographical imagination this essay considers the work of Jacqueline Kiyomi Gordon, contemplating from the participation in her installation *Inside You is Me, July/Surface Substance* a social-geography as proposed by Massey, and debating the experience of its invisible volume as a sphere of performing and unperforming the representation of geography as discussed by Nigel Thrift. Both Massey's discussion of space as configuration of movements and narratives, and Thrift's promotion of performance to challenge the abstract knowledge of geography, aid the articulation of a geography of sound as a geography of the unknown that resists the hyper-invisibility of conventional reality in favour of the real unseen of sound. I will suggest that this unseen sphere of sound is where the political possibilities of geography can be rethought, beyond the givens that underlie its representational schemata through the ephemeral occurrences that transform the landscape invisibly.

I go on to perform such invisible transformations in the anxious geography of *Uneasy Listening* (2014), a piece by Susan Schuppli and Tom Tlalim that tests the tolerance and scope of the unseen. Their work, a 5.1 composition of drone surveillance, pulls the sky, the ground and the underground into the political domain of geographical science, and brings to experience the slices of a geographical imagination as they are articulated by Eyal Weizman's politics of verticality: his notion of the landscape as a three-dimensional matrix that can be used to divide an 'indivisible territory'.[9]

By listening to and walking these works, as a doing of geography, I follow Erin Manning and Brian Massumi and run interference into the discipline: employing the outside of geography as a 'generative environment' where the notion of space and time, place and map 'is uneasy because always in the encounter'.[10] Manning and Massumi discuss philosophy rather than geography. They articulate its possibility to make art, its movement, thought and practice felt rather than cast in a predefined language. But their sense of interference, transgression and generative intentions can be employed across disciplines to regenerate the environment of geography also. Their aim is not to describe but to activate, to produce the rhythms of creative practice in philosophy. My aim similarly is to activate a geography of sound, to produce its knowledge not as maps and borders, but as rhythms, textures, materials and subjectivities.

Travelling transformations: Narratives as geographies of the in-between

I am writing this essay in Madrid, in a hotel room, performing exactly the geographical of academics who Massey, in her essay 'Power Geometry and a Progressive Sense of Place' (1996), describes as the privileged travellers, for whom movement always happens in relation to nice hotel rooms and the certainty of a home to go back to. This movement within certainty confirms Heidegger's Heim, as the functional dwelling and home that realizes the purpose of being and stands in opposition to migration and flux.[11] Thus it confirms the possibility of a geography of Heim, as land and ground; as territory and surface for an indigenous production and certainty. Massey objects that the discourse of this privileged traveller does not take into account the anxiety of enforced movement, the precarity of living in flux without the stabilizing port of home or the comfort of a paid for hotel; without the sense of authenticity and belonging afforded by the coincidence of roots and territory and their cartographic legitimation. By contrast, the geography of migration is drawn not on the map but against its stable grid, performing invisible instability and plural unseens.

In *Listening to Noise and Silence* (2010), my consideration of geography and space as timespace started from this appreciation of the subjective situation and situatedness, as a physical and political manifestation of power or disempowerment, in relation to a geographical truth. There I recognized and theorized the relativity of fixity and fluidity and sought to find a less dichotomous articulation via the agonistic and playful mobility of sound.[12]

I still agree with Massey's insistence on particularity and circumstance and with her understand geography as a sociopolitical terrain of multiple perspectives. Thus I continue my focus on listening and sounding to articulate the contingency of being in the world as a practice of its plural geographies. In fact, the current political and media manipulations towards sociopolitical homogeneity, where, as suggested by Jacques Rancière, differences are excluded and conflicts denied through 'the simple nullity of the impossibility of the impossible', render the need to consider personal positions of travel and home, enforced stasis or desperate flux, more apparent and pressing even.[13] This emphasis on personal narratives does not aim to render this a human-centred endeavour, an anthropogeography that charts the world through human movement and stasis, however. To the contrary, the particularizing of geography as contingent narratives and experiences – an 'unmapping' of territory and a 'mapping' of the variants of this world – makes room for the multiplicitous positions, fluid and static, human and non-human, that hover over, under, beside and within any visual map as its invisible possibilities.

Listening and sounding join Rancière's discussion of the consensus system of reality, where realism is managed and curbed governmentally within the order of 'police logic' – Foucault's military logic of geography – where all reality and all truth is absorbed 'in the category of the only thing possible', and provide glimpses of the impossible.[14] A geography of sound, as the geography of invisible, mobile and plural slices of the world, questions the singularity a consensual reality purports and challenges the power of its administration and governance. Therefor it includes human and non-human narratives to create not a system but a practice of knowledge that considers simultaneous, plural and potentially contradictory realities to be true, and that recognizes the truth of the simple possibility of the impossible. It does so not to be needlessly contradictory and unnecessarily anarchic, but because the continued belief in the singularity of the real is an expediency that we cannot afford if we want to understand the world there is rather than the image we have made of it.

In her book *For Space* (2005), Massey introduces the need to 'imagining space as the sphere of the possibility of the existence of multiplicity' as one of her three key propositions for a spatiality that is not always already conceptualized in relation to political power but producing it: generating it as a sphere of coexistence and plurality that 'enables in the first instance an opening up to the very sphere of the political' as a politics not of instrumentality and consensus but of process and conflict.[15] This multiplicity is simultaneous, creating a map of temporal trajectories and configuring space as the uneasy encounters that Manning and Massumi propose to lie in the generative environment of philosophy's outside. This generative outside is the outside also of my geography, and thus it is the sphere of possibility that I believe a geography of sound explores: the simultaneity of voices, rhythms, textures, noises and silences that create the geographical configurations of sonic possible worlds that bring with them an opening up to the political that is not that of the strategic and historical but is the political possibility of the invisible, the plural and the conflictual, or what Massey terms the 'simultaneity of stories-so-far'.[16]

For Massey the multiple 'narratives, stories, trajectories are all suppressed in the emergence of science as the writing of the world'.[17] The science of geography depersonalizes and denarrativizes space as the individual experience is overridden by graphs, maps, charts and facts, which are more factual but probably less true, and come to produce the truth from their own abstracted imagination. For her the notion of travel and stories rather than maps can evoke transformation and avoid the closure of spaces within representation in favour of their conceptualization as simultaneous 'time-slices' which are space's dimensions of activity.[18]

Her notion of time-slices is developed in critique of Henri Bergson's conception of the 'quantitative divisibility' of space into discreet and chronological multiplicities: 'Movement visibly consists in passing from one point to another, and consequently in traversing space.'[19] This assumes space as an always already existing whole through which we pass, applying our time to its static expanse, moving along its infinite but separate nodes without affecting its duration. Consequently, as Massey points out, space remains infinitively divisible: a discrete multiplicity without time, static and representable. In response, she suggests the perception of space more akin to Bergson's time, as instantaneous sections that possess their own vitality and duration and do not function as discreet multiplicities but in their inter-connecting. In other words, she proposes space as a 'dynamic simultaneity' of variant time-slices, which configure not an already inter-connected whole but are engaged in the process of connecting that is unfinished and open, that knows no ground or surface, but understands its multiplicity to be concurrent and mobile: producing space as the indivisible continuum of temporal activities and infra activities.[20]

Her time-slices are not identical to and yet they are thinkable as the slices of possibility, which I articulated as sonic possible worlds, as modal entities that are not worlds per se but are each one slice of the many slices that make up the world.[21] These slices generate the world as a sphere of variant activities and inter-activities, and produce not a map but an invisible and indivisible volume of what we might call simultaneous 'timespace-slices' through which we inter-are, inter-act and inter-invent a contingent geography. The travels of the refugee and the travels of the academic happen in this same volume, understood as a timespace signed not by boundaries and borderlines but as a dimensionality that has a capacity: the capacity of the world and the capacity of our living within its organization. This is an invisible geographical volume that provides us with the terminology and the imagination for the experience of the world as a mobile and viscous expanse that enables and holds our agency and that of things, without visible boundaries in a generative and reciprocal embrace. In this invisible geographical volume the lives and movements of the academic and that of the refugee meet and produce the actuality of their in-between. They inter-are, one in relation to the other, and yet this inter-agency is asymmetrical, defining very different geographies of entitlement and belonging. They narrate two different modes of being in the same world and reciprocally create two variant worlds through their being in it; and it is the invisible in-between of these two variant worlds, rather than one or the other that narrates the political actuality from the possibilities and aware of the impossibilities which that encounter brings to the fore. The refugee might be an academic and the academic an immigrant, and so the difference is not total but incomplete, a narrative rather than a fact, visually deceptive but always a politico-geographical possibility.

Writing this essay in a hotel room in Madrid is an activity that highlights this in-between, generating geography as a moving and relational field of experience that we perform and unperform, that we are performed by, enabled and limited through. In this way, a geography of sound is not the study of territory, land, visual relationships and boundaries, economic and social interests and facts, but the study of the indivisible volume of the world as a dimensionality in which things inter-are and where the in-between rather than this or that creates the political possibility of its reality.

The geography of plastic, carpets, curtains and metal

Jacqueline Kiyomi Gordon's work *Inside You is Me, July/Surface Substance* produced with dancer and choreographer Sonya Levin for 'Geometry of Now', curated by Mark Fell at GES-2 in Moscow in 2017, creates such a dimensionality in whose sphere of materialities and subjectivities the possibility of a geography of sound can be imagined and performed. The location of the exhibition is an old power station situated along the Moskva river in central Moscow. It is a vast and dilapidated building soon to be renovated into a state-of-the-art gallery, narrating a process of transformation that itself performs the mobile and consequential geography of the world.[22]

Kiyomi Gordon's installation was located on the second floor of the building sharing space with what was called the 'reading room', a corner installation of books and texts chosen by Fell and laid out on a table to invite the visitors' engagement in the background interests that motivated the exhibition programme. This reading table created an expectation of research, of process rather than outcome, which introduced Kiyomi Gordon's piece, at the other end of the space, by tuning us into its processes rather than the finished work.

Visually *Inside You is Me, July/Surface Substance* is very sculptural. Taking on the tones and materials of its environment it responds with fourteen aluminum frames that are over 2 metres long and high, and are draped with carpet, curtain fabric and transparent silicon sheeting. These frames are on castors that extend their height and indicate their mobility as a sculpture in process, on trial, rather than fixed and certain of itself, defying the notion of static architecture and building a room of potential time.

The materials that are held by these sculptural frames complete and contradict each other, reflecting and absorbing light and sound, blending in and standing out from their sparse architectural surround. They break the space and make a space, adding other surfaces and textures and creating 'in-between places' that I hear as undulations on my walk through. They bring other possibilities to the experience of this room and my movements through it, challenging interpretations that might arise from the consideration of the floorplan or the installation shot. Both of which tell me where the work is and what it looks like, but cannot reveal its depth and those elements that remain hidden in a visual or cartographic representation of its installation.

Fourteen speakers are suspended from the ceiling. Their black oblongs add another sculptural dimension to the work, responding to the shine of the aluminium frames and the transparency of the silicon sheets, and contrasting with the muted colours and textures of the beige carpet and draped curtain cloth. The sounds emanating from the speakers are composed from files recorded on a modal synth elsewhere and at another time, and are distributed and filtered here via a Max Patch. They are imported into this space and interact with its materialities to reveal a volume of reflective surfaces and the absorbing expanse of carpets and cloth. Rather than confirming the reality of walls, windows, ceilings and floors, as additive entities of the place's construction, they create a sense of the space from the invisible in-between of things: from the inter-connecting timespace slices that I hear in my walking through.

The sounds are not interactive in a technologically enabled manner, but interact and inter-invent the space by their own response to the sculptural walls, the architectural surfaces and the bodies that move around them. This interbeing of textures, material and physical rhythms is performed by dancers who move around and between the frames, following instructions and following other sounds in search for their in-between, to perform the location of its coincidence.

> Move around the space and find locations where you may hear clearly two or more different types of sounds. Chose one sound to embody Switch to another sound or combine two sounds
>
> Find another performer in space who is already embodying a sound and join them. Try to interpret the movement that they are doing. Taking the motion information but still listening to the sounds. Listening to the sound through their movement.[23]

These dancers are dressed in everyday clothes, they do not signal as dancers but as people moving. They follow the instructions written by Kiyomi Gordon and inspire my own movements. Their dancing loosens my body and I dare to perform rather than look at the work: to move and listen, listen and move to the rhythms created between things and subjects, moving and searching for points of coincidence, pleasure and its dissipation, that is not in the sculpture, the building or in the notion of an installation, but is generated from the ephemeral volume they produce together. No surface is on its own, they inter-act and inter-invent a space that is not this or that: curtains or silicon, metal or carpet, but is there in their invisible in-between, accessed by dancing, listening and moving through. It is a performing of the geography of the place of the work as a sonic possible world, as a world made from the invisible configurations of things and subjects as things, inter-inventing their possible reality by performing their in-between.

A geography of sound is a doing of geography, as a practice of the possible, defined not in opposition to actuality but as its lived expanse, as its generative environment, which is the outside of geography but not its annihilation. Instead, it is the continuation of geography in 'unseen lands' as 'unknown lands' that create a different territoriality and a different sense of boundaries and participation.[24]

This interpretation of a generative outside of geography in the possible worlds of sound draws inspiration from science fiction writing, and in particular from the detailed geographies of Ursula K. Le Guin, whose stories include descriptions of worlds and planets never seen, and a future not yet experienced, but don't insist on a future tense, but make us consider what else might be here, present now, that our cartographic language bars access to and our chronological thinking shields us from: 'I can! I can see all the stars everywhere. And I can see Ve Port and I can see anything I want! ... And there is a planet, there is too! No don't hold me! Don't! Let me go!'[25]

In her cabined solitude, Lidi felt the gravity lighten to the half-G of the ship's core-mass; she saw them, the nearer and the farther suns, burn through the dark gauze of the walls and hulls and the bedding and her body. The brightest, the sun of this system, floated directly under her navel. She did not know its name.[26]

Le Guin's worlds are not mapped but narrated, walked through, ridden across on horse back, sailed on and moved between in the future machines called NAFAL ships, and via Churten Theory 'displacing of the virtual field in order to realize relational coherence in terms of transiliential experientiality'.[27] Her writing is invested in the confusion of a plural simultaneity and the uncertainty of a relative time that allows us to revisit cultural and patriarchal norms and realities from the fiction of a future mode.

Her reimagining of the present from the future; her writing of unknown lands in the generative outside of geography, proposes a feminist equivalent to Afrofuturism: a term coined and practiced by Sun Ra in the mid-1950s and more recently elaborated on by Kodwo Eshun as the rising of plural sonic fictions that disavow all pasts to hear the subversion of the present from a black-technocultural future. Such a future science deliberately eschews the known in favour of the freedom of the unknown, to redraw the parameters and emphases of actual knowledge and gain a present possibility. It professes an unorthodox irreverence towards conventions and works with an achronological sense of time and the notion of a Futurerhythmachine, which 'operates not through continuities, retentions, genealogies or inheritances but through intervals, gaps and breaks', to gain a breakbeat rhythm for the present.[28] Thus it ignores roots and genres, the measure of time and space, by reverse engineering the direction of revolution, through the force of a science fiction, where space is elastic and time creates reversals and turns things around.[29]

The science fiction of a geography of sonic possible worlds equally makes space for a discontinuous time and practices reversals through an elastics of intervals 'where listening becomes a fieldtrip through a found environment', and where in the volume of an aquatic world 'Everything emerges from the subaudible static of underwater electrickery.'[30]

The possible worlds of sound enable the rethinking of a current geography, showing irreverence to its aims as historical and governmental regulator by creating a geographical future science. Free from its military and scientific conventions, and thus free from the constraints and expectations of the past, it is able to access the present from the future to practice its unknown variants. This geography does not produce a utopian or dystopian vision into, but a possibilist look back from the future. Its unknown is not indeterminate or chaotic, threatening or inarticulate, but is the overlooked, ignored or excluded possibility of now that has no measurement or language and thus appears impossible, but whose access is found in the sonic fiction of a future place: from all the stories-not-yet-told. From there it can provide the tools and the imagination to grasp the volume and depth of the world, rather than the measure of its surface and visible form.

Such an imagination of geography as a sonic science fiction connects Étienne Balibar's statement that 'all political practice is territorialized', qualifying people according to their ability 'to occupy a space, or being admitted to it',[31] with Thrift's demand for 'a new kind of political weave to the world ... which avoids a model of a hallowed ground of politics surrounded by a desert of quietism, in favor of "continuous" political activity woven into the fabric of life'.[32] The quotidian practice of sonic possible worlds and their narration as multiple but simultaneous stories from the future performs a political practice that deterritorializes politics. It removes its hallowed ground and denies governance by occupation and the administration of admission, and instead politicizes the mobile in-between:

I am the darkness between the suns, one said.

I am nothing, one said.

I am you, one said

You- one said- You-

And breathed, and reached out, and spoke: 'Listen!' Crying out to the other, to the others, 'Listen!'[33]

This is the political practice of Le Guin's brown planet in 'Shobie's Story': a planet that is not there, as a firm ground, but exists between material and imagination, between the individual and the crew. It has no solid surface but a depth to sink in to.

The geography of such an ephemeral place demands a 'ethics of engagement' that creates vulnerability, calls for responsibility and enables the recognition of simultaneous difference and multiplicity in the configuration of the world.[34] In this way it transforms the politics of territorialization by decolonializing its empirical, military and historical narrative to generate an outside of geography from its future in the invisible and indivisible volume of unknown lands. Kiyomi Gordon's work presents us with such a future place as a diffuse timespace that is open to the world as a cosmos of inter-existence, creating a contingent place from encounters and misses, human and non-human that create not a territory but the durational performance of its weave and undulation.

Kiyomi Gordon's sound files are 20 minutes long, but this duration cannot be found within the experience of the work whose composition changes not in time but as a timespace place. We can never find the same temporal location again but move through multiplicitous and simultaneous timespace slices as the configuration of all the possibilities of the work, reminding us of all the possibilities of the world. In this sense the work is elastic and probable rather than real. It unperforms the visual representation of its environment and articulates as its mobile depth. Agitating the aspects that remain hidden on conventional maps and floorplans, it highlights givens and points to blindspots: corners of impossibility that are activated by engaging in the tension of a connecting dimensionality rather than the representation of separate things.

This brings us back to the demands of both Thrift and Massey, that a different mode of engagement needs to be found to theorize and deal with geography not as intellectual work, abstract reason and representation in search of a totalizing system, but through constant experimentation, performance and the narrating of mobile and invisible territories as a future science worked through contingent situations and circumstance.

> Now we are finally facing up to the fact that we need new forms of more modest theoretical curiosity which are minded to overcome problems in quite different ways.[35]

Kiyomi Gordon's notes made in preparation for the work, reveal that the castors on the aluminium frames are there to enable mobility and facilitate the research of the space. They allow her to compose not sound itself but the physical material and its connecting in the production of a socio-geographical volume. The speakers too are initially placed on moveable stands and only later fixed on the ceiling. In this way everything remains mobile, moveable, and moving each other until a geography is found that is the geography of the work for me to walk and dance, listen and tell and thus to rearrange and reconfigure in my own performance. This demonstrates the deliberate uncertainty and unfinishedness of the territory her work builds. It is not an absolute terrain but a fragile and mobile imagination of territorial tensions, collaborations and conflicts that is composed between and beyond its own materiality.

It is intriguing to think from my own 'listening dancing' of the space into her configuring it by moving walls and speakers, light and sound, to compose their inter-relation as a 'voluminous score' of possibilities and impossibilities. This process of research and composition points to a practice of geography that is not as Foucault points out in the shadow of the military as a conquering science, but tries the invisible and indivisible slices of a capacious space, to grasp how else the world might be, what other image might be made of it.[36]

The interactions performed between audience and dancer and sculptural form are intimate, communicative almost. As the dancer picks up the sound of a speaker to inform her movement, I pick up her movement to pick up a different sound. We build an ephemeral map of our possibilities together, as a group of people and things who do not speak and yet generate patterns, rhythms and textures that produce an invisible place, looped through, under and over, again and again. It is a timespace place, an ephemeral volume that we inhabit and perform, whose geography is invisible and indivisible and informs a sociality based on our interbeing not on top of a certain world, but as the configuration of what the world is.

The installation does not coincide with the floorplan as map but reveals the blindspots and the invisible depth that are left out in a cartographic design. In this sense, the work creates an impossible territory and manifests a geographical subjectivity and materiality that acknowledges the invisible interbeing of things as a more truthful measure of the world's reality and demands we perform rather than view or chart the work. Performing the installation, by walking and listening, I move from the generative outside of philosophy into a different sense of geography: as the outside of its science and the possibility of a politics of groundlessness; that produces the idea at least of a social-geography and geopolitics of sound.

Socio-material volumes: Vertical geography

The geography produced by Kiyomi Gordon is a geography of sounding, listening and dancing the possible worlds generated by her work, configuring the invisible space of the building, its materials, ourselves, the dancers and anything else that plays an indivisible part: my travelling to Moscow, her residency at the Gallery, the life of local dancers, the future transformation of the building and its past use. This is a geography that accounts for the existence of multiplicities as the simultaneous performance of various agents, human and non-human. It does not chart their separate movements and articulations, however, but grasps them through their interactions: through the moments of coincidence that render their activity political, engaged in the social and material possibility of what is real even if it does not seem possible.

This geography insists on practice, on inhabiting, moving and standing still. It fails to produce a representation apart from tentative and personal accounts of its experience. In this way, it is not strategic or ideological but fragile and contingent, accessing not the actual but its possibility and reaching towards the truth of its impossibilities to create a different knowledge base from the pouvoir and savoir of sound: from its capacity as volume and its expertise of hearing the invisible.

This is a geography of social and material volumes that does not enable the study of borders and lines but of the in-between and the with-each-other: their multiplicitous simultaneity that helps us understand the world we produce together, not in political homogeneity but in practical conflict and disagreement and within its plural quotidian weave.

This socio-material volume has a dimensionality made from simultaneous and indivisible timespace slices, which are the activities and durations of encounters and configurations. In turn, this dimensionality has a viscosity within which we move and are still together, as in an unavoidably connecting but plural sphere, suggesting an intersubjectivity and interactivities that enable the imagination and articulation of a socio-material geography. We experience this viscous expanse from within its depth, not at its center but centered by it: defined by the material processes of connecting and being in-between.

This depth is the 'back' and 'behind' that Maurice Merleau-Ponty discusses in the working notes of his book *The Visible and the Invisible* (1968). According to him, it is 'the dimension of the hidden', which is the place of my looking, my simultaneity with the thing, which therefor I am too close to see but exist in simultaneity with, and thus I can hear while sounding myself.[37] I hear this sound of my simultaneity with others not as a horizon of my being but along vertical lines as the possible slices of our encounter, establishing the depth of the in-between where it does not serve theory or cartography, but the movement and configuration of a performative place.

The visual representation, the floorplan and the installation shot, the map and image of the work, goes around this depth, avoiding its distinctness; avoiding its openness onto the hidden of the work and the world. It ignores our body and that of things as they stand in its depth, in the way of its absolute view, and presents a totalizing map that gives our flesh no part. Instead it works on the surface, on the capacity of its *hyper-invisibility*: showing us that the visual carries the invisibility of a normative truth that supports a singular actuality and the unspoken reality of the map, whose investments we fail to see when we stare at its measurements but that we cannot fail to notice when we listen to its sphere. The hyper-invisibility of normative structures of knowledge and truth are ideological and strategic. They rely for their acceptance on not being seen but pervade the visible.

The map answers questions about where we are and where to go, it does not prompt us to ask about its own ideology and politics: what it leaves out, where its blindspots are, and what perspective it creates. The depth of sound's *actual-invisibility*, the demands and challenges of its unseen and plural existence, by contrast, point directly at these blindspots at the back of and behind the surface measure, and insist we participate in the performance of the unknown, and construct alternatives to the structures that kept it unknowable.[38]

The persuasiveness and limit of the hyper-invisibility of the surface is exposed, for example, in the anxious geography of *Uneasy Listening* (2014), a work by Susan Schuppli and Tom Tlalim. This piece, produced for '[Hlysnan] the Notion and Politics of Listening' at Casino Luxembourg Forum d'art contemporain in Luxembourg, in 2014, provides an account of the drone flight patterns as they overfly the Federally Administered Tribal

Areas (FATA) of Northwest Pakistan. Based on research and the account of witnesses, using generative software and the fixed frequency of 105 kHz, the work simulates the experience of what it is like to live under a drone, and imparts information on the frequency of flights and the area surveyed. The restaging of the over-flights in 5.1 surround sound, in a slightly dimmed exhibition space, is focussed visually by a back-lit image of the then US president Barack Obama, a fly buzzing about his face, which hangs officiously on one wall, and gives voice to Schuppli and Tlalim's sense of 'the injurious nature of what it means to live under the constant sonic menace of drones'.[39]

To grasp this terror of the drone overhead is to grasp the verticality of geography. The incessant circling sound pulls the sky, the ground and underground into the political domain of a geographical imagination. The above and beneath the surface become part of its discourse and challenge its conventional emphasis on horizons and territory as terrain. The drone threatens the dominance of linear perspectives, maps and landscapes, as a symbol of historical military strategy, and creates vertical lines that transverse the above, underneath and beyond, bringing them into one volume and issuing in a different military offensive that employs the timespace dimensionality of place to gain control.

The drone insists on simultaneity. It forcefully becomes a timespace slice in the multiplicities dynamic of place, and changes our performance of its quotidian weave. 'I can't sleep at night when the drones are there.'[40] Our being in the world and being with things is affected by this enforced interbeing with drones. Thus it becomes apparent that the invisible produces a possible world that holds a tangible consequence and impact for its inhabitants for whom it is an actual possible world, while for a cartographic actuality it remains impossible. It remains a blindspot that reveals the authorship of its power at 'the place of its own vision': in Merleau-Ponty's depth where we cannot see ourselves looking; where the discipline of geography cannot see the location of its own gaze or the direction of its power.

While the flight paths of drones can be captured and represented on an aerial map, the experience of a shared volume, the in-between of the drone and the listening inhabitant, remains unrecognized and needs to be considered via a geography that takes account of the world's performative contingency. The focus of this geography is not the drone or the inhabitant, the terrain or the frequency range, but the viscous expanse that connects them together and defines their asymmetrical reciprocity. This experience remains an impossible territory, a terrain without words or a map. However, a vertical listening to the in-between can hear its power lines and give recognition and a voice to those defined in the shadow of its military aim.

A geography of sound can grasp the cartographic blindspots and invisible timespace slices through its voluminous capacity and can access these apparently impossible territories through its vertical sensibility. Consequently, it can problematize the effect of the drone on the actuality of place through the knowledge of its discipline and can grasp the reality of its experience in order to engage in 'the process by which knowledge functions as a power and replicates its effects', to gain a voice and validity for its own reality.[41]

Sounds' viscous dimensionality makes the political reality of the drone thinkable and imaginable. Its cartographic impossibility becomes an actual possibility, and as such it can be drawn into language and become articulated in relation to the political possibilities and impossibilities according to whose objectives the world is being made.

Listening to vertical territories

The verticality of geography as experienced in *Uneasy Listening* is articulated by Eyel Weizman as a politics of verticality in relation to the Israeli occupation of Palestine. In his book *Hollow Land* (2012), he narrates the occupation by stealth and with the help of military antennas, of the hill tops in Gaza from where eventually ever more land is seized and colonized by dividing and partitioning space in three dimensions: the air above, the surface of the land and the resources down below.

> Latitude became more than a mere relative position in the contoured surface of the terrain. The colonization of the mountain regions created a vertical separation between the parallel, overlapping and self-referential ethno-national geographies, held together in startling and horrifying proximity.[42]

In this instance, the vertical is used to institute separation: the partitioning off of space on a three-dimensional matrix that seems to legitimize and make possible an occupation of Palestinian territory against the rules of law drawn up on two-dimensional maps. Quoting Ron Pundak, the 'architect' of the Oslo Process, from an interview in 2002, Weizman explains that the international community accepts the use of a vertical depth to divide an indivisible territory, rather than engaging in its indivisibility. The acceptance of this logic is fascinating. It is an expression of the visual's attempt to go around rather than into the depth that according to Merleau-Ponty is there, in the location of our own vision, where our flesh demands engagement and accountability. It serves to avoid reciprocity and responsibility and enables the invested separation of a land on visual terms. The technicians of this space are not architects but politicians and the military, and as Weizman points out their interests and investments are realized through a militarized geography and the scopic drive of occupation. Theirs is a visual verticality that understands space as divisible and its slices as static and discrete. It represents a visual logic of occupation and colonial rule, of total difference, of the strategies and ideologies of military power and domination that Foucault suggests linger in the shadow of geography.

Such a visual verticality makes the volume discontinuous. It renders it a simultaneity of discrete slices. This visual separation aids the colonizer and gives him a footing above or beneath the land of the other. By contrast, the sonic verticality of a continuous simultaneity makes apparent that the discrete is an illusion and that partitioning is just the admission of an insurmountable inter-existence. Against this admission, a geography of sound produces a different political imagination that focuses not on dividing but on interbeing and the sharing of the voluminous expanse of the world. Sound's focus on the in-between destroys the logic of partition, not just in Palestine but also between the United States and Mexico, in Northern Ireland, in relation to gated communities the world over, and in terms of the current attempt of 'auto-partitioning' the UK off from the EU. The sonic articulates an imagination of indivisibility and questions the logic of separation, producing a different political possibility of a cosmopolitan interbeing that acknowledges our insurmountable simultaneity.

The attempt to design a wall that could bring an architectural solution to a fluid political problem led, according to Weizman, to the construction of ever moving and evolving partitions, creating an elastic geography, whose territories represent the changing ideologies and the multiplicity of voices engaged in its construction. In relation to this notion of elasticity the movements of the occupation seem like the dancers of Kiyomi Gordon's work, instructed to 'move around the space and find locations where you may hear clearly two or more different types of sounds'. But instead of enjoying the moments of coincidence and simultaneity and trying to inter-be, to engage in a politics of the encounter, the politics of occupation builds vertical separations, and uses those moments of hearing the other to perform partitions. Thus it uses the elasticity of performing difference and its socio-material geography to build contingent walls whose flexibility is not a sign of its yielding and reciprocal intent but the strategy of its control.

The frenzied nature of this undertaking, the constant need to react and resist, to build a new tunnel, a new bridge, to change the run of the wall and redefine the rules of belonging, paradoxically attest not the divisibility of place but prove its indivisibility, confirming it as a volume of inter-connecting dimensionalities. The effort to control this indivisibility and to deny the interbeing of its socio-material terrain is bound to fail and fails but its failure is never brought back to the principle of interbeing but to the failure of the infrastructure of separation that needs to be fortified, changed, moved on and improved in military terms of occupation, power and control.

Hearing 'depth barriers'

According to Weizman, individual segments of local settlements in the West Bank that could not be accommodated into a linear border, with its significance as legitimate territorial boundary, the internationally agreed-upon Green Line, but have their separate fortifications, are referred to by the Israeli Ministry of Defence as 'depth barriers'.[43] These are islets of occupation producing 'security zones' in the midst of Palestinian territory and demanding a different conceptualization of access and the circumvention of their separation from the motherland, as ground and home, through tunnels, bridges and conduits of one form or another.[44] These 'extraterritorial islands' remain, according to Weizman, politically invisible, ignored by the international community in exchange for more transparency on the Green Line: the promise by Israel to move the main section of the wall closer to the agreed boundary in return for turning a blind eye to the barriers placed in its depth. Thus they represent physically as well as psychologically the blindspots of the vertical geography of occupation. They are the hidden elements of a regulatory production of space that 'carves out possible spaces of agency within a paralysing and powerful system of apparent impossibility'.[45]

The allusion to the 'depth' of their political location and task brings the military and governmental control of space face to face with the hidden at the back and behind their own standpoint. It confronts their project with Merleau-Ponty's depth understood as the inexhaustible depth of intertwined bodies and matter that cannot be carved out from the landscape through the synthesis of different points of view, but needs to be inhabited in its plural possibility. This depth is the psychological three-dimensionality of Merleau-Ponty's invisible vision, which elsewhere I theorize in relation to sound as the simultaneity of my sounding body with that of others and other things; as my relationship, in other words, with the world as the political possibility of the in-between and a multiplicitous interconnecting, rather than the segregation of singular things and subjects.[46]

In this sense, walls, actual or governmental, as visual 'depth barriers', obstruct access to the possibility of the in-between and represent the avoidance or denial of shared multiplicity. Their rejection of continuous simultaneity creates the visual illusion of the complete and sovereign state, the totalized and totalizing configuration of any political institution and practice, 'as the only thing possible', while denying 'the means the things have to remain distinct':[47] to tell the multiplicity of simultaneous stories and narratives that create the world from their interbeing as possible and seemingly impossible variants.

> Without it [depth], there would not be a mobile zone of distinctness, which could not be brought here without quitting all the rest – and a

'synthesis' of these 'views'. Whereas, by virtue of depth, they coexist in degrees of proximity, they slip into one another and integrate themselves. It is hence because of depth that things have a flesh: that is, oppose to my inspection obstacles, a resistance which is precisely their reality, their 'openness', their *totum simul*.[48]

Merleau-Ponty's depth confronts the governmental agenda of depth barriers with proximity and integration. His place at the back and behind things, at the place of looking, disrupts the territories of a visual depth as barrier, as a vertical line of separation, with the sound of its flesh. Sound resists separation and provides a way to understand these vertical partitions through the auditory imagination of indivisible volumes and the dynamic simultaneity of what can be heard. Its indivisible and viscous dimensionality affords the capacity to inhabit this depth and hear from the in-between of things and subjects, our socio-material simultaneity. The sonic volume becomes a geographical imaginary that resists and redefines the separation enabled by visual architecture and introduces new political possibilities for a knowledge of geography as a timespace dimensionality that includes the invisible, the indivisible and even the impossible not to control their image but to perform and unperform the configuration of their sound. Hearing I can bear witness to separation, exclusion and inclusion, and foster a different understanding of their unavoidable relationships and reciprocity. Thus a geography of sound becomes a means to understand political issues between surface, movements, ground and air, by delving into the vertical, to live at its depth and hear its simultaneity.

According to Weizman, geography can serve as a means to understand political issues. I suggest that a listening, dancing and moving geography of sound that performs its socio-material terrain rather than measuring it, can make a contribution to this understanding and maybe even provide some solutions to places where separation and segregation have come to be seen as the only thing possible when they are simply 'an image [from the past] in which the world is being made'.[49]

Conclusion: Meeting visual geography on a groundless ground

In her essay 'In Free Fall: A Thought Experiment on Vertical Perspective' (2012), Hito Steyerl discusses the downfall of the linear perspective and the anxiety of verticality as vertigo and fear of groundlessness, and concludes that,

In many of these new visualities, what seemed like a helpless tumble into the abyss actually turns out to be a new presentational freedom. And perhaps this helps us get over the last assumption implicit in this thought experiment: the idea that we need a ground in the first place.[50]

While I am not engaged in the new visuality of verticality that Steyerl talks about, and prefer to associate the vertical with sound and engage listening in the exploration of its inexhaustible depth to access the simultaneous multiplicity of the world, I share her optimism that verticality charts not only problems: the occupation of Palestine, the drone warfare in Pakistan, but also provides a new thinking and a new freedom where political practice is not territorialized and people are not qualified according to their ability 'to occupy a space, or be admitted to it' or indeed be excluded from it.[51] Instead, the vertical can tune us to an emphasis on interbeing in an ephemeral and indivisible terrain, where individual agency is acknowledged to have a shared consequence, and time and space are 'uneasy because always in the encounter'.[52]

A sonic verticality, as concept, as material and as agency, provides new tools, a new toolkit and a new imagination to access the timespace slices of sonic possibility, new solutions and new ideas about how we participate, live in and design the world. The appreciation of the world as socio-material volume, its verticality and expanse, and the actuality of the in-between that it reveals, gives form to the intangible sphere of living together. It makes thinkable the indivisibility of the world and helps to challenge its vertical partitioning and control. Thus it provides insights and understanding of the consequences of separating water reservoirs below the surface from its land above, and the effect of the occupation of the skies by drones on the possibility of life beneath. It makes their ideology, strategy and politics sensible and intelligible, and makes us better equipped to communicate, resist and respond to the norms they try to set up through a hyper-invisibility of mapped relations.

However, this is not an attempt to bring a sonic sensibility to visual geography, nor to help it map and chart the world through sound. Instead, I invite the visual geographer to consider the invisible, indivisible and (im) possible world of sound in her methodologies: to engage in the research of sonic possible worlds as a plural, ephemeral and mobile territory that can help rethink the norms and expectations of geography as a scientific and philosophical knowledge system. A sonic sensibility and approach can decolonialize geography's terrain and produce a different imagination of the world through an integrated study of its invisible and indivisible possibilities. The task is to invent a geography for possible worlds that takes account of the variants, the simultaneous plurality, the agency of their configuration and the blindspots of their mapping, to find a way to access the impossible territories and articulate their political possibilities. This might produce, as Thrift quoting Hölderlin suggests, 'an awkward perspective'. A perspective that defies the traditional vantage point of its discipline to perform and unperform its territory from a different position, not, as Thrift points out, for spurious and fanciful reasons of youthful anarchy and the wilful sabotage of the discipline, 'but out of a deep-seated conviction that securing a point of view that never goes wrong cannot add to the world'.[53] Thus we need an awkward perspective that hails from the future as the possibility of the world heard from another 'planet' understood as an as yet impossible variant that charts its possibilities from the simultaneity of a three-dimensional depth. From there it can resound the socio-material geography of the world as the configuration of a timespace of 'awkward objects': Cauleen Smith's things – discussed in the introduction to this series of essays and motivating their writing – that include their own fragility and possibility for failure and are not shaped through the necessity of their task, or the expectations of power and ideology, but inspire a (re-)engagement with the unknown. In other words, geography has to meet sound not as a historiographical continuum but from the future: as a Futurerhythmachine or a NAFAL ship moved by Churten theory, which shows the formless contours of the world in its depth.[54]

I appreciate that for a geography of sound to be valuable and make a useful and legitimate contribution to geography as an integrated science of the world, it has to find strategies and tools that can collaborate with a visual/historical geography. It has to find a consensus and a shared vocabulary to make its knowledge count: to bring its voluminous dimensionality, its indivisible interbeing, its possibilities and what seems impossible to geography's intellectual work and practice. However, in turn, for the geography of sound to contribute on sonic terms, and bring a sonic knowledge to the field of geography, geography needs to expand and engage with a sensibility of invisible volumes and the uncertainty of an aquatic world. In other words, the geographer needs to practice the moving and shifting invisibility of a world at sea, so that her imagination can challenge and augment the framework of the discipline, its value and validity, and geography can come to contain the poetic and unmappable while remaining legitimate and trustworthy. And so, this essay is not about denying geography the objectives of its discipline, but to expand what they might be by insisting on the geographical exploration of sonic possible worlds through the practice of singing and dancing, listening and walking in its indivisible, voluminous and invisible terrain, and by bringing the possibility of sound to the measure of a politics of territory, lines, borders and belonging.

For the world is very large, the Open Sea going on past all knowledge; and there are worlds beyond the world.[55]

Notes

1 Steve Roggenbuck, *LIVE MY LIEF, Selected & New Poems: 2008–15*, boost house, 2015, p. 49. Reprinted with the author's permission.

2 Arturas Bumsteinas, *Epiloghi*, Liner Notes, Unsounds, Deutschland Radiokultur, 2013.

3 Michel Foucault refers to the engineer, rather than the architect, as a 'technician of space' who controls the three great variables of territory, communication and speed ('Space, Knowledge and Power', in *The Foucault Reader*, Paul Rabinow [ed.], London: Penguin Books, 1991, p. 244).

4 Doreen Massey, *For Space*, London: Sage Publication, 2005, p. 4.

5 Ibid., p. 84.

6 Michel Foucault, 'Questions à Michel Foucault sur la géographie', *Hérodote*, vol. 1 (January–March 1976): 71–85.

7 With the notion of *hyper-invisibility*, I am referring to the unseen norms and conventions that while ideologically and culturally constructed are so omnipresent and accepted as to have become entirely invisible, their forms and functions taken for granted, they present a naturalized reality that pretends a convenient actuality that is hyper-invisible.

8 In 'Questions à Michel Foucault sur la géographie', Michel Foucault discusses geography in terms of the tension between pouvoir and savoir, and suggests: 'Hence forth one can analyze savoir (knowing) in terms of region, the domain, the implantation and displacement, the transference, one can grasp the process through which knowledge functions as power (pouvoir) and reproduce its effects' (Foucault, 'Questions à Michel Foucault sur la géographie', p. 76, my translation).

9 Eyal Weizman quoting Ron Pundak in *Hollow Land, Israel's Architecture of Occupation*, London: Verso, 2012, p. 13.

10 Erin Manning and Brian Massumi, *Thought in the Act: Passages in the Ecology of Experience*, Minneapolis and London: University of Minnesota Press, 2014, p. vii.

11 Doreen Massey, 'Power Geometry and a Progressive Sense of Place', in *Mapping the Futures*, Jon Bird, Barry Curtis and Tim Puttnam (eds), London: Routledge, 1999, p. 61.

12 Salomé Voegelin, *Listening to Noise and Silence*, New York: Bloomsbury, 2010, pp. 138–9.

13 Jacques Rancière, *Disagreement, Politics and Philosophy*, London: University of Minnesota Press, 1999, p. 133. In this context, Rancière talks particularly about the consensus system of political reality and suggests that the final truth of metapolitics is the management of reality as the only thing possible, in order to exclude those subjects and things that fall outside the parameters of its truth administration from even thinking or articulating their position.

14 Ibid., p. 132.

15 Massey, *For Space*, pp. 9–10.

16 Ibid., p. 9.

17 Ibid., p. 25.

18 Ibid., p. 23.

19 Bergson in Massey, *For Space*, p. 246.

20 Ibid., p. 23.

21 They are the private slices of life-worlds, phenomenological versions of Kripke's 'mini-worlds' that are constantly negotiated to produce contingently what the world might be (Saul Kripke, *Naming and Necessity*, Oxford: Blackwell Publishing, 1981, p. 18).

> Possibly, in the end, there might be no actual world at all, but only temporary negotiations of possible worlds between my world and your world, in moments of coincidence, where our maps might overlap affectively, with the actual world being the mirage of joint and equal access that does not exist: the pretense of a fiction of power and ideology, confirmed by a presumed and singular reality, and exposed through the plurality of possibility.
>
> (Salomé Voegelin, *Sonic Possible Worlds*, New York: Bloomsbury, 2014, p. 61.)

22 This work was originally created during a residency at The Lab in San Francisco, 1–31 October 2016, and previously installed at GON Festival 20–27 February 2017, Human Resources in Los Angeles 11–12 March 2017, as well as at SFMOMA *Soundtracks* Exhibition 15 July 2017–1 January 2018. Each time it takes on a contingent and site-specific form and finds a different performance.

23 These are two examples of the instructions given by Kiyomi Gordon to the dancers who performed the installation.

24 Nigel Thrift commenting on his notion of unknown lands in the 'Performance and Performativity: A Geography of Unknown Lands', in *A Companion to Cultural Geography*, James S. Duncan, Nuala C. Johnson and Richard H. Schein (eds), London: Blackwell Publishing, 2007, p. 121.

25 Ursula K. Le Guin, *The UNREAL & The REAL, Selected Stories Volume 2 Outer Space, Inner Lands*, London: Orion, 2015, p. 86.

26 Ibid., p. 92.

27 Ibid., p. 78.

28 Kodwo Eshun, *More Brilliant than the Sun: Adventures in Sonic Fiction*, London: Quartet Books, 1998, p. -003.

29 Ibid., pp. 136 and 076.

30 Ibid., p. 066. Sun Ra's film *Space Is the Place* (1972), a film about his travelling from a new planet in outer space into 1940s Chicago, transported by music, illustrates the spatial dimension of Afrofuturism. While sonic possible worlds are not literally parallel universes or new planets but the variants of this world, the metaphor of future and space nevertheless enable their potency.

31 Étienne Balibar, *Citizenship*, trans. Thomas Scott-Railton, Cambridge: Polity Press, 2015, p. 68.

32 Thrift, 'Performance and Performativity', p. 122.

33 Le Guin, *The UNREAL & The REAL*, p. 92.

34 Ibid., p. 128.

35 Ibid., p. 122.

36 In answer to 'Questions à Michel Foucault sur la géographie', Foucault explains that:

> la géographie s'est développée à l'ombre de l'armée. Entre le discours géographique et le discours stratégique, on peut observer une circulation de notions: la région des géographes n'est autre que la région militaire (de regere, commander), et province n'est autre que le territoire vaincu (de vincere). Le champ renvoie au champ de bataille ...

> [Geography developed in the shadow of the army. Between the discourse of geography and the discourse of strategy one can observe a circular notion: the region of the geographers is the same as the region of the military (subdue and command), and the province is the same as the conquered territory (de vincere). The field refers to the battlefield ...]

> (Foucault, 'Questions à Michel Foucault sur la géographie', pp. 75–6, my translation.)

37 Maurice Merleau-Ponty, *The Visible and the Invisible*, trans. Alphonso Lingis, ed. Claude Lefort, Evanston, IL: Northwestern University Press, 1968, p. 219.

38 This might lead us back to maps and cartography as unmapping: as an affirmative re-performance of mapping that creates an ephemeral cartography of processes and blindspots, at the in-between of things, from where the indivisible volume of the world takes its viscous shape. I am not sure we can theorize these maps, however. It might be a matter for practice, in the first instance at least, to imagine and design their changing shape.

39 Susan Schuppli, 'Uneasy Listening', exhibition handout, http://susanschuppli.com/wp-content/uploads/Uneasy-Listening-medium-dark.pdf (accessed 16 January 2018).

40 Ibid.

41 Foucault, 'Questions à Michel Foucault sur la géographie', p. 76. Translated from 'on peut saisir le processus par lequel le savoir fonctionne comme un pouvoir et en reconduit les effets.'

42 Eyal Weizman, *Hollow Land, Israel's Architecture of Occupation*, London: Verso, 2012, p. 117.

43 Ibid., pp. 177–8

44 Ibid., p. 163.

45 Ibid., p. 261.

46 Merleau-Ponty, *The Visible and the Invisible*, p. 145.

47 Ibid., p. 219.

48 Ibid.

49 Ibid., p. 84.

50 Hito Steyerl, 'In Free Fall: A Thought Experiment on Vertical Perspective', in *The Wretched of the Screen*, Berlin: Sternberg Press, 2012, p. 27.

51 Balibar, *Citizenship*, p. 68.

52 Manning and Massumi, *Thought in the Act*, p. vii.

53 Thrift, 'Performance and Performativity', p. 133.

54 Eshun, *More Brilliant than the Sun*, p. -003 and Ursula K. Le Guin, 'The Shobins' Story', in *The UNREAL & The REAL, Selected Stories Volume 2 Outer Space, Inner Lands*, London: Orion, 2015, pp. 96–7.

55 Ursula K. Le Guin, *The Earth Sea Quartett*, London: Penguin Books, 1993, p. 365.

References

Balibar, Étienne, *Citizenship*, trans. Thomas Scott-Railton, Cambridge: Polity Press, 2015.

Bech, Henning, Christian Borch and Steen Nepper Larsen, 'Resistance, Politics, Space, Architecture: *Interview with Nigel Thrift*', *Distinction* no. 21 (2010): 93–105.

Bumstainas, Arturas, *Epiloghi*, Liner Notes, Unsounds, Deutschland Radiokultur, 2013.

Eshun, Kodwo, *More Brilliant than the Sun: Adventures in Sonic Fiction*, London: Quartet Books, 1998.

Foucault, Michel, 'Questions à Michel Foucault sur la géographie', *Hérodote*, vol. 1 (January–March 1976): 71–85.

Foucault, Michel, 'Space, Knowledge and Power', in *The Foucault Reader*, Paul Rabinow (ed.), London: Penguin Books, 1991.

Kripke, Saul, *Naming and Necessity*, Oxford: Blackwell Publishing, 1981.

Le Guin, Ursula K., *The Earth Sea Quartet*, London: Penguin Books, 1993.

Le Guin, Ursula K., *The UNREAL & The REAL, Selected Stories Volume 2 Outer Space, Inner Lands*, London: Orion, 2015.

Manning, Erin and Brian Massumi, *Thought in the Act: Passages in the Ecology of Experience*, Minneapolis and London: University of Minnesota Press, 2014.

Massey, Doreen, *For Space*, London: Sage Publication, 2005.

Massey, Doreen, 'Power Geometry and a Progressive Sense of Place', in *Mapping the Futures*, Jon Bird, Barry Curtis and Tim Puttnam (eds), London: Routledge, 1993, pp. 59–69.

Merleau-Ponty, Maurice, *The Visible and the Invisible*, trans. Alfonso Lingis, Evanston: Northwestern University, 1968.

Rancière, Jacques, *Disagreement, Politics and Philosophy*, trans. Julie Rose, London: University of Minnesota Press, 1999.

Roggenbuck, Steve, *LIVE MY LIEF, Selected & New Poems: 2008–15*, boost house, 2015.

Schuppli, Susan, 'Uneasy Listening: The Chronic Sonic of Life under Drones',
    in *[Hlysnan] The Notion and Politics of Listening*, Berit Fisher (ed.),
    Luxemburg: Casino Luxembourg, 2014, pp. 80–90.
Schuppli, Susan, 'Uneasy Listening', exhibition handout, http://susanschuppli.com/
    wp-content/uploads/Uneasy-Listening-medium-dark.pdf.
Smith, Cauleen, Visiting Lecture at Pacific Northwestern College of Art (PNCA), 2
    November 2016, https://www.youtube.com/watch?v=-1mwULFTXRk.
Steyerl, Hito, 'In Free Fall: A Thought Experiment on Vertical Perspective', in *The
    Wretched of the Screen*, Berlin: Sternberg Press, 2012, pp. 12–30.
Thrift, Nigel, *Non-Representation Theory, Space Politics Affect*, London:
    Routledge, 2008.
Thrift, Nigel, 'Performance and Performativity: A Geography of Unknown Lands',
    in *A Companion to Cultural Geography*, James S. Duncan, Nuala C.Johnson
    and Richard H. Schein (eds), London: Blackwell Publishing, 2007.
Weizman, Eyal, *Hollow Land, Israel's Architecture of Occupation*, London: Verso,
    2012.

Work

Bumsteinas, Arturas, *Night on the Sailship*, from Album 'Epiloghi', Unsounds,
    Deutschland Radiokultur, 2013.
Kiyomi Gordon, Jacqueline, *Inside You is Me, July/Surface Substance* produced
    with dancer and choreographer Sonya Levin for 'Geometry of Now', curated by
    Mark Fell at GES-2, in Moscow in 2017, 20–7 February 2017.
Susan, Schuppli and Tom Tlalim, *Uneasy Listening*, exhibited as part of '[Hlysnan]
    the Notion and Politics of Listening' at Casino Luxembourg Forum d'art
    contemporain in Luxembourg, curator Berit Fisher, 17 May–7 September 2014.

Morality of the invisible, ethics of the inaudible

This essay does not write a text, but a score, a set of instructions to listen, do and read. In this way, it deliberately derails a singular meaning and interpretation by inviting participation in what is heard, done and read. During a performance, such instructions inform and trigger actions. After the performance their format, as a readable score, gives permission and the opportunity to reperform its content, and thus to revocalize and reauthorize the theoretical ideas presented in its content and materiality.

The shifting authorship and vocal textuality that is proposed and enabled by a score, considered in the context of this particular topic, *Morality of the invisible, ethics of the inaudible*, responds to the idea of a participatory ethics and the morality of its entanglements. Thus it signals an acknowledgement that 'what ethics is' is not definable as a list of rules or guidelines, but *is* forms of behaviour, actions and interactions, responses and gestures, which are entirely contingent, a matter of what it does rather than what it is. Therefor what follows here is not a study that oversees and judges action but is the engine of the action itself: the moral impetus and rhythm of doing things, which the performative approach gives opportunity and articulation to.

Consequently, in this particular performative frame, the score enables participation in the invisible mobility of sound to practice and trial how listening to its unseen processes might contribute to the articulation of a contemporary morality, and how it might be able to bring the unheard, understood in the sense of Rancière's 'sans-part',[1] 'those that have no part',[2] into an ethical framework not as a simple inclusion but, as Étienne Balibar suggests, as 'an enunciation of the principle of radical democracy as the power of anyone at all'.[3]

To enable this inclusion of anyone at all, this score reimagines ethics through the lens of a sonic sensibility of indivisible volumes, in whose viscous expanse we hear not 'this' or 'that' but the contingent in-between of things and subjects that are not autonomous but are as interbeings, existing together through the movements, stillness and causalities of an interconnected world. This sonic understanding grasps the world not as an organization of things, hierarchized by a symbolic lexicon and ordered by cultural signification, but as a simultaneity of actions, visible and invisible, indivisible in their consequences and meaning. The ethics of such a sonic world is consequently not a rule-based ethics, separate from and a priori to the movement, the doing and organizing of that world. Rather, it is its very essence. Sound's lack of signifying distance collapses ethics, being and doing, into one synchronous move. Thus ethics is not an attribute or a description that can be complied to, but is the energy of our actions and our being in the world itself that needs to be attended to while doing.

This score invites the performance of an ethics of entanglement between morality and its practices. As a set of instructions, it invites to perform the conventions of aesthetic and everyday processes – the conditions of artistic and social production – as well as the conventions of language and representation – the conditions of its communication and institution, and it helps to unperform, understood as an affirmative mode of working on the outside of norms, their ethical and moral givens through a contingent but shared doing. In this way, the score functions as an emancipatory and political force and method as well as a participatory and collective capacity to practice the value and validity of an entangled sense of things.

To contextualize this collapse into practice, and articulate this shift from ethics as rules for action to ethics as the doing of things, we can look to Karen Barad's move from agency to agentiality. To the way in other words that she moves from the noun and the attribute of agency, the actant and enactment, to the verb to agitate, and ultimately defines a being agential. Her agency is the action of doing, it is a material practice of being in the world. Equally, ethics as ethicality is a verb, is the doing and being in the world and at the same time an expression of participation and generation of a contingent ethical weave. It 'is an ethics that is not predicated on externality but rather entanglement'.[4] Its performance is an ethical engagement with the instructions provided and the textual materials offered. This does not preclude conflict and disagreement, or indeed the possibility of rejecting the score altogether, but it frames its performances, or the performances of its rejection, within the morality of action rather than prejudice and rule. Further, it focuses morality not on a static context but on the contingent in-between of things and subjects, that, as agential interbeings, read the world 'through one another for their various entanglements, and by being attentive to what gets excluded as well as what comes to matter'.[5]

In this sense, ethics does not rule but is part of the configuration of the real. Without ethics there is no activity and no being, and no activity and no being exists without ethics. Thus ethical discourse cannot be found outside of action, articulation and being, but only within it, as part of it, construed as a participatory and an entangled practice. This inside is not the inside of a discipline or institution however, but the outside of disciplinary and institutional boundaries at the inside of doing things.

Such an 'agential ethics' also implies that being ethical is not good per se. When positing ethics as the engine and essence of doing and doing nothing, we have to differentiate further, outside the binary of ethical and unethical, to allow for a more detailed, non-partisan and culturally more pluralistic discussion on the premise of the ethical performance of the world. The unethical cannot just be what is not ethical. That is too diffuse and dialectical a definition, granted by a singular authority that might not be God or theology anymore but which in refusing to investigate further and seek articulation on the nature of the unethical, becomes its own dogmatic position. Thus we have to name them both, beyond the binary, to articulate their actions contingently as not simply oppositional, but inescapably interrelated, expressive of actions and activities that are taking place within the same indivisible world. This contingent calling demands our engagement and participation, through which we constantly re-evaluate our actions on the basis of an entangled practice.

To write a score for you to perform, with your voice and body, as a physical activity of your interbeing existence, means to engage you in actions whose ethicality is your engine of doing them. In this way, the score enables a performative morality that is not an inculcation of preexisting rules but a challenge to your participation. The score offers not a moral and intellectual instruction but an instruction without rules to do an agential ethics. It does not instruct to think but to do in order to rethink contingently, through the simultaneity of the material and speaking it. As the instructions loosen your control, they bestow you with the ability to observe while doing, where the ethical engine of doing, its 'subjectivity engine', is.

Holger Schulze interprets Kodwo Eshun's term 'subjectivity engine', his 'machine of subjectivity that peoples the world with audio hallucinations'[6] as 'a material engine, that is connected to your body, to your incorporated idiosyncratic imagination, your sonic *corpus*'.[7] It is from the materiality of this sonic *corpus* that we interact with the materiality of the score, performing inter-actions as a way to start differentiating beyond ethical and unethical, to rethink the agential reality of both terms and dig deeper, physically and intellectually, beyond the binary into the complexity and participatory demands of an ethics of doing. This implies an acknowledgement that ethics is contingent, the matter of an agential in-between that needs to be performed in a material practice, rather than rules made about.

The essay score

This text does not follow the format of the other essays in this book and yet it sits at its centre, in terms of layout, theme and as its engine. Equidistant between *Writing Fragments*, which explains and situates the book's writing as a writing in fragments of essayistic experiments that produce awkward objects and promote the legitimacy of contradiction, and *Reading Fragments*, which suggests an approach and methodology of how all these essays could be read as vertical lines of words that do not come together on the horizontal, but dig into the material and into the practice of writing and reading to find an understanding that is that of sound rather than its mute theorization.

Responding to this context, these instructions to perform don't aim to create a first principle of ethics and neither do they hope to promote its final principle. Instead, they position ethics as the performance of things, subjects, texts and words, from their fragile and contingent in-between, in an indivisible cosmos, where the question of value, validity, right and wrong is collapsed into practice, into an entangled agential ethicality rather than held in the order of abstraction.

Therefore, here, the score is a 'performative essay', an essay that is not written but instructs on the possibilities of its writing not as a finishable text but as a formless possibility of doing rather than knowing the ethical dimension of one's own actions and inactivities. This format has the capacity to forge connections and set up tensions in order to explore the simultaneity of doing as a doing of an ethical practice in-between texts, questions, actions and thoughts. The 'essay score' rejects a complete assessment and opinion, and instead highlights the subjective processes and the responsibility of being as accountability through the practice of the material scored. It invites to perform its essayistic trial by giving only the building blocks of research: the things I gather around me when writing and in whose performance an essay that enacts the ethics of its making can be generated.

In this sense, the essay score is a DIY effort that rejects conventional critical registers and technologies, and responds to the idea that we could do things differently. It is the methodological answer to the demand stated in the introduction to this book: to produce in writing, sounding and listening awkward objects and speculative artefacts that engage in a concurrent representational crisis by shifting expectations of perception and inspire a re-engagement and participation in what things might mean. In other words, the score enables misalignment and purposeful inarticulation in the ephemeral between-of-things. It creates from ambiguity and from what is not there, in the rhythm of a contingent doing, new possibilities for the academic artefact, for theory, for language and for the political, and thus for the ethical entanglement of what they could be.

Its format and practice relates to a remark made in the introduction, via the writing on *The Essay Film* (2016) by Elizabeth A. Papzian and Caroline Eades, suggesting that the essay is the perfect format for a crisis 'as it longs for utopia – that is, for an impossibility'.[8] Thus it is the perfectly incomplete and imperfect form to write about the possibility and impossibility of a practical morality and ethics at a time when we lack imagination to think beyond the ideologies of neo-liberal capitalism and its violent singularity. In the absence of alternatives, the performance essay as essay score allows us to unperform this singularity and reimagine its violence without engaging in the circularity of its sublation.[9]

While the essay enables us to engage in the possibility of ethics through a do-it-yourself desire that embraces a connected and collaborative world, the score allows us to put the body in the breach and perform alternative interpretations of its invested territory.

What follows is an adapted and developed version of a score for a performance produced for and realized at *Sound, Ethics, Art and Morality*, at Tel Aviv University Faculty of the Arts, Tel Aviv, Israel, 29–30 May 2016.

Action 1: Listen to the sound
of a washing machine

Read 'Listening to the Stars' over its cotton wash cycle:

Listening to the Stars

Make new acquaintances: listen to learn their methods of attaining success

(19 November 1952, Sagittarius)[10]

We have lived here for a while. Third floor, nice views but no garden. I always resented that, no garden. And the stairs, particularly with the buggy and the children. They are older now but still. Then came the mudslide, all of a sudden, I really do not know where from. But the long and short of it is that now we are on the ground floor. No more stairs, no more dragging up of shopping, no more lugging of buggies and heavy children up and down three sets of steps. Just a nice ground floor entrance, and of course the garden is ours now.

Sometimes we can hear the noises from down below. Screams and banging, smashing of furniture against the walls and the ceilings no doubt. We try to ignore it. I am sure it will stop eventually. The mud is drying, we have sown some seeds, by summer it should have become a nice green lawn to play on.[11]

Question 1: What floor do you live on?

Read *Morality of the Invisible* quietly to yourself:

Morality of the Invisible

Sound, as material and as concept, illuminates the unseen processes of the world and invites us to see things in a different light. Listening, we access the possibility of the world from the possibility of time and the possibility of space, participating in the plurality of reality and challenging the singular actuality it is presented as. The invisible mobility of sound informs and incites this exploration and invites the listener to enter into slices of possibility to understand the heterogeneous construction of the real and participate in its reconstruction: to build a timespace world of its ephemeral possibilities and make it count within current notions of actuality.

The morality of this sonic engagement is the morality of the invisible. It does not produce the totality of the image, and neither does it fulfil preexisting normative codes, but responds to the demand of the dark when we have lost our anchorage in visual things and rules, and are forced to suspend our habits and values, to listen in order to see the complex plurality of the real as simultaneous possibilities that include also impossibilities: that which has no part in its singular actuality; and it makes us reconsider also the part we play ourselves.

Action 2: Open a window and make a cuckoo sound

Read the following excerpt from 'Are we staring down on a doomsday clock getting closer to midnight or merely looking out of the kitchen window?'

vi

(speaks into microphone) We have just spotted rabbits and we are just following them, because they have gone down a hole underneath the tree. We are just gonna see if we can see the rabbit hole.

We do not want to scare them. We just want to see the hole, see where they live.

Fantastic, there, look!

It's like three holes …

Isn't that fantastic, fantastic! What a sight …

Okay let's leave them be …

Oh my god, there is a whole load of rabbits …

No, that's a squirrel

But mostly I see rabbits

I just discovered another hole

I see, yes, you got another

That's where it came from

A whole warren, a labyrinth

These are like the best sightings ever

(speaks into microphone) This is really very exciting

We are walking upon a network …

Look at the parakeet. Look at them, sitting on the ground, walking on the ground

Ring-necked parakeets, a woodpigeon, rabbits

We are walking upon their ... along the roof of their warren

They can hear us probably going bumpf bumpf on their roof

That is why they are all gone

They are all hidden, gone down their holes

(speaks into microphone) And we are leaving to the sound of a green woodpecker

A distant sound of a woodpecker

Wonder what all of these humps are

The rabbit's place

It's amazing this is a very memorable moment, memorable area, isn't it? This is fertile ground ... (speaks into microphone) Small area, no bigger than a ... four tennis courts. Fertile.[12]

Question 2: What are you excluded from? – What is your story?

Go for a walk in the street and read *The Value of a Fluid Sound* aloud while moving along:

The Value of a Fluid Sound

For Étienne Balibar, the cornerstone of political activity is the tension of equaliberty, the pull between freedom and equality, which is a seat of conflict that enables and calls for participation, and which thus represents the political as the possibility of politics: where rupture happens and transformation can occur; where the excluded can find a voice and make themselves count and where inclusion can become pluralized.

Capitalist neoliberalism neutralizes this tension and renders the conflict insignificant, banal in the light of an undifferentiated flow of things and people reduced to the purpose of economic utility and worth. In its sphere things, goods, people, borders and identities, become moveable. They are in the flow, however, they are not fluid themselves. They have no power to transform and be transformative. They are not things thinging as conceptual and actual sonic things that make a sound of their own, to be heard and to contribute to the plural composition of actuality. Instead, they are reduced to the articulation of a harmonized flow to which they are not even an audible discord. Therefore, they are not self-determined agential subjects, but identities defined by the measure of their utility.

Balibar calls this within 'the development of a new ethic of self-care, whereby individuals must moralize their own conduct by submitting themselves to the criterion of utility maximization or the productivity of their individuality'.[13]

The result is a negative individuality and a negative community or what Balibar terms 'the dark face of ethics', where solidarity and social security are dismantled and the subjects are disaffiliated from the community to live as entrepreneurs of their own circumstance. I understand this as a negative fluidity, a fluidity bound up in the dichotomy between fixed, coerced belonging, and desperate flight. As such it has no autonomous agency but represents a reactive mobility dependent on what else moves and stands still.

By contrast, the fluidity and predicative nature of sound, its transformative agency and imaginary potential, can contribute to the critique of this entrepreneurial precarity and its concomitant internal and external exclusions. Investigating the capitalist mobility through a sonic sensibility can grant us access to the coercive dynamic of its forced and homogenous flow and entice us to interrupt the monochord of neo-liberalism and make it sound as polyphony: 'composed of differences, themselves formed by crossing visible and invisible borders'.[14]

Action 3: Turn a bolt 10 times to the right and 10 times to the left. Listen intently to the tightening and untightening of the space between bolt and screw.

Question 3: Who and what are you excluding?

Read 'Poem' from *Poetry of the Taliban*:

Poem

Who am I? What am I doing?
How did I get here?
There is no house or love for me;
I am homeless, without a homeland.
I don't have a place in this world;
They don't let me rest.
There are shots fired, and gunpowder here,
A shower of bullets.
Where should I go, then?
There is no place for me in this world.
A small house
I had from father and grandfather,
In which I knew happiness,
My beloved and I would live there.

They were great beauteous times;
We would sacrifice ourselves for each other.
But suddenly a guest came;
I let him be for two days.
But after these two days passed,
The guest became the host.
He told me, 'You came today.
Be careful not to return tomorrow.'
Najibullah Akrami[15]

Lie on the floor, arms stretched up in the air and read *A new God for a Possible World*:

A new God for a possible world

Neither a sonic possible world nor the negative fluidity of personhood and materiality of a neo-liberal context can rely on preexisting moral principles, shared emotions, or God. Commandments, rules, cultural codes or a higher power do not attach to the invisible mobility of sound and neither do they guide or safeguard the territories of belonging and identity in transnational capitalism.

The tautological reality of neoliberalism eschews conventional ethics of solidarity and sociality. Balibar's phrase 'the dark face of ethics' recognizes a disincorporation of the individual from the practice of the social contract, where notions of solidarity and security are negotiated by the conflict of different interests. In its place comes a humanitarian rights not based on positive identities and the negotiation of differences, but controlling and unifying the heterogenous (the young unemployed, the migrant, women, gays) into 'an odd multiple, in which the uncounted are counted',[16] but crucially they cannot make themselves count, cannot make their voices heard and thus are not allowed to participate and make that participation impact on the reality of the actual, which remains the tautological possibility of reality, whose God is the neo-liberal flow and whose ethics follow the moral code of efficiency and utility. In other words, the humanitarian rights of global capitalism outline the post-moral and post-ethical rights of an absolute possibility, which inscribes those rights into its image and prevents the inscription of anything else.

Action 4: Shout *your name* again and again into the bottom of a cup or a glass until you feel the rim tight around your mouth.

Question 4: Are you audible?

Action 5: Listen to the murmur of an internet hub

Read 'Ethics of Listening' (edited excerpt):

Ethics of Listening

Recently I was away, in another country. It looked and sounded not unlike this one, with streets, trees, houses, people and their dogs. The people had eyes, ears and mouths, just like us. They looked, listened and spoke as we do. But since I could not recognize what I had heard in the acoustic environment around me from the way they talked about it I had to assume that they heard it all very differently.

Their focus was on process and the notion of existence as doing, which meant that what was described was the motion, the present doing of being, not its material totality nor the conglomeration of past occurrences and achievements. This focus on process privileged and was privileged by the ear, which steered the eye away from the material onto its thinging: onto the possibilities it proposes as a thing, as an object existing in time.

The material of this world, while seen and heard by me the same way as that back home, was clearly appreciated in an entirely different way by the indigenous population. And so it *was* different: its materiality, its status and what it could do and enable in terms of understanding, imagination and purpose was very different. The resulting consideration of value and reality was completely different, and so while from the outside this world looked and sounded just like ours, the thinking that manifests the invisible layer of its processes and results in the sense of actuality and morality lived by, was very different indeed.

It is difficult to imagine, harder to describe, but I came to understand that what their eyes saw was unfocused movement. Like looking at a photograph taken on a slow shutter speed, they saw indistinct motion that was given definition by sound. But this definition was not concerned with size, location, outline or distance, but was the fluid defining of its possibility: what it proposed to be at this moment in time, producing its own contingent situation. Thus what became clear is that their auditory process of definition is not concerned with sizing up, with ordering the heard into a hierarchy of use-value and identity, nor of placing it in a pre-given space. Rather listening rephrases definition as a contingent activity of defining, of drawing the thing in the fragility of what it could be continually rather than what it shows permanently.

My hosts laughed at me when I talked to them of my exhaustion to try and see and hear the world their way. They mocked my desire to place myself, my fears of getting lost, my need to dominate the object to know myself. They retorted how difficult it must be to have the eye, rather than as a freely roaming motion, captured by the immobile object, to be thrust up against it all the time; to have to have a position against another form rather than enjoy shared formlessness. They felt it must be such a burden to own things, to either have them or want them, when you could just partake in their existence with you.[17]

Question 5: What are you included in?

Stand on a chair and read *Ethics of the Inaudible:*

Ethics of the Inaudible

While the neo-liberal disincorporation of social rights ignores the tension between equality and freedom on which political activity as the possibility of politics relies, sound makes this tension sensible and thinkable, and invites into participation also those that have no part not as a *sans part* but as 'a part of everyone at all'.[18]

For this 'everyone at all' to truly be everyone at all, it needs to include also the inaudible: that which for physiological and cultural, but also for ideological and sociopolitical reasons we cannot and do not want to hear. Thus once we are attuned to the invisible and practice listening as the negotiation of mobile differences and unseen possibilities, we need to lend our ear to what as yet remains inaudible: those 'that have no part', the erased and overheard voices, that cannot make themselves count in the constitution of a current actuality or its possibilities.

The inaudible is the possible impossible of this world. It is its sociopolitical horizon beyond which we pretend not see anything even once we start to hear it rumble. The ethics of this inaudible is an ethics of practice, the practice of listening out for what sounds too but we do not want to hear, in order to grant it access to the sphere of influence.

Action 6: Take a passport close to your ear and listen as you flip through its pages

Question 6: Are you hearing the inaudible?

Action 7: Put your ear against a window and listen to whatever is outside

Read 'Fractal Geometry' from *Crystallography* over the heard outside:

Fractal Geometry (excerpt)

Fractals are a pretty knotty
way to say: the length of any
coastline depends upon the
lengths to which a ruler goes.

A lost vacationer who strolls
along a beach patrols a spatial
breach between dimensions

Christian Bök[19]

Action 8: Put your mouth against the window and try to voice *hello*

(This works particularly well with secondary glazing.)

Notes

1 Jacques Rancière, *La Mésentente: politique et philosophie*, Paris: Galilée, 1995, p. 28.

2 Rancière, *Disagreement, Politics and Philosophy*, Minneapolis, London: University of Minnesota Press, 1999, pp. 38–9.

3 Étienne Balibar, *Equaliberty*, Durham and London: Duke University Press, 2014, p. 297.

4 Karan Barad, interview in *New Materialism: Interviews & Cartographies*, Rick Dolphijn and Iris van der Tuin, Ann Arbor, MI: Open Humanities Press, 2012, p. 50.

5 Ibid., pp. 52–3.

6 Kodwo Eshun, *More Brilliant than the Sun: Adventures in Sonic Fiction*, London: Quartet Books, 1998, p. 121.

7 Holger Schulze, 'How to Think Sonically? On the Generativity of the Flesh', in *Sonic Thinking: A Media Philosophical Approach*, Bernd Herzogenrath (ed.), New York: Bloomsbury, 2017, p. 237.

8 Caroline Eades and Elizabeth A. Papazian (eds), *The Essay Film, Dialogue Politics Utopia*, New York: Columbia University Press, 2016, pp. 2–3.

9 In *Violence and Civility*, Étienne Balibar identifies the belief that violence can be eliminated as fundamental to our idea of politics, which is legitimized in its aim of order and control, its political institution, by the attempt at sublating violence. He suggests that this attempt at control becomes a force that suppresses the possibility of politics in an infinite circularity between violence and antiviolence, through which politics takes on an antinomic logic trapped in the imagination of violence and its opposite (Balibar, *Violence and Civility, On the Limits of Political Philosophy*, trans. G. M. Goshgarian, New York: Columbia University Press, 2015, p. 5).

10 Theodor W. Adorno, *The Starts Down to Earth*, London and New York: Routledge, 2007, p. 145 [1950].

11 Salomé Voegelin, 'Listening to the Stars', in NOCH VOLUME, *What Matters Now? (What Can't You Hear?)*, anthology on expanded listening, http://www.nochpublishing.com/, April 2013.

12 David Mollin and Salomé Voegelin, 'Are We Staring Down on a Doomsday Clock Getting Closer to Midnight or Merely Looking Out of the Kitchen Window?', in *THIS I THAT IS ALL OF YOU*, Brian Shabaglian (ed.), New York, 2017.

13 Balibar, *Equaliberty*, p. 26.

14 Ibid., p. 32.

15 Najibullah Akrami, 'Poem', in *Poetry of the Taliban*, Alex Strick van Linschoten and Felix Kuehn (eds), London: Hurst, 2012, p. 156. With permission and thanks to Hurst Publishers.

16 Rancière, *Disagreement, Politics and Philosophy*, p. 121.

17 Salomé Voegelin, edited excerpt from 'Ethics of Listening', *Journal for Sonic Studies*, vol. 2, no. 1 (2012).

18 Balibar, *Equaliberty*, p. 297.

19 Christian Bök, 'Fractal Geometry', in *Crystallography*, Ontario, Canada: Coach House, 2003. With permission from the author.

References

Adorno, Theodor W., *The Stars Down to Earth*, London: Routledge, 2007 [1950].

Akrami, Najibullah, 'Poem', in *Poetry of the Taliban*, Alex Strick van Linschoten and Felix Kuehn (eds), trans. Mirwais Rahmany and Hamid Stanikzai, London: Hurst, 2012, p. 156.

Balibar, Étienne, *Equaliberty*, trans. James Ingram, Durham and London: Duke University Press, 2014.

Balibar, Étienne, *Violence and Civility, On the Limits of Political Philosophy*, trans. G. M. Goshgarian, New York: Columbia University Press, 2015.

Barad, Karen, interview in *New Materialism: Interviews & Cartographies*, Rick Dolphijn and Iris van der Tuin, Ann Arbor, MI: Open Humanities Press, 2012.

Bök, Christian, 'Fractal Geometry', in *Crystallography*, Ontario, Canada: Coach House, 2003.

Eades, Caroline and Elizabeth A. Papazian (eds), *The Essay Film, Dialogue Politics Utopia*, New York: Columbia University Press, 2016.

Eshun, Kodwo, *More Brilliant than the Sun: Adventures in Sonic Fiction*, London: Quartet Books, 1998.

Mollin, David and Salomé Voegelin, 'Are We Staring Down on a Doomsday Clock Getting Closer to Midnight or Merely Looking Out of the Kitchen Window?' in *THIS I THAT IS ALL OF YOU*, Brian Shabaglian (ed.), New York, 2017.

Rancière, Jacques, *Disagreement, Politics and Philosophy*, Minneapolis, London: University of Minnesota Press, 1999.

Rancière, Jacques, *La Mésentente: politique et philosophie*, Paris: Galilée, 1995.

Schulze, Holger, 'How to Think Sonically? On the Generativity of the Flesh', in *Sonic Thinking: A Media Philosophical Approach*, Bernd Herzogenrath (ed.), New York: Bloomsbury, 2017, pp. 217–42.

Voegelin, Salomé, 'Ethics of Listening', *Journal for Sonic Studies*, vol. 2, no. 1 (2012), http://journal.sonicstudies.org/cgi/t/text/text-idx?c=sonic;sid=b04cc09b4 814ce9b29744216a2f1ee52;view=text;idno=m0201a08;rgn=main.

Voegelin, Salomé, 'Listening to the Stars', in NOCH VOLUME, *What Matters Now? (What Can't You Hear?)*, anthology on expanded listening, Daniela Cascella and Paolo Inverni (eds), April 2013, http://www.nochpublishing.com/.

Hearing subjectivities: Bodies, forms and formlessness

NO SKIN
Christopher was born without skin. He slid from his
mother all organs barely held in with muscle and sinew.
Naked at 35 he is still covered in a wide net of scars from
the unconventional patchwork grafting the doctors did.
Like the skin quilt they sewed onto him. Like Edward Scis-
sorhands. Like Herman Munster. Christopher loves it. It
makes him feel like a superhero who could at any minute
discover his powers. He has seriously considered getting
tattoos at all the scars' intersections. Little points of black
ink all over his body emphasizing the thin white lines.
Maybe cryptic symbols. Something badass. Maybe he
should shave his head.

Moss Angel[1]

The sonic flesh has no dermis, no skin, but inhabits the possibility of the
world with its own formless possibility. It is organs without a body, without
social boundaries and etiquette, and merges into the volume of the world
with its own capacity to be as volume a mass of plural things: unidentifiable,
half hazard and fluid.[2]

The shape of me is not revealed in my image but in my movements, in my
rhythm and my participation in the world's mobile form. My sound is part
of other sounds and they are part of me: we inter-are, objects and subjects
as things that define each other contingently, without creating complete
pictures and final identities, but as fluid approximations, converging towards

contingent shapes and dissolving again. There is a tyranny in the visual form that holds us in a certain place and demands a certain name. By contrast the skinlessness of sound allows the play of all the elements we are made of and puts the form on trial. In this formlessness, we get a chance to reinvent and reimagine the source and form of named identities, to listen for the cause and consequence of their delineation and make a noise to disrupt their naturalized shape. Thus we can fabulate on other possibilities, other forms and shapes to take, and other ways to live and speak. What 'thin white lines' would we make visible, what scarred intersection would we hide?

When Jean-Luc Nancy asks about the secret that is at stake when we truly listen, when we focus on the sonority rather than the message of a sound, he points to a 'cut in the un-sensed [*in-sensée*]', where we do not hear the source as a quasi visual and complete appearance or sign, as skin making a certain shape, but hear the scars and intersections that make a fragile form.[3] Sound provides an incomplete picture and brings signifiers into doubt: it is not 'this' or 'that', as things defined against each other, a matter of differences and similarities; and it does not offer us a certain form, but is the moment of production of what the thing and the listener are. This demands participation and offers an investment in its possibilities: to be in its encounter not its source or recipient, but the improbable identity of their 'interbeing', their being, according to Thich Nhat Hanh, as a relation of each other and of everything else.

Nhat Hanh's term acknowledges that there is no independent self but that every 'I' and everything is made of non-'I', non-thing elements.[4] I will be using this notion of interbeing to stress the perceptual focus on the in-between: the invisible process of production where things have no a priori and distinct meaning or definition, but are, in their contingent co-relationality, sensed at the cut in the un-sensed. This stretches a phenomenological intersubjectivity, the reciprocity of sensing subjects, into the realm of things, and shows their incomplete and formless form in the indivisibility of their 'interobjectivity'. Following Nhat Hanh we cannot define a thing or a subject by its source but by the complexity of its being as a being in the world and have to accept the interdependency and incompleteness of this existence.

> Suppose we try to return one of its elements to its source. Suppose we return the sunshine to the sun. Do you think that this piece of paper would be possible? No without sunshine nothing can be. And if we return the logger to his mother, then we have no piece of paper either. The fact is that this sheet of paper is made up only of 'non-paper elements'. And if we return these non-paper elements to their sources, then there can be no paper at all.[5]

The source delivers an arbitrary outcome and shape, which belies the complexity of its production and thus hides the cause and consequences of its definition, naturalizing it in a lexical sign. By contrast, in sound we exist transiently and contingently not as signifier or definition, but as the agitation of the between-of-things. Thus listening does not find its actuality in a source but performs the interrogation of what that might be. It questions the complete and its finite appearance and instead involves itself in the invisible and mobile connecting that creates the real as a cosmos of possibility. Consequently, subjectivity according to listening promotes an attitude of doubt in the complete, in the representation, in what we think we see as a persuasive whole, and what we think we do and want to look like.

In her essay 'A Thing Like You and Me', Hito Steyerl asks:

> What happens to identification at this point? Who can we identify with? Of course, identification is always with an image. But ask anybody whether they'd actually like to be a JPEG file. And this is precisely my point: if identification is to go anywhere, it has to be with this material aspect of the image, with the image as thing, not as representation. And then it perhaps ceases to be identification, and becomes participation. I will come back to this point later.[6]

I will come back to this point of participation later too, but for now want to contend, with Steyerl, that the image is not an ocular object but a material thing whose depth is not reached with a cultural eye but with an expanded ear. The image seen produces a representation, the pretense of a complete reproduction and the allusion to an authentic source. The image felt through its quasi audition, through its interrogation via a sonic sensibility, by contrast, brings us to the interbeing of its materiality, to comprehend how things converge on its surface without finding the certain form of the represented. The ear does not receive the complete representation of an actual thing, but works as process of interrogation and participation that does not recognize and see, but doubts the seen and senses something else: another way that I could be me, and you could be you. This admits that representation is an ideology rather than a possibility of the real, and that what we want to be needs to be invented rather than aspired to or copied.

Listening we experience the possible slices of this world, what might be and what else there is, behind and beyond the façade of a visual reality that trades in complete images, absolutes and certainties, and produces the neo-liberal interests of consensus and homogeneity constructing a realism and an identity which, in Jacques Rancière's terms, 'is the absorption of all reality and all truth in the category of the only thing possible'.[7] Reality as the only thing possible, is not a sonic possibility that is part of and opens up towards all the variants of this world. Instead, it is a tautological possibility as legitimacy of the absolute where those who have a part need to play a role, and those who have no part have even lost the right to appear as not counted. Rancière describes the absolute possible reality of a current political age as a community that is reduced to the sum of its parts, where singular voices are made speechless in a consensual amalgamation, where they have lost the power to interrupt and the opportunity to be interrupted, and where the noise that might pluralize reality has been muted.[8]

Identifiers such as gender, race, class, religion, which are potential seats for disruption and heterogeneity, are muted into certain forms, categories and lexical givens, whose representation we follow or are disabled against. The formlessness of a sonic subjectivity: my noise, my words, my song and my silence can disrupt this 'heterogeneous-homogeneity' and question bodily, through invisible inhabiting as resistance, the legitimacy of its consensus. The sonic possible subject exists like the sonic possible world in slices that are variants of its identity, as all she could be, indexical rather than absolute. This indexical position is formless, fluid and ephemeral and answers not a visual grid but the invisible and intersubjective practice of listening and making noise. Thus on the fabulated grid of a sonic index I can dance a different identity. My own formless form can take on shapes that transgress expectations, social parameters and norms. I can call myself anything and enter, via Saul Kripke's realist philosophy of language, into a counterfactuality that keeps its name even once it changes its form. Because his language does not affirm but questions the reference points and criteria that set the name in a lexical system.[9] And I can with Hélène Cixous rupture the norms of meaning and identity to disrupt and unravel what it is possible to write and what it is possible to be: 'sweeping away syntax, breaking that famous thread, (just a tiny little thread they say) which acts for men as a surrogate umbilical cord'.[10] To cut the stranglehold of canons, values and conventions and write not inside identity, confirming its limits, but apart from it, out of it, expressing its inexhaustibility and transitory nature.

In that sense sound, a sonic sensibility, offers the imagination of a trans-subjectivity that expands beyond the conventional identification of trans-gender into the realm of trans-technologial, trans-object, trans-political bodies who realize their contingent shapes in collaboration with others and other things rather than in the terms of or against an a priori definition. This is not a colonial stance, a taking over of the female by the male, the male by the female, of the body by technology, the individual by the community, as a violent act of redefinition, or what Étienne Balibar terms the 'ultraobjective' violence that reduces humans to the condition of things, or the 'ultrasubjective' violence that creates 'the fantasy representation of the Other as a mortal threat operating from inside the community: as if an inassimilable Foreigner had penetrated the Self'.[11] Rather, it is an acceptance of the other as part of the self to reach what Balibar terms an 'internal multiplicity', 'without which no self could exist'.[12] Sound stretches this capacity for multiplicity beyond internality and the intersubjective into a broader and open cohabitation of subjects and materials in a possible world – to form new shapes from contingent collaborations between my sound, yours and that of things.

This essay explores the formless, skinless body of listening as the basis of a sonic subjectivity and considers how it might restage visual notions of identity and belonging and their corresponding representation and use as a political and capitalist resource. It recognizes with Steyerl that the subject might not be the exclusive seat of emancipation anymore, and that it is in a meeting with the object as thing that a new sense of identity might emerge.

> Generations of feminists – including myself – have strived to get rid of patriarchal objectification in order to become subjects … But as the struggle to become a subject became mired in its own contradictions, a different possibility emerged. How about siding with the object for a change?[13]

Therefore, here I develop a subjectivity that takes account of itself as an identity with others, as a transitory and contingent interbeing that lives on the cut, in the invisible in-between of things where its agency does not produce representation, 'this' or 'that', but the ambiguity of the incomplete; and where it pursues via Kripke and Cixous the possibility for an identity that is not called into a system of givens and a priori criteria, but performs its own name and its own body to produce 'indispensable ruptures and transformations'.[14] In this way, I come to acknowledge with Balibar the violence of identity, and gain as Rancière aims to, an ear for the voice that is not heard.

I will deliberate on the possibility of such a transformative sonic subjectivity by listening to the work of Evan Ifekoya and Pamela Z, which invite us to sing, move and breathe together; to lay a different track from our bodies into the world, to connect not through references and givens, and to proffer ourselves not through the channels of identity, representation and actuality, but from the possibility of being everything with everything else.

Gender Song (2014) and *Disco Breakdown* (2014)

Evan Ifekoya dances, moves the body, hands and words in different clothes and different shoes, with wigs and hairdos, accessorized and unadorned. The songs are catchy and memorable, their tunes stay in your head, make you move and find a rhythm with the patterns, colours and things that move on screen. The voice sings in speech song without technique, which makes it unpretentious and easy to join in: and so I enter the work by its sound, rhythm and words, and participate in the flow of its transformations.

While the visual as image keeps the potential for distance and the opportunity to read the body as form and representation, the sound makes us converge in the material aspect of the seen, whose body is there, doubles up, triples up, quadruples and finds a way back to one through video editing techniques and effects that are no doubt digital but in their undisguised simplicity bring an analogue sense to the work. The fades and pop ups, split screens and overlays, highlight the materiality of the seen rather than what it represents, and make the image a thing that is malleable and transformable rather than the stable representation of the original subject.

The effects are collaged, superimposed and brought next to each other; edges are sought and juxtapositions created whose reality is performed in sound. Listening we hear the work's dimensionality that expands its frame and gives us access to its movements where it is not about what is seen but how it is agitated and agitating its own reality between hands and bodies, things and words, that are not separate constituents of one seen but are the invisible material of the image-plane heard from its depth. In listening the image escapes its borders and preconditions. Sound confronts my gaze and preconceptions with an invisible rhythm that beckons participation and questions the visual parameters of negotiation by demanding a more self-conscious reflection: the words singing about gender, work, identity, dancing and expectations become mine to resing and reimagine, to own and speak rather than receive, and I have to, as Ifekoya demands, practice self-reflection:

> When I am performing I tend to think less about …, or even in my video work, I kind of feel like I am an avatar in a way. And actually, I think in an ideal world maybe what I'd have is like some kind of mirror. Like my face would just be a mirror in a performance, like that is what I am trying to do in a way. I am more interested in putting up these things that encourage a self-reflection.[15]

The voice is the mirror on Ifekoya's face and throws my gaze back at me. I can hear myself looking at my own skinless formless form projecting another. Hearing the artist's voice reverses my gaze to see how I look, not as an image but as an agency, and it reveals what I see in a new light. Its sound invites the performance of different forms and shapes, transitory and transforming, dancing to a syncopated rhythm without recourse to virtuosity, a right way to sing, a right way to dance.

Most of Ifekoya's work is accessible online and lives very well in the fluid vernacular of the virtual where categories between art and commentary, fact and fiction, work and leisure start to break down and where the certainty of their meaning and authority starts to dissolve, and their definitions take on other forms that get their signification not from one source but from the cross referencing of different sources and contexts.[16] This presence online enables the work to critique and reframe the boundaries and interdependencies of old knowledge and to perform new points of views, new bodies and new identities that might not settle on a certain form but keep on dancing their own transition between places of history, identity and belonging.

Online the artist's work starts to converse beyond defined spaces across the realm of commerce, politics and fashion, and finds a relevant association in pop music, listened to and streamed. In that way it gains the ability to interfere in the naturalized look of commercial representations and becomes able to introduce other possibilities. It manages to engage in the discourse of representation and identity by performing alienation and its alternatives in the awkward space between expectation and what is really there.

But it is not only the placing of the work online but also the placing of the artist within the work that is particular to this task of reimagining identity, representation and self. The two works that inspire this writing, *Gender Song* and *Disco Breakdown* and the work-cum-interview *Genuine. Original. Authentic* (2015) feature Ifekoya prominently, not as subject but as material agent, dancing and singing, talking and moving: as a sound image that holds the dimensionality of interaction and agitation, and the potential to be without a source at the edge of the invisible.

The artist's body is part of this complex audiovisual-image-thing. It participates in its production and generates itself as an aspect of its material. Rather than remaining an authentic represented, it performs its contingent subjectivity as a skinless and mobile identity. Even as the visual image pretends a separation between the reproduction and its source, the subject and the object of representation, and offers us a gap, an absence, to step into and define them both, the sonic image knows no original and does not defer itself to a source, but generates it. The visual 'gap' nourishes the idea that we can truly understand things, assign them names from a lexicon, and define ourselves in relation to those names as stable subjects, as identities. It purports a knowledge that is not produced in practice but received as abstracted facts by identities that are not producing themselves but are a product of historical, economical, racial and gendered identification. By contrast, in sound I am simultaneous with the heard whose identity I am too close to see but have to negotiate in this blind encounter. No gap is left from which to guide the work back to its symbolic register and to give the body its lexical name. Instead, a new lexicon needs to be produced that can name invisible things and bodies as things in transition that have no desire to arrive or to stand still.

The ear works not along the lines of reproduction as the recreation and making up for the absence of the real, but generates the real from what is heard, which is always absent; and it does not hear the complete but practices fragments, edges, visible and invisible slices of what things are or what they might be. In this way, it injects possibility into the apparently finished form, and invents its 'malformation' as a legitimate identity:

How about acknowledging that this image is not some ideological misconception, but a thing simultaneously couched in affect and availability, a fetish made of crystals and electricity, animated by our wishes and fears – a perfect embodiment of its own condition of existence?[17]

Ifekoya *is* the image in sound, there is no real Ifekoya, as a substrate or 'norm', which here is only performing its own aberration. Listening to the work I see the generative fiction of the body as material presence that is all there is and that gains significance in its performative 'condition of existence' rather than as its author, subject or object. The sound as the physical agency of singing and as the concept of a performative self demands inhabiting and participation. The sonic body dances within the material of the image, taking part in the temporal flow of its production within which it abandons a clear sense of autonomy but grasps what it is from what they are together. Sound opens the relationship between rhythm, lights, movements and words into whose between the body disappears as a clear identity and within which it reappears as an interbeing: a subject made of things.

Referring to a remark by Elisabeth Lebovici, Steyerl suggests that,

Traditionally, emancipatory practice has been tied to a desire to become a subject. Emancipation was conceived as becoming a subject of history, of representation, or of politics. To become a subject carried within it the promise of autonomy, sovereignty, agency. To be a subject was good; to be an object was bad.[18]

She goes on to remark that 'the subject is always already subjected' and therefore another way, another autonomy might need to be found that does not hold the tyranny of a name and identification, which might offer the certainty of a historical determination, but which also carries the limits and prejudice of this certainty and the consequences of its name, and which holds the potential too of its imminent abuse as a political and capitalist resource: to be as woman the target of your desire, the consumer of your product and the recipient of exclusion and lower pay. The lexical definition categorizes us, it overrides our actions and agency and determines, before we can move or dance, what we are.

A Kantian philosophy of language, according to Howard Caygill, still today totally and almost imperceptibly so, pervades our conception of language as a lexical resource and represents the cornerstone of Western thought, decisively influencing the organization and possibility of our thinking, speaking and writing. Although, according to Caygill, Kant's own views on language were more open-ended and discursive than some would come to interpret and use them, or indeed criticize them for, what is relevant here is that its analogical definitions lend a hand to structures, networks, taxonomies and lexicons and thus set the parameters of the possibility of knowledge, identity and thought, and delineate as unthinkable and impossible what falls outside its grammar and logic.[19] The pervasiveness of his conception of language means that it is not only within the remit of philosophy but also across the larger cultural consciousness, its sense of signification, truth and worth, that a Kantian language frame influences the definition of the real and thus delimits the mobility of knowledge and identity: what a woman, a man, a child, a chair or a table can be is determined by their correspondence to criteria associated with that word, and while those criteria may develop over time, they still represent a definition that precedes and determines our living those names.[20] In a Kantian worldview, the description 'justifies' the name as a word that refers the object or subject to a set of lexical givens, which it needs to fulfil to be called thus. Once the object or subject stops to comply with those givens it stops being called by its name. A chair is a chair because it fulfills the function, criteria and expectation of what that is. If it fails in its function, if it breaks down, changes shape, loses its legs, it ceases to be a chair as it cannot fulfil its criteria anymore, or it becomes a 'broken chair'. This seems a relatively harmless distinction in relation to a chair but reveals itself to be much more consequential when translated to a human or an animal, a fact that ought to make us think about the possibility for a more mobile identity and its performance in language.

Kant's conception of language enables taxonomies of abstract knowledge and creates structures about what things are and how the world is. They grant legitimacy, enable consensus and communication, but at the same time they disable the transformation and contingency of the subject and object who cannot change for fear of losing the 'autonomy, sovereignty and agency' of their name. Language thus applied names not the fluid 'condition of existence' but the stable body of subjects and objects within an etymological and symbolic frame that grants their image a visible form, but hides their skinlessness and the scars of a contingent identity that could make them 'feel like a superhero who could at any minute discover his powers'.[21]

Evan Ifekoya

Evan Ifekoya performs a different philosophy of language, where the name remains but the form changes, is transitory, in process and on trial, without ever ceasing definition. 'Dance is all I want to do'. This refrain in *Disco Breakdown* voices repeatedly the desire not to work, not to function, but to dance instead and is juxtaposed with 'I should' 'I should' as a reminder of what is expected and what criteria have to be fulfilled. The artist sings the wish not to engage in the functionality of work and of identity, and to instead perform a mobile existence, while crafting a disco ball from small mirror plates, glue and hands. The piece at once addresses racial stereotypes of the entertaining body, and engages the work ethic and the commensurate identities of neo-liberalism in a bodily critique. It denies work and the name of work through dance, becoming a subject through the autonomous movement of the body rather than its lexical definition and an abstract reference to work.

The moving body is the name in sound, and performs a Kripkean naming of a subjectivity that keeps its designation whatever its form. Saul Kripke's philosophy of language advanced in *Naming and Necessity* (1972) articulates against a Kantian background a realist philosophy that does not refer words to a lexical structure but names, as in baptizes, objects and subjects, which then remain named so in all counterfactual situations, even if their function and form, what they are doing and look like, or what we might think of them, change. The named is certain of who it is: a dog, a cat, a mouse, but there are many variants of how it can be so without ceasing to be itself.

With recourse to Aristotle's pre-enlightenment philosophy, where concepts and thoughts are not tied to words, Kripke overturns Kant's analytical philosophy and recognizes a different relationship between words as names that acknowledges the mutability of the named and references the context of naming rather than a lexicon of names. His language does not discover correspondences and does not organize things according to lexical givens but calls them within 'rigid designators' that identify the name without corresponding criteria but through the testimony of its context. It eschews historical necessity, ideal references and absolutes, and instead focuses on the circumstance of definition, the contingent, ahistorical associations that enable designation as the condition of existence, and that give the name its credibility and legitimacy. The best example to illustrate this lived condition of a given name can be heard in Kripke's lecture on the unicorn in which he suggests that even if the bones of a thing fulfilling all the criteria of the fabled beast would be found, these could not be retro associated to the unicorn as they exist not in the context of the flesh but live in the circumstance of their own invention as fabled beasts. Instead, these bones would have to be given a new name, in recognition of their autonomous existence.[22]

Kripke's philosophy of language, as a cultural consciousness, has the potential to rethink knowledge, the authority and subject of knowledge as well as its object, and leaves room to debate the circumstance and agency of its definition: who can participate in its production, what histories and canons determine its legitimacy and what about those that cannot be found in history and those that come from the future; what about the invisible and the inaudible?[23]

The name in sound moves Kripke's baptism into the designation of the unseen where it does not find confirmation in a visual form, but articulates the agency of the predicate, which generates a mobile world that keeps on changing its look under cover of its designation. Sound brings to Kripke's logic the phenomenon of the invisible that functions not as entity but as the between of things, and challenges him to name the ephemeral and the passing. In this way, a sonic philosophy of language takes from Kripke the contextual action of designation and the variability of the named, and adds to it the contingency of its call, which performs rather than structures or defines the heard and names, unnames and renames it again and again. Thus adapted, Kripke's realist philosophy is useful to grasp the mobility of a sonic world and to give autonomy and authority to the invisible subject, without subjecting it to the definition of its name, but by instead listening out for its fluid designation, and empowering it to call itself through its mobile relationship with others and other things. And so to hear Ifekoya's voice and sound, is to hear the artist's fluid condition, which refuses a lexical definition and invites participation and self-reflection instead.

In this way, a sonic practice and philosophy escapes taxonomies and historical determination and gains identity as a transitive potential that is reciprocal and does not have to arrive back in a lexicon, however contingent and contextual. Instead, it can move on and through, and therefore it can perform the possibilities and even the impossibilities of its skinless body. As Ifekoya sings in the *Gender Song*: 'Female hemale shemale don't matter ... gender is not sex, so don't get it twisted.'

Thus I give up on the lexical definition and call myself by my own name, so I do not have to look for myself in history, where according to Hélène Cixous and Catherine Clément I cannot be found anyway. 'What is my place if I am a woman? I look for myself throughout the centuries and don't see myself anywhere' ... 'Where to stand? Who to be?'[24] So instead of looking for an image that even if found would only represent what I am supposed to be rather than what I am, I have to invent myself, as Ifekoya does, singing and dancing, without fear of definition, in the certainty that the song will let me transform and change. In sound I am becoming a subject not through the name but through the movement of the body that calls itself and can take on any form without losing authority.

> The future must no longer be determined by the past. I do not deny that the effects of the past are still with us. But I refuse to strengthen them by repeating them, to confer upon them an irremovability the equivalent of destiny, to confuse the biological and the cultural. Anticipation is imperative.[25]

Ifekoya's dancing and singing body ruptures the power of the past, its lexical name and definition, conventionally understood as a point of strength and self-assertion, but which is always also the locale of repeated subjugation. Thus she brings a new emancipatory force into play. This new emancipatory force does not rely on history and conventions for its authority but on the present condition of existence that becomes visible in its own song. The rupture of the past, through the performance of the voice, translates Cixous's request for women to write in order to achieve 'the indispensable ruptures and transformations in her history' into a request for women to sing; to perform a feminine subjectivity in song.[26] Ifekoya performs the rupture by singing, and by considering femininity without its pronoun she fast-forwards into the future of Cixous's 'unknown women' that can be found in the undefined spaces, the in-between, where names do not define but generate, transform, grant agency and autonomy without histories, lexicons or grammar. From there we can update Cixous's feminine writing into a writing of trans-subjectivity.

> Her language does not contain, it carries; it does not hold back, it makes possible. When it is ambiguously uttered – the wonder of being several – she doesn't defend herself against these unknown women whom she's surprised at becoming, but derives pleasure from this gift of alterability. I am spacious, singing flesh, on which is grafted no one knows which I, more or less human, but alive because of transformation.[27]

Ifekoya is the unknown singing flesh, alive because of transformation. The feminine rupture without a pronoun is the sensibility and agency of a skinless sonic body that has the power to take on any shape and form and to sound against a dominant masculine logic the potential of the undefined as 'a multiple and inexhaustible course with millions of encounters and transformations of the same into the other and into the in-between'.[28]

Even though 'The Laugh of the Medusa', Cixous's 1976 text on a feminine writing from which I quote above and glean the 'unknown women' whose libido is cosmic, whose language denies the grammar of masculine logic, who are defined by an infinite and mobile complexity and who perform their bodies in writing, does not mention as name or grammatical possibility the idea of trans-subjectivity, her essay suggests that writing is precisely the in-between and the undefined that finds contingent definition in its performance and produces the circumstance of a different definition not tied to physiology or history but to the desire of a present existence.

I take Cixous's call to woman to 'put herself into the text – as into the world and into history – by her own movement', to assert a femininity that can 'by her own movement' transform 'the same into the other and into the in-between', and take on any role it wants, any look it desires.[29] This is not to deny the feminine, the specificity of 'her' neglect and discrimination, but to accept with Steyerl that a historical subjectivity has lost the promise of agency with which to fight for autonomy and sovereignty, its right to make itself count and to be reflected in the world's design. Since, in a neo-liberal context 'her' pronoun is used as a political and capitalist resource, as site a of a social mythology and territory for colonialization that shuts her performance down, a more powerful emancipatory force lies with a sonic designator that offers the subject its transformative potential and gives access to the in-between, as the refusal of definition and the play with the possible from which to 'go right up to the impossible'.[30]

The critical agency of the avatar-I

> I kind of feel like I am an avatar in a way. And actually, I think in an ideal world maybe what I'd have is like some kind of mirror.[31]

The authority of a normative identity can exist in the impersonal. It needs no particular interface to see itself. Its form is omnipresent and recognizable. It is evidenced and mirrored in what counts as actually real and it expects to see itself mirrored in my gaze. Therefore, it needs no device of self-reflection to articulate its subjectivity or agency, it *is* their definition and sees itself reflected absolutely. Its reality is not experiential or transitory, generated in the heterogeneity of a doubtful 'I', but presumes certainty and stability in the only reality there could possibly be, whose singular status is so pervasive as to be transparent, and whose identification so absolute as to need no contrivance for an alternative reflection or a different agency.

The sonic mirror of Ifekoya's voice by contrast is the articulation of absence, where the lack of a pronoun does not signify omnipresent transparency, but a void in language and in our imagination to account for a transitory subjectivity and its possible reality. It does not assert the demand to represent but invites self-reflection. The mirror-voice breaks my gaze and makes me audible to myself in my relationship with the artist. It presents actuality as an intersubjective possibility within which we negotiate as contingent differences, through whose tensions the transparent 'I' loses its hegemony and discipline, and the world gains its sociopolitical dimensions.

The 'I' that is audible to itself acknowledges other 'I's and at least knows of if not hears their audibility. The 'I' of authority by contrast only hears itself without being audible to itself. Without, in other words, the humility or responsibility for the difference and conflict that makes the self doubt itself and the other count. That is why the focus on the body is not the privileging of an immersive, pre-reflective physicality, an anthropocentrism run riot, but the acknowledgement of a fragile subjectivity. The sonic self as 'avatar-I' deflects norms and provides representation to the inaudible and grants it the opportunity to make itself heard and its listening gain influence.

The avatar-I performs not a certain identity but presents a sonic mirror that allows the 'I' to maneuver and reconnect, illuminate and articulate what from the third, the impersonal person remains too dense and immobile and what in the first person appears too emotive and closed-off. Thus, the avatar grants movement and agency, while the 'I' keeps a focus on the humility and openness of the subjectivity that is the locus of that agency.

The conceptualization of the avatar-I provides a means and location to hear the world beyond that which is mirrored in the singular actuality of the perceived real and its normative language. It stages the artist not as a referent but as a portal into a possibility where plural and less audible subjects and things sound, and it enables the performance of unknown subjectivities and things through the reflection of my gaze. In this sense, the avatar-I performs the 'I' not for itself, but for its agency to illuminate less audible and even inaudible subjectivities and things, and applies its sensitivity to the articulation of the overlooked and the ignored. In the mirror of the sonic avatar the listening selves function not simply as alternative centres of power and determination, but as things among things, with the humility of their own doubt and the responsibility to listen out for what cannot make itself heard: that which has no name or that which wants to fall out of its historical name and definition. The sonic mirror reflects another space where things find other relations and my own gaze gains a different view.

Instead of becoming a subject of history, subjected to the consequences and causes of my name's subjugation and neglect, or categorized within the descriptions of lexical givens, I can look into the mirror of Ifekoya's voice, dance with the artist, and sing with the autonomy of things, in the in-between, in the undefined spaces where we are not 'this' or 'that' but 'inter-are', transient and transforming, a thing of other things, comingling and forming part of skinless bodies that are the material rather than the representation of what we see.

> I just like to be in these in-between spaces, these like undefined spaces. You know, I just do not want to have to be one or the other, I am quite happy to be inbetween, but I just don't want to be put into a box that I didn't chose. And all I can do is keep making work that just moves and shifts in different places.[32]

Breathing (2014, solo version)

> We must kill the false woman who is preventing the live one from breathing. Inscribe the breath of the whole woman.[33]

Pamela Z is breathing, her body breathes into the microphone, into technology that amplifies and multiplies the invisible material of her breath, while her voice is singing 'I was breathing' and 'I am breathing', again and again in operatic gestures and spoken lines, as whispers and as sounds. The movement of her right arm activates and changes the articulation of her breath and of her voice via a MIDI-controller that is strapped to her wrist and reacts to muscular movements and contractions; other sounds and manipulations are produced by her fingers passing by an ultrasound-activated box, placed on a little stand next to her laptop that sits on the other side of the microphone that started the cycle of action and interaction by recording her breath.

The track is seven minutes long and forms part of *Carbon Song Cycle* (2013), a longer rendering of the piece that includes accompaniment of bassoon, viola, cello and percussion. The one I am listening to is the solo version, shorter and voice only. However, this voice does not remain singular but produces the proliferation of Pamela Z's body through her breath and song, which is conducted by the gesture-activated controller on her right wrist and the ultrasound activated box on the stand. The wrist-attached controller resembles a bionic appendix, whose power at once recalls an archaic notion of occultist magic, of moving things by gestures and the mind alone, and conjures a futuristic vision of bodies with technologically facilitated super powers that transcend the limitations of the human form and prejudice. The microphone, the laptop, the MIDI-controller and the ultrasound box, cords and sockets, BodySynth™, VST plugins and so forth, enable the plural materializations of her body in the invisible utterance of her breath, and 'operate' on its texture and spatiality.[34] In this way her breath comes to inscribe the whole woman beyond her physical form, as a libidinal force, as an inexhaustible and complex expansion, whose voice generates an as yet impossible subject that gains corporeality through the poetry of the invisible and comes to suggest its possibility by her own movements.

This technological operation produces her work as an infinite end of plural means that articulates as the coincidence of both languages: that of technology and that of the body; the machine and the physical, converging in the sound of her breath in which they are extended invisibly into a multiplicity of voices that meet pre-recorded word samples – 'humans', 'orang-utans', 'little shellfish', 'exuding carbon dioxide', 'oxygen' – which syncopate the flow of her ephemeral plurality to create an unseen and fleeting assemblage.

Pamela Z creates her multiplicity through a trans-technological practice, which brings all the variants of her body together in her breath, and proliferates them outside of her skin, the outline and border of her objectivity, in a fantastic imagination of her skinless form and possibility. However, the air does not always flow steadily. Sampled sounds pick up and generate the catch of her own breath and play with the consonants of its material where the air does not flow unhindered but makes a stutter, meets an obstacle and seems to suffocate. All the while her voice reassures us 'I was breathing', 'I am breathing'.

Her trans-technological body is complex and concentrated. It is generated from the virtuosity of her performance with technological tools that respond through a network of electrodes to every movement in her arm. But it is not idealized, in the sense of instrumentalized and perfect. Instead it is physical, libidinal and material. It does not create the representation of the subject as a techno-body, colonialized and repurposed by the machine, but forms a trans-technological subjectivity sensitive to her biology and practicing their shared capacities. The technology strengthens her voice rather than giving her another. It amplifies and extends her body that resources itself. Pamela Z is not taken-over and she is not erased, but asserts her autonomy, sovereignty and identity through the performance of her invisible body made possible by technological means but not to their ends.

Her performance is visual, it is a spectacle of physical concentration performed between her body and the technology that surrounds her and around which she moves to articulate her breath. Its articulation is not limited to this gaze however, which in some way is only the concession she pays to the needs of a live audience. Instead, the intrigue and pluralizing energy lies in the invisible performance: the unseen workings of muscles and synapsis up and down the conducting arm; the invisible between of body and technology where ultrasonic waves trigger the breath that came from her lungs; and the dark mobility of sound from where between intent and technology a different body emerges that has the capacity to become an 'impossible subject' demanding to be heard, demanding we imagine at least an aesthetic and social framework within which she might become possible and even real.

This sonic invisibility complicates the potential awe and wonder at the technological capability and its virtuous use, and offers an alternative focus that hears interactions and co-productions, forming a 'techno-subjective' environment rather than showing its tools. I am not staring at the bionic man but hear the invisible materializing of a bionic femininity. I hear a new body a new poetry of the breath that is the material of Steyerl's emancipatory image, which eschews representation and has Cixous's transformative capacity and power of eroticization, not to manipulate but 'to dash through and to "fly"'.[35]

To fly in French, as Cixous points out, is *voler*, which at once means to fly and to steal, and thus in this context connotes the ability to lift off, to lose the gravity of the human form and its physical and societal constraints and to steal a different definition: to call myself by my breath.

Trans-technological subjectivity: Listening to the unicorn breathing

The breath is the poetry of the body; it is where its invisible and mobile plurality lies and where it performs the acceptance of the other as part of the self, to reach what Balibar terms an '"internal multiplicity", all *différence* in the self (the "us") and its others without which no self could exist'.[36] In this passage from *Violence and Civility* (2015), Balibar talks about the tyranny of an idealized identity, *an identity identical to itself* (national, religious or racial) that believes itself to be exclusive, and that seeks to oppress and eliminate all otherness and to effect the suppression of all difference, to attain its own realization. This dialectical and absolute self is acted out through 'ultrasubjective' violence, the frenzied hatred and irrational cruelty against all otherness even if it involves hurting or killing the self: 'one's own death is preferable to any mixing, intercourse, or hybridization, the threat of which is perceived at the fantasy level as worse than death.'[37] It manifests a desire for a false autonomy and a false sovereignty, and stems from an *idealized hatred* of the other, which, according to Balibar, paradoxically presents an obliteration of the self, since, the self cannot exist without its internal multiplicity: it cannot exist without 'humans', 'orang-utans', 'little shellfish', 'carbon dioxide', 'oxygen'.

This need for the other to exist as part of the self, articulated in relation to violence and identity, reframes the philosophy of interbeing, articulated by Thich Nhat Hanh within a political perspective. Nhat Hanh's belief that there is no independent, self-sufficient self but that every 'I' and everything is made of non-'I', non-thing elements meets Balibar's pronunciation of the tyranny of a reified and absolutized identity manifest in the denial of any trace of otherness in the self. In juxtaposition and superimposition, they confirm the political possibility and dimension of interbeing as a critical and generative subjectivity that confronts the violence of the absolute through a mobile and transitive 'I': a political trans-subjectivity.

I have earlier located the agency of this interbeing in sound, which calls not 'this' or 'that' but the in-between, and names, as in gives a fluid designator to the invisible co-production of things. Through Balibar we come to appreciate the political nature of this interbeing as an alternative to a homogenized and fetishized definition. Consequently, sound, as an access point to and as material of this political dimension of identity in interbeing, attains an emancipatory force, and listening, as a focus on and participation in the invisible agency of such an in-between, attains a political possibility: the possibility to critically hear not just the historical representation of identity and its commensurate sublimation and suppression, but to recognize also the undercurrents of what Balibar calls the psychotic cast of idealized hatred, which sees the other as an enemy who is both 'potential victim and mimetic persecutor'; who at once threatens the self through his otherness and needs to be threatened.[38] This listening must be attentive to the violence of an ideological identity and its representation, and it must aim to hear another possibility in the contingent encounter between the self with the other, with the world and with things. This consideration assigns listening the responsibility and task to see into the sociopolitical actuality of the world, to illuminate its intersections, overlaps and co-productions; and demands sound making as inter-action and inter-invention of alternative possibilities of definition, value and form.[39]

The sound of Pamela Z's breath, amplified and conducted, transforming into song, meeting words, changing shape, becoming a stutter and confirming itself again, is the invisible agency of her interbeing with technology, with other subjects, with things and with language. Her *Breathing* performs her '*différence* in the self': her plural and complex identity with others, whose autonomy does not define an absolute identity and location, but practices a diffuse being that is a being of the other as being part of the self. Her performance reveals sonic subjectivity as an identity that is contingent and in process, certain not of itself but produced in a transformative exchange with another that is not threatening or threatened, but inter-invents their formless form.

Pamela Z's performance focuses not on the voice but on the breath that enables the voice, and enables the body, through its interbeing with an oxygenized world. The breath is our silent base-rhythm that illustrates our inability to self-sustain, to be anything without being with others and other things. It keeps the body alive through its reciprocal and renewing bond with the world, and performs subjectivity as an invisible exchange with other beings that thus become part of our selves. Her breath sounds her own multiplicity as the simultaneous plurality with others that expands her body and her capacity, and realizes invisibly the political possibility of a sonic subjectivity that is capable of political participation and the effecting of change.

Breathing is at once a necessity of life and the fantastic extension of the body. It is its fabulation and creates the invisible performance of a mobile and multifold self that transgresses a normative representation and function and makes a formless form that conjures possibilities and impossibilities and opens up to different interactions. It breaks through the limits of actuality of what Rancière identifies as 'the community of speaking beings' and makes 'the invisible visible, to give a name to the anonymous and to make words audible where only noise was perceptible before'.[40] While this breakthrough of silence as a break into audibility performs a violence, this is not a dialectical but an emancipatory violence, predicated by the violence of a political reality that has limited the inaudible voice to the condition of things.[41] It is a violence that does not seek to silence or suppress but to sound itself: to participate and to listen in order to unthink a singular reality that insists on the impossibility of the impossible, and to unthink the oppressively close relationship between logic and language, the lexical contract between identity and name, and perform other possibilities.[42]

The transformation of the body through its breath is powerful. It unthinks and unperforms the actuality of the body, expending of its form and certainties. Thus it thinks and performs contingent and reciprocal shapes that enter the political order and question the management of its structure and the limits of its reality. The breath confronts political speech with its noise and generates a different interface, a different plane on which to interact, to listen, to speak and to be heard. This demand is physical and erotic. The breathing body seeks an intercourse with the world, it demands for the scars and stitches of its skinless body to be sewn into the body politic, for it to sing and dance with its language and form new intersections that can grow together and become parts of a complex and fluid entirety.

In some ways, Pamela Z's *Breathing* is the invisible equivalent of Rebecca Horn's *Einhorn* (Unicorn), her wearable sculpture of a unicorn dress and work made between 1970 and 1972 from bandages, a wooden horn and metal clasps, which was worn by a woman who Horn had chosen for her upright posture. She was filmed walking through the empty landscape in the early morning: 'Her figure mirrors the tall foliage surrounding her, but her pale skin and long white horn separate her from her environment, conjuring images of the fabled creature the title references.'[43] The work creates a generative trans-subjectivity between the human form and the fabled beast, created in the interbeing of flesh, fabric, metal and wood, which together perform the possibility of a different subjectivity and a different being in the world.

Both works engage the body in an encounter with technology, the technology of sonic reproduction, sampling and diffusion, and the technology of cloth, wood, feathers as well as large bandages and prostheses. Both dress the body and augment the body, give it extensions and bring it into motion to test and try a different outline, a different intersection where the scars and stitches between the Einhorn suit, the biosynth wristband and the body are not seen but their transforming potential takes place; and where the body meets the world and transforms its view.

The *Einhorn* and *Breathing* perform, against what Rancière terms a 'governmental curbing' of politics, the limiting of an administration's accountability and action within the realm of a designated real, a pluralized economy of erotic extensionality.[44] The transformation of the body through both the breath and the wooden horn is erotic, empowering, and self-generating. Its eroticism ruptures a designated real and practices through the fabulation of bodies and movements contingent possibilities, creating the self in a fantastical form and sharing its creation through the mirror of the avatar-I. In this way, the extensionality of the prosthesis and the breath becomes our shared erotic possibility, as a political possibility of desire that uncurbs politics.

According to Rancière, current governments delimit politics within a humanitarian frame that grants universal and thus universalizing human rights but eschews the rights of the individual as citizen as a singular person and formless voice, and thus denies the possibility of the impossible, not because it is really not possible or true but because its truth disables consensus governance. By contrast, *Breathing* and *Einhorn* produce the extension of the body into its impossibility, not by simply appropriating something, nor˙by being overtaken and controlled by another thing, but by coming together with technology and things to realize subjectivity as an interbeing that resources the self and amplifies its as yet unheard voices. But while the images of the *Einhorn* have become iconic, they have come to *be* Horn's work in representation, which limits its generative and transitive force, the invisible interbeing of sound keeps on refreshing Pamela Z's trans-production. It keeps on breathing, constituting the body between the source and rhythm of its life. Sound avoids representation, and remains invisibly the inexhaustible source of the body's renewal and fabulation. Therefore, we have to consider the *Einhorn* with the sound of Pamela Z's breath in our ears, to re-perform, again and again the faint calling of its invisible self as a conceptual sonic subjectivity that avoids the identification with the image and continues to participate in its materiality.

> Back to the heart chambers,
> back to the bloodstreams
> resembling branches of energy outside the body,
> Flowing from one person to another,
> Like a web of electrical currents.[45]

This coming together with the other to become a proper and powerful self, that is neither colonializing nor colonialized, that is not reified and absolute, but open and open-ended, demands the responsibility and humble generosity of the avatar-I: the sonic subjectivity that remains invisible but reflects, agitates and inter-invents and makes available connections, realities and possibilities through which it creates the space and condition of existence as multiplicity.

> If there is a self proper to woman, paradoxically it is her capacity to depropriate herself without self-interest: endless body, without 'end', without principle 'parts'; if she is a whole, it is a whole made up of parts that are wholes, not simple, partial objects but a varied entirety, moving and boundless change, a cosmos where eros never stops trailing, vast astral space.[46]

This 'depropriated woman' as varied entirety, moving and boundless, articulated by Cixous and Clément, suggests a feminine subjectivity that refers us not simply to a biological gender or its categorization and appropriation within politics and neo-liberal capitalism, but to a fluid calling of femininity, as the name of a sensibility, agency and attitude. This femininity acts and interacts as a mobile trans-subjectivity, that realizes itself in the between of the body and the world, its things and technology, without suppressing or sublimating anything or itself in the process. The idea is not to become the technology, the MIDI-controller or the prosthesis of wood, metal, fabric and bandages, or to deform, delimit, abuse and use them, but to perform and understand that subjectivity is the interbeing with these things in their entirety and in hers, 'without "end"', without impossibility and silence.[47] It is their reciprocal production that is not body or technology but is their trans-formation. This trans-formation articulates as verb and as noun. It articulates an identity of interbeing that is not rigid but transitory, and that is not an idealized destination, but calls into being a moveable locale of reciprocity and shared production. Thus it is the locus and action of the political possibility of a sonic subjectivity that agitates against representation, discrimination and exclusion.

Unperforming identity and knowledge

In *Genuine, Original, Authentic*, Evan Ifekoya talks about unperforming the representation of the black body as an ever performing and entertaining body by moving against its frame: re-singing, re-dancing it to erase its image and to rupture the historical definition that reduces its identity to the condition of its representation. Instead, the artist's movements generate a different language of this body and a different imagination of its name. Similarly, Pamela Z unperforms an idealized instrumentality and the functionality of technology with her breath, and thus she unperforms an idealized and instrumentalized subjectivity. She 'breathes' through tools for making sounds, or what Tara Rodgers, alluding to the military history and purpose of sound technology, terms the 'interface to ghosts of technoscientific projects past', and breathes out a body without expansionist purpose and ideal form, but of an extensional and shared existence.[48]

Pamela Z's work does not use technology to overcome human inadequacies, or to attain an idealized virtuosity. Her 'MIDI-appended' body does not enter into the dialectic of strength and sublimation, suppressing individuality into a generalized condition of instrumentality, but realizes the body and the technology in their particular existence together. This is an emancipatory unperforming of a technological necessity that does not follow its own chronology in the service of perfection and with an expansionist zeal, but enables an interbeing and co-production of the possibilities of the impossible, both of the body and of the tool; and it is an unperforming also of a feminine subjectivity that is not caught in the place of her history but enacts and invents a different future. Just as Ifekoya reclaims a performative subjectivity that cannot be stereotyped, bought or sold, but moves to be as alterability unrepresentable; the expanded breath does not overtake and suppress Pamela Z's identity, but realizes it, makes it possible beyond a visual frame and capacity, as a variable interbeing.

Both artists unperform normative positions and given expectations by performing a 'feminine song' that is not gendered but physical and cosmic: dancing a 'vast astral space' where the noun's trans-formation is an inexhaustible predicate that does not tie itself into the neo-liberal drive of a phallocentric organization and taxonomy, but expands, boundlessly into anything it could be with anything that could be and even things that cannot be, or seem impossible, at least for now. Their works pursue libidinal extensions into an invisible economy of being everywhere with everything without hierarchy, discrimination or the neo-liberal thrust of profit and the devaluation of the apparently worthless.

> Woman does not perform on herself this regionalization that profits the couple head-sex, that only inscribes itself within frontiers. Her libido is cosmic, just as her unconscious is worldwide: her writing also can only go on and on, without ever inscribing or distinguishing contours, daring these dizzying passages in other, fleeting and passionate dwellings within him, within the hims and hers whom she inhabits just long enough to watch them, as close as possible to the unconscious from the moment they arise; to love them, as close as possible to instinctual drives, and then, further, all filled with these brief identifying hugs and kisses, she goes and goes on infinitely. She alone dares and wants to know from within where she, the one excluded, has never ceased to hear what-comes-before-language, reverberating.[49]

The profits of the couple head-sex, as Cixous and Clément call it, are the profits of the spectacle technology, its neo-liberal function, drive and aims. It does not have to think about what comes before language as it is transparent to itself in language. It 'speaks' in the language of words, grammar, things and technology that design the world and that are its pervasive force. It is part of and creates its norms, and forms the infrastructure and organization of its knowledge through which it confirms and solidifies the transparency of its articulation. This cycle is tautological, seemingly unbreachable, and reflects the visual ideology of identification as a closed off reality and history that is self-certain and justified in its own taxonomic methodology. Therefore its critique and disruption cannot come from the visual but must come from the possibilities of the invisible, from sound, which is not drawn from the taxonomical rhetoric and knowledge base inscribed within its frontiers, but is cosmic and infinite, ungraspable but sensible and thus can critique necessity and the deceit of reason: stretch it, transform it through the diffuse knowledge of a sonic sense expanding as reverberation from 'what-comes-before-language'.

This before of language is not a primitive primordiality, a naïve apperception before reflection, but is Maurice Merleau-Ponty's 'ouverture au monde', his 'openness to the world', that carries the French connotation of reciprocity and agency towards the world's invisible depth, and lets us uncover the process of perception itself, revealing the ideologies and dynamics of knowledge and inviting a different effort of reflection that does not settle on the image but reaches the infinite and inexhaustible process of its sonic materiality.[50] Thus it allows us to rupture knowledge's transparent tautology through the opacity of a mobile sound and drives us towards knowing as a sensorial and physical engagement.

The digital accelerates Kant

This need to rupture the transparent tautology of rational thought and truth as the guarantors of identity and possibility, becomes amplified in the digital. Networked technology extends the Kantian consciousness of the lexicon into the acceleration of a digital world: producing from a thinking in analogies and references the reality of algorithms, numerical categories and the consequent necessity to fulfil their criteria instantly. The digital-lexicon is a visual pursuit that pre-determines and limits knowledge and colonializes bodies and things through numbers. It makes the subject into a worker or a consumer, defined culturally and ethnically as well as along lines of gender and class, against algorithms and the mathematical accuracy of statistics and definitions. The lines of that technological body are rigidly drawn rather than loosely extended. They construct pixilated media profiles of ultrasubjective violence, Balibar's articulation of the violence of a reified and absolutized identity, that psychotically 'acts out' against the mythologized other from its own fetishized self and in the process kills them both.[51] And they are deformed through the systems of representation, which enact Balibar's ultraobjective violence: a state- or system-sponsored violence that reduces the subject 'to the condition of things, beginning by supressing their individuality and treating them 'as quantities of residual "pieces"'.[52] These pieces are partial objects not a varied entirety, and are derogatively perceived as 'Stücke'. Balibar's mention here of the German term refers to its use by the Nazis to describe the individuals in the concentration camps, illustrating the linguistic and thus quasi-technological effort of fascism at depersonalization as part of the systemic, ultraobjective violence perpetrated against the Jews. Balibar goes on to articulate its current use in global capitalism and the way it eliminates its superfluous population: those that neither work nor consume, those that do not have the capacity to fulfil the role assigned to them by the system.[53]

The global reach of the digital network, the speed and connections of online identities and culture exacerbate the conflation of logic and language and make the pervasiveness of the analytical colonial. They rob the local of the facility of its own language and thought, which it needs to nourish its internal multiplicity. Instead its subject becomes a subject without agency, muted and deformed into the rationality of a global system that is not sensitive to *différence* in the self, and represents its identity in the form of the JPEG file as its visual representation: 1.6 MB, rather than its materiality.[54] The digital file, as measure and size rather than material, produces and affirms the singular possibility of the real and assumes creative authority over its soul.

The digital infiltration and consequent (forced) global adoption of a taxonomical consciousness into everything everywhere, brings to the surface the ultrobjective violence implicit in its systems of knowledge and truth. The speed of the network, its acceleration of conversion, the rapid elimination of difference in thought and articulation, illuminates its causes in rationality, and begins to bear consequences on individuality and collective identity. Its algorithmic certainty and unfailing definition reduces humans to the condition of things, and reduces things to the condition of objects, and both to the condition of technology and language that describe and instrumentalize them, rather than enabling their interbeing, their thinging and autonomy, sovereignty and identity.

In the sphere of mathematical categorization and virtual networks online, we take our role simply as pieces, as Stücke, determined in our identity by the algorithm of the search engine, and tasked to fulfil the criteria assigned to us on the basis of the system of a neo-liberal economy that masquerades the individualist 'ethos of self-care' as the new welfare state: propelled forward by the availability of 'technologies of the self'.[55]

The digital gives a Kantian consciousness the technological and conceptual infrastructure that augments the ultrasubjective and the ultraobjective violence of which Balibar talks and which finds consequences in the lack of a plural reality, and the impossibility of varied identity as outlined by Rancière. Those that have a part, need to play a role – be defined and definable – to be a consumer or a worker, a piece in the machine of capitalism, and those that have no part do not even have the right to appear as not counted. They might not, as Balibar suggests, be eliminated by genocidal means, their obliteration might be more insidious, slow and by neglect, through the consequences of climate change, terror attacks or the individual and collective social tragedies of the welfare state under austerity, but their voices will nevertheless be eliminated, their possibility denigrated to the impossible, 'pronouncing the word "silence" … and writes it as "the end"'.[56]

Viewing and listening to the work of Pamela Z and Evan Ifekoya online 'unends' this silence. Their moving, dancing and singing unperforms and unthinks the measure of the digital file and the homogeneity of its environment. They refuse the acceleration into the taxonomy of a lexical digitalization with its purposeful algorithms, resisting not only the representational reduction of the image, but also its material's reduction into data, and proliferating another consciousness, where the body performs new connections in the truly virtual sphere of sound, and where identity participates as an avatar-I in the boundlessness of a transitory subjectivity that does not show a 'profile' but enables self-reflection. Thus they unperform a Kantian consciousness on which the universal measure of reality relies and from which the digital has accelerated its actuality.

Conclusion: Sonic Stücke

'Realism claims to be that sane attitude of mind that sticks to observable realities. It is in fact something quite different: it is the police logic of order, which asserts, in all circumstances, that it is only doing the only thing possible to do.'[57] Against the singular reality of such a totalising belief, the *Breathing Einhorn* performs the mirror of the normative structure's own insanity and unperforms its limitation, prejudices and tautologies while celebrating the possibility of the impossible.

The trans-technological subject unthinks and unperforms ultrasubjective and ultraobjective violence by transforming itself into fabled beasts, the poetry of ephemeral breath and the fluidity of a dancing body. It does not pause in a graspable form as Stück, merely a piece, but generates itself inexhaustibly as a complex entirety made from inter-actions and inter-inventions with all there is. It at once unperforms the military heritage of technology and the instrumentality of its aims that have influenced musical discourse and practice towards the notion of ideal performances, beauty, and the correct piece of work; while also unperforming subjectivity as a historical and political category and definition: unsinging and undancing with Ifekoya the representation of the black body as the image of entertainment and of a polar sexuality, and unmoving with Cixous the phallocentric organization of sculpture, of writing and of music, through the ephemeral breath of Pamela Z that produces the in-between in a reciprocal process of exchange.

In this way, the trans-technological body ruptures chronology and necessity. It starts not from the past but from an undefined future point on a moveable index of sonic reality, and generates a current transitory and transforming relationship with technology and with things. Ifekoya's singing and Pamela Z's breathing are their 'ouverture au monde', their opening to the world, to live with it symbiotically, to understand its reverberation not through a preexisting language but by creating it contingently in the negotiation of their interbeing. My breathing and moving is my taking part in this cosmos, its phenomenology and economy. Through the invisible air of my breath I participate and get a voice, even if just a whisper. And from this emancipatory impulse I can forge a different place in the community as a collective of breathing subjects, aware of our interbeing with the environment, its circumstance and shared air.

The sonic trans-subject performed by Ifekoya is not a transcendental subject, it does not follow a predetermined path to its ideal destination, it does not come from language, but from before language, from a reverberating openness towards the world. It does not shut subjectivity down in categories and definitions but sings as a subject in process on trial with other things, unfinished and unfinishable but inexhaustible and expansive. This subject on trial is always signifying never a sign, dependent on the contingent contact, on the encounter with the other who looks at it with a mirror in its eyes within which it meets its own internal multiplicity.[58] This subject steps into the order of things, thinging, signifying without an aim or end. It is not reduced to the condition of things but elevated to their interbeing.

Sonic Stücke unperform the violence of pieces. They are mobile and invisible, they cannot be organized in the order of things, in the taxonomies of purpose, use and uselessness but generate with the things a different order, the disorder of possibility and the erotics of impossibility. They are a refuge and a transformative locale, a noun and a verb, and as agency they hold the political possibility of a sonic subject that can break through the tautological frame of its narrow definition as a pre-given role or as silence. The sonic piece can shout and generate, it can find connections and associations that visually remain unseen.

The political possibility of this sonic subjectivity lies in its capacity to disrupt the violence of the lexicon, its consciousness and politics in its analogue and its digital accelerated form. It can disable the taxonomical project of definition by sounding as dark mobility a name that is beyond its structure, that transforms and is transformative; that is inexhaustible, without silence, and thus 'without "an end"'.

Notes

1 Moss Angel, 'No Skin', *Untoward Magazine*, vol. 2, no. 12, 22 October 2012. With permission from the author.

2 'These organs without a body can take on any form they please: shrill points and buckled flesh sticking out of a certain shape to assert singularity within a plural nest. Producing the movement of many heads and many tongues, voices and breaths meeting and dissipating in sound' (Salomé Voegelin, *Sonic Possible Worlds*, New York: Bloomsbury, 2014, p. 80).

3 Jean-Luc Nancy, *Listening*, New York: Fordham University Press, 2007, p. 27. This 'cut in the un-sensed [*in-sensée*]' describes his definition of listening as an openness to meaning, as the possibility of sense: 'a friction, the pinch or grate of something produced in the throat, a borborygmus, a crackle, a stridency, where a weighty, murmuring matter breathes, opened into the division of its resonance' (ibid.)

4 'To be is to inter-be. You cannot just *be* by yourself alone. You have to inter-be with every other thing. This sheet of paper is because everything else is' (Thich Nhat Hanh, *The Pocket Thich Nhat Hanh*, ed. Melvin McLeod, Boston and London: Shambhala Pocket Classics, 2012, p. 57). While not adhering to the Buddhist context of Nhat Hanh's philosophy, I will be developing his notion of interbeing in relation to sound and listening, to bring the idea of the in-between into my deliberation on a sonic subjectivity.

5 Thich Nhat Hanh, *The Pocket Thich Nhat Hanh*, pp. 57–8.

6 Hito Steyerl, 'A Thing Like You and Me', in *The Wretched of the Screen*, Berlin: Sternberg Press, 2012, pp. 49–50.

7 Jacques Rancière, *Disagreement, Politics and Philosophy*, London: University of Minnesota Press, 1999, p. 132.

8 Ibid., p. 123.

9 Saul Kripke, *Naming and Necessity*, Oxford: Blackwell, 1981, p. 55.

10 Hélène Cixous 'The Laugh of the Medusa', *Signs*, vol. 1, no. 4 (Summer 1976): 886.

11 Étienne Balibar, *Violence and Civility, On the Limits of Political Philosophy*, New York: Columbia University Press, 2015, pp. 69–70.

12 Ibid., p. 61.

13 Steyerl, 'A Thing Like You and Me', p. 50.

14 Cixous, 'The Laugh of the Medusa', p. 880.

15 Evan Ifekoya, *Genuine, Original, Authentic*, interview by AQNB Productions, 2015, https://www.youtube.com/watch?v=pObx57o0gmQ (accessed 7 June 2017).

16 While both works were accessible without password at the time of writing, just before the book came to publication *Disco Breakdown* (http://evanifekoya.com/work/) had become password-protected.

17 Steyerl, 'A Thing Like You and Me', pp. 51–2.

18 Ibid., p. 50.

19 Caygill Howard, *A Kant Dictionary*, The Blackwell Philosopher Dictionaries, Oxford: Blackwell, 1996, pp. 1–7. Clearly himself infected by lexical thinking, Caygill's book is a dictionary of Kantian terminology, which interestingly does not contain the words 'language' or 'grammar', but does define the word 'logic'. It is the synonymity or overlaid character of language and logic, as the grammatical structure of thinking, that does not even need a separate entry, that makes the dictionary as an organization and as the foundation of thought possible and that demonstrates in the context of this *Kant Dictionary* an understanding of language as the form and expression of thought: 'Kant would accommodate both the traditional logic based on forms of judgement and inference and the modern logic stemming from the Cartesian cogito and based on self-consciousness and apperception' (Caygill, *A Kant Dictionary*, p. 282).

20 Michael N. Forster quotes Kant as saying that our cognition needs the means of language, and that 'A Judgment (Urteil) is a proposition (Sprache)'. He suggests that it is in the Vienna Logic, that Kant's long-standing mere analogy between logic and grammar turns 'into the picture of an intimate connection between the two' (Michael N. Forster, 'Kant's Philosophy of Language', *Tijdschrif voor Filosofie*, vol. 74 [2012], p. 489).

21 Moss Angel, 'No Skin'.

22 'Lecture I: January 20, 1970', given at Princeton University and published later in *Naming and Necessity*, Oxford: Blackwell, 1981, pp. 22–70.

23 As long as we took for granted Kant's notion that we structure the world by representing it, the study of the nature of representation (of Mind in the 19th century, of Language in this century) took pride of place. For in studying the activity of representation philosophy takes itself to discover 'formal', 'conceptual' 'structural truths' – truths higher and purer than those produced by science. If we lose our grip on the Kantian picture, this structure-content distinction begins to evaporate. So does the notion of philosophy as the armchair study of the nature of representation.

(Rorty, 'Kripke versus Kant', *London Review of Books*, 4 September 1980, p. 5.)

With this evaporation of the structure-content distinction and its focus on representation, a new thinking of knowledge, truth and subjectivity becomes possible that might be able to grasp what finds no form, what has no name and does not fulfil the taxonomies of rational thinking but produces a possible reality of which we have to learn to speak.

24 Hélène Cixous and Catherine Clément, *The Newly Born Woman*, London: I. B. Tauris, 1996, p. 75.

25 Cixous, 'The Laugh of the Medusa', p. 875.

26 Ibid., p. 880.

27 Ibid., p. 889.

28 Ibid., p. 883.

29 Ibid., pp. 875 and 885.

30 Ibid., p. 886.

31 Evan Ifekoya, *Genuine, Original, Authentic*, interview by AQNB Productions, 2015, https://www.youtube.com/watch?v=pObx57o0gmQ (accessed 7 June 2017).

32 Ibid.

33 Cixous, 'The Laugh of the Medusa', p. 880.

34 In an interview with Cathy Lane, published in *Playing with Words* (2008), Pamela Z lists in detail all the technology she works with. She does not elaborate on why or how, but makes a point of a comprehensive inventory, mentioning also the people who have developed these technological interfaces and instruments for her and with her. To me this seems very interesting, particularly in relation to the idea, which I develop a little later on via Cixous and Clément, of woman as a complex whole made up of physical and technological parts that extend the self and expand into the parts of others, with others.

35 Cixous, 'The Laugh of the Medusa', p. 887.

36 Balibar, *Violence and Civility*, p. 61.

37 Ibid.

38 Ibid., p. 60.

39 In *Listening to Noise and Silence* (2010) I discuss listening as the invention of sound and describe auditory perception as a generative process that does not recognize or receive but creates the heard from what is there and even from what remains unheard. This inventive and generative capacity of sounding and listening becomes, in the context of interbeing, first an inter-vention and then an inter-invention: the action in the between-of-things, the inter-action of generating the heard as the complexity of all there is together.

40 Rancière, *On the Shores of Politics*, p. 85.

41 Instead, it is more akin to Nancy's violence at the 'cut in the un-sensed [*in-sensée*]', where we do not hear the source as a quasi visual and complete appearance or sign, as skin making a certain shape, but hear the scars and intersections that make a fragile form: an tentative opening towards meaning (Nancy, *Listening*, p. 27).

42 In the French version Cixous's word at this place is dé-penser, and in a footnote the translater makes us aware that this term 'Dé-pense', is a neo-logism formed on the verb *penser*, hence it is a de-thinking, it 'unthinks', but it is also 'depenser': to spend ('The Laugh of the Medusa', translator's note, p. 882). I read the de- as my un-, as an affirmative unthinking not as deconstruction but to think anew, to dispense and expense with old thought and thought structures. Thus the spending is an investment in new thinking, an affirmative renewal of its restrictive meaning in a Kantian frame.

43 Alex Kittle, 'The Body Extensions of Rebecca Horn in Art, Film and Over-Enthusiasm', 11 February 2014, http://alexkittle.com/2014/02/11/art-the-body-extensions-of-rebecca-horn/ (accessed 13 March 2018).

44 Rancière, *Disagreement, Politics and Philosophy*, p. 133.

45 Rebecca Horn, *Tailleur du Coeur*, texts and drawings Rebecca Horn – Notebook, Zürich, Berlin, New York: Scalo, 1996.

46 Cixous and Clémente, *The Newly Born Woman*, p. 87.

47 Ibid.

48 Tara Rodgers, *Pink Noises, Women on Electronic Music and Sound*, Durham, NC: Duke University Press, 2010, p. 6. These ghosts are the ideologies and sociopolitical interests of military and technoscientific projects, which according to Rodgers still pervade and influence the current use of electronic tools and technologies that enable the making of electronic music and sound art. And while the sound of a current use of those interfaces within the context of art and music might only hold a lingering radiation of the technoscientific purposes that drove their design, it is, according to Rodgers, enough to keep them within the belief systems that gave rise to them, and within the political and philosophical sense that organizes their conception. In this instance, Rodgers points to the link between audio and military technology in the United States, a connection that can be assumed to hold globally.

49 Cixous and Clémente, *The Newly Born Woman*, pp. 87–8.

50 The *ouverture au monde,* describes a practical and applied openness to the world through the reconsideration of the relationship between knowing and its object. It does not simply indicate a passive opening, a noun, but prompts opening as verb, as a predicate that makes the world open (Maurice Merleau-Ponty, *The Visible and the Invisible*, Evanston, IL: Northwestern University Press, 1968, pp. 35–6).

51 Balibar, *Violence and Civility*, p. 69.

52 Ibid. This state- or system-sponsored violence of making into Stücke is perpetrated by the search engines and facilitated by social media interfaces revealed as systems of ultraobjective violence. The online exchange and social media networks are also fora for an accelerated ultrasubjective violence, facilitated by distance, representation and anonymity.

53 Balibar, *Violence and Civility*, footnote 11, p. 175. This notion of the elimination of a superfluous population, meets Rancière's distinction between those that have a part but need to play a role, and those that have no role to play, quoted at the beginning of this essay, which now finds a clearer articulation in the relationship between online and offline communities.

54 Online, Steyerl's image as material, articulated in critique and rejection of representation, discussed at the beginning of this essay, becomes again disabled as a resisting object. The digital platforms and networks render the image not a material but a measure of its size.

55 Balibar suggests that the withdrawal of the welfare state happens on the rhetoric of an ethos of self-care (*souci de soi*) where 'individuals must moralize their own behaviour by submitting it to the criteria of maximum utility or the future productivity of their individuality'. He identifies this via Manuel Castells, as the development of negative identities, where social security and thus social solidarity is destroyed (Balibar, *Citizenship*, Cambridge: Polity, 2015, pp. 111–12).

56 Cixous, 'The Laugh of the Medusa', p. 886.

57 Rancière, *Disagreement, Politics and Philosophy*, p. 132.

58 This subject on trial, always signifying never a sign, is Julia Kristeva's subject of the fourth signifying practice of the text, and is exposed to impossible dangers:

> relinquishing his identity in rhythm, dissolving the buffer of reality in a mobile discontinuity, leaving the shelter of the family, the state, or religion. The commotion the practice creates spares nothing: it destroys all constancy to produce another and then destroys that one as well.

> (Kristeva, *Revolution in Poetic Practice*, p. 104.)

59 This is a recording of the work from the concert with Joan La Barbara as part of the 2014 ROOM Series at Royce Gallery in San Francisco.

References

Balibar, Étienne, *Citizenship*, Cambridge: Polity, 2015.

Balibar, Étienne, *Violence and Civility, On the Limits of Political Philosophy*, trans. G. M. Goshgarian, New York: Columbia University Press, 2015.

Caygill, Howard, *A Kant Dictionary*, The Blackwell Philosopher Dictionaries, Oxford: Blackwell, 1996.

Cixous, Hélène, 'The Laugh of the Medusa', *Signs*, vol. 1, no. 4 (Summer 1976): 875–93.

Cixous, Hélène and Catherine Clément, *The Newly Born Woman*, trans. Betsy Wing, London: I. B. Tauris, 1996 [1975].

Forster, Michael N., 'Kant's Philosophy of Language', *Tijdschrif voor Filosofie*, vol. 74 (2012): 485–511.

Horn, Rebecca, *Tailleur du Coeur*, texts and drawings Rebecca Horn – Notebook, Zürich, Berlin, New York: Scalo, 1996.

Ifekoya, Evan, *Genuine, Original, Authentic*, interview by AQNB Productions, 2015, https://www.youtube.com/watch?v=pObx57o0gmQ.

Ifekoya, Evan, interview with J. D. A. Winslow for YAC, Young Artists in Conversation, May 2015, http://youngartistsinconversation.co.uk/Evan-Ifekoya.

Kant, Immanuel, *Critique of Pure Reason*, trans. Friedrich Max Müller and Marcus Weigelt, London: Penguin Classics, 2007 [1781].

Kittle, Alex, 'Art: The Body Extensions of Rebecca Horn', 11 February 2014, http://alexkittle.com/2014/02/11/art-the-body-extensions-of-rebecca-horn/.

Kripke, Saul, *Naming and Necessity*, Oxford: Blackwell, 1981 [1980].

Kristeva, Julia, *Revolution in Poetic Language*, New York: Columbia University Press, 1984.

Merleau-Ponty, Maurice, *The Visible and the Invisible*, Evanston, IL: Northwestern University Press, 1968.

Moss Angel, 'No Skin', *Untoward Magazine*, vol. 2, no. 12, 22 October 2012, https://untowardmag.com/you-are-actually-a-baby-deer-and-im-not-going-to-let-that-get-in-the-way-of-our-potential-future-ec2874ba654.

Nancy, Jean-Luc, *Listening*, ed. Charlotte Mandell, New York: Fordham University Press, 2007.

Nhat Hanh, Thich, *The Pocket Thich Nhat Hanh*, ed. Melvin McLeod, Boston and London: Shambhala Pocket Classics, 2012.

Pamela Z, interviewed by Cathy Lane, in *Playing with Words*, Derbyshire, UK: CRiSAP, RGAP, 2008, pp. 34–6.

Rancière, Jacques, *Disagreement, Politics and Philosophy*, London: University of Minnesota Press, 1999.

Rancière, Jacques, *On The Shores of Politics*, London, New York: Verso, 2007.

Rodgers, Tara, *Pink Noises, Women on Electronic Music and Sound*, Durham, NC: Duke University Press, 2010.

Rorty, Richard, 'Kripke versus Kant', *London Review of Books*, vol. 2, no. 17 (1980): 4–5.

Steyerl, Hito, 'A Thing Like You and Me', in *The Wretched of the Screen*, Berlin: Sternberg Press, 2012, pp. 46–59.

Voegelin, Salomé, *Listening to Noise and Silence: Towards a Philosophy of Sound Art*, New York: Continuum, 2010.
Voegelin, Salomé, *Sonic Possible Worlds: Hearing the Continuum of Sound*, New York: Bloomsbury, 2014.

Work

Pamela Z, *Breathing* (2014, solo version), part of *Carbon Song Cycle* (2013), https://www.youtube.com/watch?v=j7AZsQoD630.[59]
Rebecca Horn, *Einhorn* (Unicorn), 1970–72 (bandages, a wooden horn and metal clasps)
Evan Ifekoya, *Gender Song* (2014)
and
Disco Breakdown (2014)
http://evanifekoya.com/work/.
At time of publication this work was not accessible without a password anymore.

Sonic materialism: A philosophy of digging

When night comes
I stand on the stairway and listen,
the stars are swarming in the garden
and I am standing in the dark.
Listen, a star fell with a tinkle!
Do not go out on the grass with bare feet;
my garden is full of splinters.

Edith Södergran[1]

The poem 'The Stars' by Edith Södergran articulates in seven short lines the dilemma of realist philosophy: the calculable existence of a star autonomous of human perception, the tension between the knowledge of astronomy, the human foundation of its discipline and the inability to reach its materiality without a body and without a mind, whose uncertainty falsifies the star's calculable existence. For realist philosophy, whose aim is to grasp the unthought, the '*absolute* outside' reality of 'pre-critical thinking' this falsifying body and mind is the weakness of phenomenology and reason, who can only see a 'relative outside', an outside of our own existence that is only our absence, the void signed by our not being there rather than its being by its own what it is.[2]

For Quentin Meillassoux, this relative outside is the outside of the correlationist, the phenomenologist for whom reality is an intersubjective mode of being in the world, and of the idealist, for whom reality is transcendental, a matter of reason and necessity, bound to general laws of nature. Accusing them of religious fanaticism and ideological dogmatism,

Meillassoux suggests that both produce a 'fideist obscurantism' of a proper truth by relating knowledge to the body as flesh and the rational mind respectively.[3] In response, he proposes that the stability [of the laws of nature] must be established as a 'mind-independent fact', 'which is to say, from a property of time which is indifferent to our existence', which is not thought or experienced within our actuality but as the absolute possibility of a mathematical reality.[4] Thus his aim is to reach the unthought via ancestrality, the exploration of the pre-human world, without referring it to human experience or theorization, but through mathematical calculations, not tampered by human 'corrections' to get to an 'irremediable realism': where 'either this statement has a realist sense, and *only* a realist sense, or no sense at all'.[5]

I will meet the irremediable reality of Meillassoux's ancestrality with a material sound. I will listen to its calculations and inhabit its numerical world to gauge what a sonic phenomenology might contribute to the understanding of the speculative materiality of the world, and how it might help to reach a proper truth that includes the outside of experience, while also accounting for the asymmetries and responsibilities of the inside.

Phenomenology, at least the psychological phenomenology of Maurice Merleau-Ponty, which informs my thinking on materiality, does not deny the desire to know the world without us, its unthought material substance and possibility, but it understands and accounts for difference, the contingency of our individual life-worlds, that inform our thinking of the unthought. Discounting a higher power or mathematical dogma, we have access to the real only from our own positions and positionings in the world. Phenomenology, its strategy of reduction and the reciprocity of its intersubjectivity, helps us to consider how these positions define us as embodied materialities and how they realize our political condition: the cultural, economic, ideological as well as physiological and educational particularity that opens the world to us in different and not entirely symmetrical ways. Thus a materialist phenomenology might enable a thinking of the unthought materiality of the world while accounting for our own materiality, including a human unthought, and baring in mind also what appears unthinkeable: those manifestations of human and non-human existence that lack representation to make themselves count.

Therefore, I agree with the principle of Meillassoux's project and that of new materialism and speculative realism at large and in its many guises, namely the desire to think the non-human matter of this world before its representation, or 'correction', in language and rational thought. And embrace the desire to speculate on the real from its actual materiality rather than its (Kantian) definition or concept. However, I believe with Rosi Braidotti and Karen Barad that the human too is matter, the mind is matter and the body is matter, and steer towards the possibility of an embodied materialism that does not seek to simply disavow the body in favour of the calculation of the ancestral, but re-engages the body and mind's own materiality in order to be with that of things, thought, unthought and unthinkable.[6] Consequently objectivity, the standard of scientific truth, is not qualified through (temporal) distance from an ancestral real, but denotes the responsibility to be a social and connected subject, to understand the reality of the world through, as Barad suggests, being entangled in its processes of materialization.[7]

While Meillassoux's statement makes it clear that he does not want to compromise between a realist and a correlationist world view, I believe that we get the clearest sense of reality if we acknowledge our human impotence to be anything other than human, but still try to see beyond a relative outside, even if we might never comprehend it, by considering it from our own embodied materiality, rather than assuming a transparent identity in a mathematical process of facticity. Thus, in this essay I want to try my fascination with Meillassoux's mind-independent reality, his notion of an absolute outside, not in order to reach it necessarily but because in the process of trying, philosophical questions on parity, materiality, agency and autonomy can be asked and discussed that address access and objectivity and give us some insights into whose unthought the absolutely real of the realist actually is.

To engage this question, this essay considers realist and new materialist ideas via sounding and listening. It finds as its starting point much agreement and some disagreement with Christoph Cox's 2011 essay 'Beyond Representation and Signification: Towards a Sonic Materialism', from which it returns a verdict on new realist philosophies as overstating the culture nature dichotomy and overlooking entirely its visuocentric tendencies on which such a dialectic depends in the first place. To elaborate the consequent notion of sonic matter, reality and possibility I turn to Luce Irigaray, Karen Barad and Rosi Braidotti, and profit from their ideas of the feminine, the agential and the creative respectively to come to a different materialism that questions representation, linguistic, mathematical or otherwise, by embracing an embodied materialism that thinks the matter of the world through the matter of the flesh and the mind, and reads objectivity as accountability rather than as distance and thus does not come to an 'irremediable realism' of absolute ancestrality, but to the radical realism of practice, to the doing of philosophy as 'spacetimemattering'.[8]

From there the question arises whether in new materialism philosophy has found its end. Whether, in other words, in the finitude of the ancestral and the practice of mattering, philosophy becomes obsolete and the post-anthropocentric has to, by necessity, be a post-philosophical. We might have to go gardening, digging and turning the earth to understand the world instead; to practice and perform the unthinkable in-between rather than think about it as the unthought.

This proposal for a radical post-philosophy of practice is inspired by *Naldjorlak I*. A work for solo cello, by Éliane Radique written in collaboration with cellist Charles Curtis, not as a score of certain instructions, but on the body of the performer and of the instrument, who search in the in-between of bow, space, flesh and audience the material reality and possibility of their relationship. It is in the performance rather than the reading of the work that a political possibility of difference as diffraction and entanglement, in Barad's sense, becomes imaginable, and that Braidotti's affirmative, mobile locationality that can stand up against the commodified pluralism of neo-liberal capitalism becomes thinkable, and that we are able, with Irigaray, to write in caresses and gesture-words: to 'appeal to language as a path towards sharing the mystery of the other'.[9]

Sonic matter – sound matters

Christoph Cox's 2011 essay on sonic materialism charts an interesting relationship between sound and philosophy by considering the relative lack of scholarly attention given to sound art. He states that:

> The open-ended sonic forms and often site-specific location of sound installations thwart artists musicological analysis, which remains oriented to the formal examination of discrete sound structures and performances, while the purely visual purview of art history allows its practitioners not only to disregard sound art but also to gloss over the sonic strategies of Postminimalism and Conceptualism.[10]

He continues by explaining that the reason for this oversight or ignoring of sound arts and sonic strategies is the prevailing theoretical models' failure to grasp the sonic. He places the blame for this inability with cultural theory that refutes meaningful existence outside the text and which thus divides the world into two domains: the meaningful cultural sphere of the symbolic and the domain of nature and materiality that remain unintelligible. Refusing to accept the presuppositions of symbolic meaning and thus refusing to critique sound art for not making itself available to discourse as a textual form of thinking, he presents a critique of representation and attempts to 'eliminate the dual planes of culture/nature, human/non-human, sign/world, text/matter' by pursuing a 'thoroughgoing materialism that would construe human symbolic life as a specific instance of the transformative process to be found throughout the natural world'.[11] He suggests that it is a materialist philosophy that could take account of sonic practices and could furthermore rethink art theory in general.

What follows is an interesting proposition towards such a sonic materialism working against the representational preconceptions of Pierce's structuralism and edging via Schopenhauer's notion of music as a direct expression of the will, and Nietzsche's naturalistic view on music towards

Gilles Deleuze and Félix Guattari, Isabelle Stengers and Manuel DeLanda to present a materialist and realist philosophy that appreciates matter's creative and transformative capacity and that thus can theorize sound art on its own transforming terms.

What makes this essay valuable is its critique of the nature/culture, text/matter, human/non-human split through a focus on sound. Through this particular emphasis, Cox identifies the more general realist and new materialist complaint about dualist structures of knowledge and locates the motivation against representation, idealism, and mind-dependentness that drives the materialist and speculative project, in the oppositionality of dialectical thinking, which relies on distance and a visual language to define things against each other.

Cox develops, through sound, the theoretical concerns about representation and figuration that I recognize from Braidotti's writing; and addresses in the particularity of sonic production Barad's unease about the term critique and the reading of objectivity as (critical) distance. In this way, and while not agreeing with him on his eventual articulation of a sonic materialism via Deleuze's notion of the virtual, as Dyonisian excess, and the flux of a sonic becoming, he makes it possible for me to focus on the dualism at the core of the materialist project and to think its causality in reverse.

Dualism is not in the world but in theory and in philosophy. There it appears not as the cause but as the symptom and consequence of visuocentrism instituted through the devocalization of thought by the logos as the right joining of words: 'Freed from the acoustic materiality of speech, this pure semantic – which is the privileged object of *theoria* – occupies the place of origin and rules over the phonetic.'[12] What Adriana Cavarero points out here is the muteness of Western philosophy since Plato. His logos is visual and mute and promotes a visual and mute thinking of the world. It is a visuocentric undertaking that is not caused by but causes the dualism, as its vision divides the world in signs and symbols, 'this' or 'that', from which theory produces ideas 'connected with "right" links in the totality of the intelligible order that the soul's eye contemplates'.[13]

Taking account of this origin of philosophy in muteness, the focus on the complaint of the materialist on the dualistic nature of thought has to be shifted from the dualism itself to its causes in visuocentrism. I propose that it is not because of the dualist split between nature and culture, language and thing, that we have to rethink matter to understand sound. Or rather it is not the dualist split, which causes our inability to grasp sound within discourse. Instead, dualism becomes apparent as a mere symptom, albeit with consequences, of a visuocentric philosophy. Thus it is the preference of Western philosophy for the visual, the essentializing of the world in a visual paradigm, textual and pictorial, that creates a dualistic thinking and promotes differentiation and thus establishes a hierarchy between things that reveals an anthropocentric view: producing the duality of human and non-human signs, creating a chain of differences and similarities.

Cox's emphasis on the cause of sound art's lack of articulation allows me to think sonic materialism not against duality, but as 'anterior' to duality, avoiding its dividing ideology by accessing philosophy in the invisible simultaneity of things, before language and culture assert their superiority and determine their organization. This is not a going back, however. It is not a primitivism that precedes the dualistic thinking of the world, as a naïve primordiality overcome through the truth of modernity. Rather, it is an acknowledgement of the unthought sonic variable of the world that exists without our thinking it. Thus reaching its truth implies a going forward into the future of a sonic sensibility, to reddress from its 'science fiction' a past philosophical turn against the invisible and indivisible sphere of sound and retry its path in the present. This anteriority is then not a chronological and patrimonial ancestrality but a simultaneous possibility of a different world, a variant whose philosophy was always there but remained unthought, inarticulate, practiced in sound only.

Therefore, while the new materialist project might help sound art to its recognition and theorization, and I appreciate the radical nature of Cox's project in this regard, what appears more relevant and striking is that a sonic thinking and sensibility as the revocalization of the logos, makes possible a new materialism and speculative realism that exists outside a dualist world view and reaches the truth of the world before its assertion in the sign. Thus a sonic materialism proceeds not as continuation but as an alternative philosophical practice without the semantic linkages of vision, and the objectivity of its distance, and thus without dualism and anthropocentrism, from a 'future world'.

To access the thinking of this unthought, invisible variable of philosophy, I read Meillassoux's writing as a mathematical fiction about a non-human anteriority that invites us to rethink our present understanding and co-habitation with materiality, science, human and non-human things, from a discontinuous future. The intention is not to relegate his project to a mere fiction, but to appreciate that his strategy of accessing the ancestral to get to the real and irremediable truth of the world, provides, beyond his own particular aims, a useful imagination of an inaccessible place from which to rethink and reaccess the theorization and valuation of the materiality and reality of this place. In the same sense I propose that sound, a sonic thinking, affords us the science fiction of an unthought variable, which helps us think and agitate the present in a different way: without representation or measurement, and without the values and validities provided for by the historical chronology of philosophy.

The suggestion is that, inspired to find a theoretical 'language' capable of integrating and addressing sound art, we do not need to work around the visuocentric nature of Western philosophy and its requisite hierarchies and values, bending its canons towards invisible and indivisible matter. Rather, we can acknowledge the dualistic tendency of thought as a consequence of its visuality and fostering anthropocentrism and come to practice a different variant in the unthought of sound. Thus we can engage in the new materialist project as a quasi-sonic project. In listening to sound we are always already in matter: an embodied ear that sounds and hears through its own simultaneity with 'what sounds' as an unseen and inter-existing 'what is'. From there we can come to understand matter and meaning in a different way, diffracted and simultaneous, invisible and indivisible, not as excess and not as becoming, but as a practical interbeing in the world not of signs and symbols, texts and culture, but of inarticulate intensities, indeterminate and indivisible, contingent and transforming.

Therefor we do not need to build materialism on modern thought, which will always and inevitably remain caught in the dualism at the heart of its history, and will thus always already entail the exclusion of other stories. Instead, we can recognize the visuocentrism that determines this historical dualism and can appreciate how the anthropocentric is tied up with visuality, in order to find the unthought not in philosophy but in the thought of sound, which opens vision maybe not to truth but to its plurality. In other words, I take Meillassoux's ancestrality from which according to him an 'irremediable reality' accessible only via science and the mathematical can be drawn, as a cause to articulate the nonhereditary of a sonic science fiction, from which a contingent and simultaneous reality can be performed that does not differentiate but acknowledges difference and the in-between.

However, sonic materialism does not propose to replace one essentialism with another only to create its own dualism. Rather, it seeks to offer the sensibility of a dark and mobile unthought to host a multisensorial engagement and entanglement with what there is, and to trigger also the 'vocalized' theorization of the unthinkable: that whose not being thought is neither a measure of its impossibility and abjectness, nor of its separate existence, but of our ignorance and desire not to think it.

In this way, the aim to find a theoretical register for sound art leads to a consideration of dualism's historical tie with visuality, and resets the new materialist project from shifting 'the dualist gesture of prioritizing mind over matter, soul over body, and culture over nature that can be found in modernist as well as post-modernist cultural theories' to shifting the material and conceptual hierarchies and preferences that produce the dualisms of its historical and methodological framework.[14] This in turn, and in line with Cox's ideas, leads to a broader rethinking not of art theory only, but also of other aesthetic and quotidian practices and materialities that do not get a voice within the visual regime of philosophical thought.

In this way, the project of materialism and realism gets focused on the issue of visuality, its processes of differentiation and distancing, inclusion and exclusion, as well as its intrinsic anthropocentrism manifest in the visibility of my own body and the invisibility, to myself, of my location of looking: my blind totality. Thus new materialism and speculative realism come to focus on the question of hierarchy and ideology: whose authoritative gaze determines the invisible, and what can make its processes of differentiation and valuation visible, as in recognizable and intelligible, within a visual regime and politics? And from there they can ask how we can grasp this regime and its politics to see a different distance.

Sound, as a sonic sensibility and concept, pre-empts and cancels these questions by remaining unseen and offering the real another truth: not that of 'the "right" links in the totality of the intelligible order',[15] what is in and what is out of its visual regime, but of the in-between of listening not to 'this' or 'that' but to what they do together. It produces the truth of the mobile and the inaudible simultaneity of interbeing that cannot be observed from a distance but has to be generated in the encounter, not to hear what I think of it, but to make room for its own voice. Sound performs this inarticulate encounter from which the thing's own language might be heard. In this way, sonic materialism serves the recognition and theorization of an inarticulate sound (art), while also presenting the possibility for a materialism that starts not from the dualism of a visual philosophy but from the unseen simultaneity of things. This is a materialism of sonic possible worlds that are the simultaneous and plural slices of this world, which are not burdened with the history of its visual definitions, categories and language, but are free to explore the unthought and the unthinkeable on its own terms.

Masculine and feminine realities

In the total invisibility of my point of view, in the unchallenged visuality of philosophy, there is another dualism that opens itself in the contemporary project of new materialist and speculative thought: it is the split between masculine and feminine theorizations of the real, the speculative and the material. Whereby the terms feminine and masculine, following Hélène Cixous's notion of a feminine writing, her *écriture feminine*, purposefully avoid the notion of male and female to acknowledge this difference not as an issue of a physiological sex and category, but of the performance of a gendered subjectivity and its position in relation to canonical discourse, power and powerlessness, and to encourage towards a plural empowerment: 'Woman must write her self', she 'must put herself into the text – as into the world and into history – by her own movement'.[16] Here she adds, 'when I say "woman," I am speaking of woman in her inevitable struggle against conventional man.'[17] And thus I read her woman as the feminine, and interpret her writing insertions as inclusive of a general marginality, 'their territory is black', their language is 'impregnable'.[18] Woman in this sense is what is not grasped in discourse and what remains untheorized, and thus it is what has no part in the reality of a philosophical and a political real without being an essentialized other.

Philosophy's history is not only visual it is also masculine. And this asymmetry finds expression in the self-certainty of the philosophical subject, his location and relationship with a material reality in which he finds himself mirrored and therefor represented in sameness and similarity. Masculine distance is relative to his correspondence with a representational truth. It is distance in the certainty of coincidence, which creates a dominant language. Thus it is a 'conquered distance', whose reach is relative to the masculine vision at the centre. Like a retractable and extendable lead, it is a controlled expanse that snaps back at the owner's command, who never loses hold of its actuality and power in the first place.

A masculine new materialism continues this dominant vision into its disappearance creating a *hyperrealism* of its historical truth. As Braidotti remarks, a hyperrealism does not wipe out class relations, racism or sexism, it intensifies them, increasing disparities and inequalities, through what I would argue is their *hyper-invisibility*: the invisibility of normative relations and values that represent unseen the unquestioned reality of an absolute view.[19] To move towards a materialism of ancestrality and distance means to continue and intensify the hyper-invisibility of a masculine philosophy, its extreme visuality and dualism that cannot see the historical ideology of its point of view. It is power signed by absence, transparency and the certainty of a calculable real, whose speculation is not that of actual uncertainty and precarity, but of factuality: the notion that the thing and the world could be other than they are, but that this 'other than they are' is a calculable probability rather than a contingent, differentiated and differentiating other of unknown matter. Therefore, the engine of a masculine speculative realism is not doubt but mathematics, numbers and measurements. And so, for example, Meillassoux, Manuel DeLanda, and Graham Harman pursue the mathematical, causation and calculations to reach beyond duality into the existence of a mind- and body-independent real in *Ancestrality*, *Possibility Spaces*, and *Object-Oriented Ontologies* respectively. Each in their own way holds that to find what things/objects really are, we need to withdraw from them, and measure their interaction, free of human influence. They read theorization as objectification in the sense of sublimation to a human-representational scheme, and in response remove the body and the mind from the encounter of materials to find 'the reality of things'.[20] This reality is that of bones and stones, of the hard facts and facticities of the world that make a picture of a calculable real, of a science with speculation but without doubt, ascribing nature existence according to laws rather than contingencies, even if the laws remain contingent. Their project does not include a conscious consideration of whose body and whose subjectivity needs to be withdrawn to attain this measured view. The term human is taken as a homogenous frame, standing directly and consistently opposite the non-human, and lacking any appreciation of the asymmetries united therein. In this way, they are deconstructing the power at the centre of an anthropocentric worldview without however critiquing its origin in a masculine visuality, its authority as a hyper-invisibility, and without therefore losing their power to articulate the very deconstruction pursued in their own image of correspondence and control.

By contrast, Irigaray, Barad and Braidotti are seeking caresses, entanglement, creativity and agency, to reach a non-hierarchical, non-dualistic world that accounts for the variability of the human and the non-human, and that comes to breach the dualistic nature of knowledge by performing its differences. Their materialism manifests the feminine body's own precarity in the negotiation of the real, and makes it apparent that the term human is not symmetrical or same, but is itself a matter of its performance and valuation as different and distant. And that therefore not all humans are ready to deconstruct the position from which to gain the voice they have not yet had: 'How can we undo a subjectivity we have not even historically been entitled to yet?'[21]

The feminine materialism, they are collectively but differently articulating, acknowledges the materiality of the body and the mind as well as of language and representation. 'It is a materialism of the flesh that unifies mind and body in a new approach that blurs all boundaries.'[22] It starts from the premise of being 'proud to be flesh', an affirmative attitude towards the visceral and sexual body, from where it meets animate, inanimate, technological, digital, and analogue others to configure the world in reciprocity and contingency.[23] Thus it pursues an 'embodied and sexually differentiated structure of the speaking subject', which is motivated by the desire to make human influence on matter accountable rather than have it disappear in the hyper-invisibility of its power.[24] To this end it seeks difference not through (visual) distance and separation, but through 'diffraction'.

Following Donna Haraway and adding insights from quantum physics, Barad proposes the practice of diffraction as a reading diffractively rather than reflectively: as a careful reading of difference and detail rather than a looking for sameness and outlines. Diffraction eschews distance and recognizes through an entanglement with the world how patterns of difference bring about what she calls 'inventive provocations' that illuminate 'the indefinite nature of boundaries:'[25] the lack of clear lines and outlines that allows disciplines and territories to be read through one another and whose absence invites a re-imagination of their cross-overs and interbeing.

Diffraction is a performative reading of the world from its interactions and interferences that allow us to see 'differences that make a difference'.[26] It describes a practical engagement with the world understood as a heterogeneous entanglement of plural patterns rather than as a singular meeting of defined shapes. Barad describes the shift from a focus on connecting similarities, the visual shape of things, towards 'differences that matter', the patterns of inter-activity that is matter, through the shift in emphasis from a geometrical optics to a physical optics.[27] Geometrical optics, according to Barad, does not pay attention to the particularity of light but only to its being light, as an approximation of a known shape, reliant on distance and comparable sameness, whereas a physical optics, enables us to 'see' the difference and knowledge that is in matter: its own voice that transcends knowledge boundaries, its disciplinary frameworks, by highlighting the simultaneous plurality of its origins and truth, which enables us to appreciate 'what gets excluded as well as what comes to matter'.[28] The first is a theoretical optics of measurements and calculations, the latter an experiment, without grammar, based on doubt and the engagement with the material as an inter-activity, or what she calls an intra-activity: the action between things and subjects that 'enact the differentiated inseparability that *is* a phenomenon'.[29] That is the phenomenon of their co-constitution and entanglement that includes inseperably also the apparatus and the material of observation: its grammar and shape.

This feminine speculation on the reality of the world, its material knowledge and knowledge disciplines, is based on doubt about the shape drawn around things, their grammar, as well as the doubt about the shape drawn around one's own location, one's historical, material and political position and positioning. Therefore, it entails a 'situated politics of locations' that takes account of our lived experience and is able to engage in different modes of mobility and stasis.[30] Acknowledging, for example, within the premise of *Nomadic Theory*, Braidotti's theorizing of material and subject in complex motion, that there is no equality of mobility; and to consequently articulate a nomadology that considers movement as the central premise of critical thought, in order to 'actualize multiple ecologies of belonging'.[31] Accordingly, her situated politics of location is not the practice of an isolated or fixed place, but its mobile and contingent configuration by the inter-activity of human and non-human matter producing the reality of their in-between as an entangled social and material place. It is based not on certainty but on doubt about language as mediator and representative of one's location, matter and subjectivity. This doubt about language as mediator but trusted as an agent of the in-between, working through the entanglements of matter rather than its articulation, resonates with Irigaray's sense that language is not a guarantor of fact and truth, but a caress that 'makes a gesture which gives the other to himself, to herself, thanks to an attentive witness, thanks to a guardian of incarnate subjectivity.' This embodied and mattered subjectivity is co-constituted temporarily in the 'call to be us, between us'.[32]

Irigaray, Barad and Braidotti each formulate their individual critique of the ability of language to grasp a plural truth, and question its trustworthiness to be inclusive, open and willing to accommodate things beyond the ontological reality of its own medium. Barad follows Nietzsche in warning against 'allowing linguistic structure to shape or determine our understanding of the world'.[33] She discusses the dominance of language and acknowledges its 'always already' meaning and reality. In an affirmative response, Braidotti considers the nomad as polyglot, who works not on the sign but its arbitrary nature, not to be cynical and endlessly relative and deferring about meaning, but to keep speech in transit and work on its constant transformation.[34] And Irigaray makes a language from caresses that as gesture-words produce a world full of neo-logisms of the feminine that do not produce a certain sense but are the material of expression itself, which is driven into speech by my inability to grasp the other in language.[35] All three propose a performative criticality: the practicing and doing of linguistic and cartographic matter to challenge the representational and figurative sense of the real, to contest its power, and to break 'humanities' own captivity within language'.[36]

In such a garden resonates the song of the birds, those who celebrate the present moment, who assure the passage between here and there, between earth and sky.

Messengers, they announce if the site is livable. When the universe is not habitable, the birds, if only for a time, are mute. As soon as the danger draws away, they again communicate the celestial: nearby, they tell the distant.[37]

A feminine sonic materialism

I understand sonic materialism to be feminine materialism. Both the feminine and sound do not speak in the dominant tongue, whose representational schema falsifies their material reality. They are both failed by the prevailing theoretical models and have to forge a different sensibility to promote the inclusion of the invisible and make themselves count. The feminine, just like Cox observes in relation to sound art, has been 'undertheorized', under-appreciated in the knowledge stakes. Its voice has not been heard or it has been marginalized as 'goofy', poetic, or sentimental.[38] Its body is ignored by conventional theory and thus its material speculation is not that of the probable unthought, but of the excluded and of alterity that is unthinkable.

Its marginality and unthinkability is one of the reasons why Braidotti insists on the situatedness of the feminine subject even in Nomadic mobility, and why she appreciates that the minority subject needs to go through a phase of 'identity politics', claiming a fixed location, to find a voice, a name and a body of its internal differentiation that has the control of its own situation to articulate itself in the flow.[39] It is why Barad is diffracting, looking for differences and the indefinite nature of boundaries, rather than finding sameness. And it is the reason also while against much criticism of its definition, and the talk of disbanding with its label, I still see value in protecting the invisible practice of Sound Art by calling its name. It too has not yet had a voice enough to deconstruct itself. So, before we disband with its name and thus with its claim to be heard on its own terms, in difference and through diffraction, we have to develop a language or a performativity, as a mode of engaging in its material practice that is 'able to grasp the nature of sound and to enable analysis of the sonic arts'.[40] Not to build a discipline and definite disciplinary boundaries, but to give a voice to its patterns of difference on whose rhythms it can meet, inter-act and intra-act with others without being subsumed into their shape and grammar, so that it can articulate itself in the flow of an entangled difference.

A sonic sensibility lets us think a different materiality that is not virtual, distant and mathematically probable, but possible as inhabited plurality, reached through the caresses and gesture-words of Irigaray, generated from the nomadic creativity of Braidotti, and performing the diffractions of Barad, to create a being in the world that articulates through the encounter, the conflict and difference that are the engine of its material reality. To me their projects are intrinsically sonic, in the sense of a sonic sensibility and concept. They are in in their differing ways pursuing a philosophy of the invisible, that does not calculate but revocalizes the object and the subject, which, as matter, sound through their difference the complex simultaneity of the world and assert a space and a practice for a nondualistic knowledge. As feminine sonic materialists they might make us hear, innovate and imagine different political possibilities and a different socio-material consciousness of reciprocity and care.

I suggest it is in the new materialism of a feminine practice, where physical optics that 'make up diffraction patterns that make the entanglements visible' enables the thinking of a sonic visibility of indivisible vibrations, connections, patterns and differences that are not either resonant or dissonant but produce the experience of reality in the between-of-things.[41] In turn, listening makes diffraction thinkable as a material experience. Its invisible and intangible sphere lends a blind imagination to a physical optics that avoids the dominant regime of representation to delve into its physics as an entangled concept of mattering rather than a line of mathematical calculations. Diffraction entangles the object and the subject, and makes knowing a direct material engagement. It brings us to the notion of objectivity not as distance and detachment but as a practice of difference to which we are held accountable. Rather than deferring its value to a quantitative measurement, which in any event, according to Barad, 'disturbs what you are measuring', we are responsible through our entanglement with things:[42] 'Objectivity, instead of being about offering an undistorted mirror image of the world, is about accountability to marks on bodies, and responsibility to the entanglements of which we are a part.'[43] Listening performs this responsibility, and practices accountability between sounding, listening and hearing things.

> Responsibility, then, is a matter of the ability to respond. Listening for the response of the other and an obligation to be responsive to the other, who is not entirely separate from what we call the self.[44]

In this way, knowledge is performative and non-representational. It is able to grasp the other in its invisible difference and to articulate our mattering in a sonic visibility that breaks our captivity with the historical determinism of language and instead grants voice to an entangled movement of things: to those who 'celebrate the present moment, who assure the passage between here and there, between earth and sky' as the between of a sonic sensibility that does not think in 'this' or 'that', but senses and participates in their inter-being as an embodied and creative materialization of the world.[45]

Objectivity as responsibility: Ethics of a modest collaboration

Meillassoux's critique, referred to at the beginning of this essay, of the strong correlationism of phenomenology and other metaphysical philosophies that he understands to develop from the criticism of the absolutism of transcendental idealism but which, according to him, result in equally dogmatic fanaticism and fideist obscurantism, drives his project towards the unthought of ancestrality: the absolute outside of a pre-human world, whose material configuration is a mind-independent fact, whose fleshlessness grants it the objective truth of distance.

Arguing that the world 'is there', rather than that the world that is there 'is there for me', he does not want to compromise his realism of the (ancestral) unthought through a correlationist subjectivity, but pursues the absolute possibility of a mathematically conceivable world.[46] To this end Meillassoux develops facticity, the pure possibility of what there is, into the notion of factuality understood as the speculative essence of facticity: the fact that what there is, cannot be thought of as a fact but is a matter of non-dogmatic speculation, a speculation of mathematical probability rather than human doubt. Critiquing phenomenological intersubjectivity, which according to Maurice Merleau-Ponty is based on doubt and practiced through the sensory-motor actions of perception, Meillasoux suggests that its

> consciousness and its language certainly transcend themselves towards the world, but there is a world only insofar as a consciousness transcends itself towards it. Consequently, this space of exteriority is merely the space

of what faces us, of what exists only as a correlate of our existence. This is why, in actuality, we do not transcend ourselves very much by plunging into such a world, for all we are doing is exploring the two faces of what remains a face to face – like a coin which only knows its own obverse.[47]

Contrasting this apparently expected and expectable world with Braidotti's sensibility for the marginal, whose body, moving towards the world, is not faced with 'merely the space of what faces us' but with its own exclusion, and whose 'plunging into such a world' is a plunging into the world of the dominant other, in which she is not mirrored and thus in which she does not recognize herself but is alien to: not situated and without words, absent not by choice but through the partisan homogeneity of its design; and comparing his sense of objectivity as distance with Barad's notion of objectivity as responsibility and accountability, it becomes apparent that Meillassoux's project of a calculable world anterior to human experience, is 'merely the space of what faces' *him* as a gendered and racial subject, culturally and historically privileged with access to definite forms of representation: performing his own recognition of himself in a world of calculations, represented in the possibility of a language of numbers articulated in the face of a canonical philosophy. Thus his realism creates, from a place at the centre of knowledge and truth a fiction about an absolute outside, and while he appears to be deconstructing his own embodied authority on the way there, he can only do so because his subjectivity has been historically entitled and matters on in the obverse of his total absence as a hyper-invisible and absolute transparent presence.

However, once we acknowledge that his realism is a realism from the centre and turn to the margins, where according to Braidotti all the action takes place, we can unread his ancestrality not as objective as in truthful because disembodied and distant, but as another location to think the possibility of the real: a remote 'planet' of the unthought; a sphere configured from the speculative essence of the pure possibility of what there is without really being what there is but providing access to the thinking of the unthought as a fiction for thinking the unthinkeable. Thus his notion of an 'after finitude', of a place without the defined finitude of humanity, can help us think about the absolute outside as an otherwise unthinkable possibility of the inside, inviting the creative performance of an unthinking of the centre from the plurality of the margins. In this way, Meillasoux's non-human ancestrality, considered from the margins, from 'the real-life minorities':[48] the women, blacks, youth, postcolonial subjects, migrants, exiled, and homeless of Braidotti, and those whose 'territory is black: because you are Africa', as discussed by Cixous, lines up interestingly with Afrofuturism, which seeks to find a space without mirrors of the past in the future to rethink the unthought and the unthinkable of the present.[49] At the same time, Meillassoux's notion of the absolute outside as the only place from which the real can be thought, brings to mind also the outside of philosophy as discussed by Erin Manning and Brian Massumi: their location outside the discipline that is opened by movement and practice rather than representation and language, to 'challenge philosophy to compose with concepts already on their way in another mode, in the mode of artistic practice, in the mode of event formation, of activism, of dance, even of everyday perception', to generate the impossible.[50]

Through this shift from the unthought to the unthinkable, I recognize the benefit of the ancestral as a place of renewal and invention, where practice can gain ground on theory, revocalize its representational matter and contribute to a different knowledge. Thus I will try to reach that space of the absolute outside not through thinking the unthought but through moving, listening and sounding towards it. To practice rather than think ancestrality so that the uncertainty of my body does not find comfort in a relative outside, the outside of my simple absence and 'correct' its vision, but can plunge into the truly unknown of what is generated in the contingent configuration between my body as matter and that of other subjects and things. In this way, I won't come back with a calculation that terminates all speculation about the outside in its probability, but with the need to keep on practising, as a constant prizing open the entangled space between the matter of my body and mind, that of other things and of the representational scheme that pretends their objective distance and thus absolute knowability. In this performance we do not grasp each other, but entangle temporarily, practising the in-between, and get to understand the world as diffractions, mobile differences, where distance enables a breach with history, and objectivity is responsibility: 'being accountable to marks on bodies'.[51]

In this materialist agitation of thought through creativity, practical knowledge bares the responsibility of the physical encounter. It does not come from a pre-given place at the centre but emerges from the sides and in another mode. According to Braidotti, 'the center is void; all the action is on the margins'.[52] This is the void that masculine materialism takes as its transparency and these are the margins from where a feminine materialism is active, changing the conceptual scheme through creativity: the 'retelling, reconfiguring, and revisiting the concept, phenomenon, event, or location from different angles, so as to infuse it with a nomadic spin that establishes multiple connections and lines of interaction'.[53]

I get to this retelling and reconfiguring of new materialism by listening to a performance of *Naldjorlak I* by Éliane Radique, composed for and with the cellist Charles Curtis, between 2004 and 2005. The work invites an engagement in the reality of embodied matter and the entanglement of things, and is what prompted and informed my investigation into the possibility of a sonic materialism as a feminist science fiction. It is a piece produced without a score, the language of music's disciplinary erudition, but in collaboration, where the grammar of composition is not representational, a semantic code, but a matter of working together, from a tentative drawing of the shape of the piece, to a work that performs the entanglement of composer, cello, cellist, bow and breath.[54]

Listening and writing about this work I try not to represent but to continue its entanglement. To understand what it does not by finding a visual figuration but by finding access into how its processes of interactions produce a creative and performative reality of the work.

Naldjorlak I (2005/2017)[55]
Éliane Radique, Charles Curtis

The work is a composition in real time without a traditional score, produced from the collaboration between the composer, the performer and the instrument of which it sounds all their parts not as separate things but in their interbeing: their being together as the configuration of the reality of their performance. It plays as a single gesture of different voices that sound in one movement their creative transformation of which none seems a leader and through which each articulates itself to become not a singular whole but a complex sphere of inter-action.

The beginning is faint but insistent, a tuning in to the instrument and the body, and in to the work that the tuning-in starts to create: exploring between them the material, the scope and scale of their meeting. They are measuring in sound the possibility of their work together before growing in insistence to know more about what could sound. This tuning-in is not the start of this sonic collaboration however, rather it is preceded, materially and conceptually, by the tuning of the instrument to the 'wolf tone': a tuning not to a referenced pitch, an inter-musical orientation, but to the cello's own resonance, its intra-activity, as it sounds the context and condition of its play. Thus it is a material reference, which is unstable, contingent and changes depending on the space, its humidity and temperature: its 'weather' and other factors that affect the cello's material sound. Curtis suggests that this tuning to the outside of music is named wolf tone to account 'for the unpredictability, danger and acoustical wildness that it stands as the herald of'.[56] Elaborating on its practise he goes on to explain that

> This 'tuning' is a days-long process, which attempts to combine a very high degree of precision in brining as many of the cello's resonating elements as possible into unison, with the essentially impossible task of matching all elements to an amorphous pitch-complex which is additionally a moving target.[57]

I read this tuning to an amorphous pitch-complex of resonating elements that remain mobile and impossible to unite, as an interesting allegory, beyond the preparation of the instrument, for the performance of *Naldjorlak* itself. The work seems to continue this tuning effort outside the resonating spaces of the instrument in those of the concert hall: tuning it to the wolf tone of *its* resonance. Thus it presents a useful image of how the playing of the instrument activates a composition between the different resonating bodies of the space, the performer, the cello and the audience, working on an impossible and yet aimed for unison. Tuning them in to a mobile complex, opening their resonances not in harmony but as their unpredictable in-between; creating the invisible volume that they sound together and in which we can sense their existence as simultaneous vibrations, as mobile materialities that are not 'this' or 'that', but are the resonance of their indivisible interbeing. Thus we hear the reality of each element in practice, in their resonating together, producing the composition as a viscous and indivisible shape of different things that are in conflict and even contradictory, searching for a vibrating line that never unites.

From this first low vibration, this hoarse breathing of the instrument and the body, the space and the bow, the sound is becoming a piece that clearly draws a shape, started possibly by the form of Radique's initial drawing shown to Curtis at the beginning of their collaborative composing, but soon producing its own contingent configuration in the viscous volume of its fraying sound. And so a space is made between bow and cello, body and sound, forged through the continuous movement of their performance. In this formless form they lose their definite shape as nouns, and transform into what they are together, as actions rather than as things, producing what Barad terms an 'agential realism' of their formless form.

With agential realism Barad describes her notion of agency not as a property of persons or things, but as an enactment of difference, 'a matter of possibilities for reconfiguring entanglements'.[58] Barad's idea of an agential realism as a realism of intra-action: of the action between things and subjects that reconfigure entanglements through difference, is useful here to elaborate on the relationship of instrument, body, bow and weather not as an inter-action of static and similiar objects but as the action in-between of active things that are at once the apparatus and material of their production and that perform the reality of their meeting by opening different resonant spaces in listening, in architecture and in music.

In relation to my articulation of sound creating the world as an indivisible sphere of interbeing and inter-activity, made earlier in this text, Barad's realism of intra-activity permits me to recognize and confirm this sonic interbeing as an interbeing not of static things but of mobile bodies, whose resonant vibrations, the sonic sign of their molecular activity, co-produce and co-constitute the formless complex of an indivisible world. In this sonic world we hear the mobile and transforming interconnectivity of things, and have to think through their porous motility rather than through the significance of autonomous and stable objects, to understand what matter does together in difference rather than in the sameness and oppositionality of separate things.

Curtis in his essay 'Éliane Radigue and *Naldjorlak*' (2010), discussing the work and the process of its collaborative composition, talks about the need to become Radique 'in order to make this work, in my performance, hers'.[59] He understands the continuous motility of the sound's vibration to reflect on Radique's hearing: 'she hears sound as a spatial, and constantly moving, entity'; and he compares the method of composition but not its sound, to her tape pieces, which were 'written' in real time on the tape, in the movement between two machines, alternating between decks to create a continuous duration, and developing a single gesture that had to be restarted if an unwanted sound or a sudden volume change or other 'false' move occurred.[60] Since, although there is no traditional score, *Naldjorlak* is not an improvisation but a composition produced in the act of performance that is determined by the act of collaboration between Radique and Curtis, the drawing of the work, the tuning of the cello to the wolf tone, and the playing of its allegory through the elements that affect its tuning.

According to Curtis, for Radique the instrument is the score. He develops this interpretation and suggests that the score is the drawing on the instrument: the physical action of creating the sound from its resonant body, its strings, wood, bridge, and bow, articulating a composition through the agitation of the instrument's physical design, as well as its location, temperature and the body that plays its sound to create the temporary form of its score. The score then is a site of collaboration. It is a temporal enactment of impulses and instructions given by the initial drawing, through conversations, and ultimately of the actions that the instrument teases out of Curtis as Curtis teases the resonances from its body.

In this reciprocal play between body and instrument every possibility for resonance is explored, excited, brought out and made to sound: to perform its capacity and the capacity of the cellist to perform it. The instrument is the contingent location of a drawn score that gives instructions and parameters to this process that the body, the bow and the breath follow and perform while in response and as iteration they expand what this drawing out of possibilities might be and reinstruct the process.

The sound grows ever more insistent, its diffuse vibrations catching ever more tones to swing along. Broadening its texture and reach, it extends beyond the limits of the instrument and excites the resonance of my listening body. The cello's sound transforms from rasping vibrations into deeper tremors that expand into the unlit volume of the place, gaining in import and ferocity, taking hold of its invisibility and transforming through the oscillating continuity of its diffracted pitch the sense of sitting in the dark.

The light is focused on the performer and the instrument only. We were under strict instructions to switch off mobile phones. And now I understand why. Their light and sound would have broken the piece, we would have had to start again, as Radique had to start again every time a 'fault' or unwanted level and sound occurred in her tape works produced in an effort not unlike this one, but staged as a performance without audience and between decks, on the movement of a rolling tape.

In this unbroken darkness we move together without breaking the tone: Moving forward and backward to see through the bodies of a packed audience sitting on wooden benches in the Moscow cold of an old turbine hall in February, the body of Curtis, that of the cello and that of the bow moving to produce the sounds we are moving to and towards. His play is agile and focused, the effort clearly visible. The rapport between cello and cellist intimate and muscular. He has to get up and move to reach and communicate with the resonances that are available in the instrument. In turn the tonality of his moving body finds resonance in the motility of the sound that moves around him. But this is not an effort of similarity or harmony but a slow and patient differentiation and diffracting of sounds and bodies into the precision of their specific formlessness together. The work performs the intra-activity of all the elements involved in the composition, and unperforms their certain form as human or as music, as bow and architecture, body and breath. Their sounds are Irigaray's gesture-words, the caresses that do not seek to grasp the semantic but to make a musical speech that 'longs for the existence of a between-us'.[61]

At their agential in-between my listening too becomes diffracting: a reconfiguring of the 'material-discursive apparatuses' of hearing: the nature of the apparatus of observation and its material object, which are the discursive and material conditions of music, of performance, of the score and of audienceship.[62] This reconfiguring listening reads them as patterns of difference, beyond a disciplinary language, in the infinite openness and volatile material of sound from where it allows us to engage in the possibilities of its expression beyond what we think it is as music.

This effort of listening ignores the line of harmonic development, the grammar of music, and the authority of performance, and grants access to the work's complex and simultaneous interbeing in difference: In the difference of each other and the complexity of their in-between, as a site not of unalterable or negative conflict but of an affirmative conflictual generation of what is in the invisible realm between things in motion. And from this invisible realm the definition of each thing can be resisted, rethought and recomposed. Thus a new music arises as a temporospatial production of wild and transforming things, enacting the differentiated inseparability that is a heterogenous music without origin.

This sonic diffracting moves the unheard and the inaudible into music. It produces a rhythm of deep vibrations and probing sweeps, a concentrated scanning for difference and particularity, growing ever more insistent and forceful, until at one point we seem to reach a plateau, a moment of balance on which the piece continues in a simpler voice but equally demanding. Swerving still in the dark. Closing in, loud and intense: a mobile horizon, static in terms of its verticality. Here the sound is extremely focused in an unplaceable pitch. Unhalting it makes pulsating connections between places on the body and the cello, performing an impenetrable but elastic core between the two that does not find a certain form but tunes itself to the movements of what either is. It is a narrow band with a plural throw, expanding how long a sound can be and extending the infinitude of listening and the reach of our ears.

Once more the intensity rises and I can feel the tremors of bow and cello reach my body and impact on its molecular shape, carrying it into the intra-activity of the composition to become part of its reality, entangled in its invisible configuration. But then the work starts to slow down, and on its ways into a quieter register it opens up the frequencies and vibrations it held together in the faster movement of a louder volume, to give them up to our listening in a slower, broader drone. Frayed and open they vibrate as formless forms until the sound collects itself, becomes slimmer, transparent almost, and the bridge, the strings and the fingerboard become visible, clear, a form in silence.

This is a point of rest. We take a breath with Curtis, the cello and the room, until with a low sound of uneven harmonics we start in a play of intense to and fro along the whole bow and in the middle of the instrument where sound becomes the rhythm of its own time. The movement starts slowly, broad and searching: a fog light in the dark space, illuminating its different resonances, while bringing them into play.

> Le lien entre le rythme et le sujet vient de ce que j'entends par pensée poétique une invention du rythme, au sens où le rythme n'est plus une alternance formelle mais une organisation du sujet.[63]

I hear with Henri Meschonnic how the work becomes the invention of this rhythm, not as a vacillation of tones, but the configuration of the work itself. It is not a metric of things but a wild engine from which the work grasps its material possibility. Thus the work becomes slowly the steady oscillating movement of body and bow articulating between tones and overtones. This movement reaches out and brings into the work what there is that can sound on its undulant weave. Its muscular performance erases any sense of an original note or common musical ground. Instead, we are in the throw of surging textures as an alternative to the tonal line, growing ever more intense, faster, more insistent. This is a choreography of unperforming as an affirmative reconstitution of musical possibility. There is nothing else now, just this movement, this rhythm that configures the room in the timespace of its material sense. This is not even really sound but is time as all there is, intense plastic and infinite. 'La notion de rythme permet précisément d'infinitiser le sens, de fragmenter infiniment l'unité, la totalité. De montrer l'enjeu du discours.'[64] To show the heart of discourse. *De montrer l'enjeu de la materialité.* To show the heart of matter: to fragment, diffractively, the unity and totality of the work.

The sound as broad and textured rhythm is the agential reality of the work's reconfiguring the space, the instrument, and music, the body playing and the body listening, in an alternative shape. This shape is visceral, muscular, agentially real. It is a predicative shape that brings us into the materiality of time, reminding us that we are with the work and that its time is our joint material duration. It is thus not a chronological measure but a viscous and voluminous expanse in all directions. It is the time of honey grasping me when I grasp it, demanding and sweet.[65] It is ahistorical time with regard to musical conventions and writes backwards from the instrumental performance into what music can do, what its material might be, and how its language might articulate.

This nonmeasured time denies distance and insists on intimacy while not revealing its form. It is a sustained but intangible formlessness that highlights the in-between, from where it grants glimpses of what is, and where we have to meet it to hear our joint configuration of what that is. Thus the work produces a doubtful measure of a feminine sonic materialism that insists we inhabit it if we mean to say anything about how it passed, to be accountable and take responsibility for what it is we think we saw.

This time is what carries the reciprocity and collaborative nature of the work's production: 'the move to composing for acoustic instruments now means working with musicians, being with them for extended periods of time, sharing the difficulties of creation and the hopefulness of the new piece evolving'.[66] And it sustains this reciprocity into perception as participatory listening that creates a durational co-production, sharing the difficulties and hopefulness of a musical possibility.

The time of this material rhythm, inhabited by me on a cold February night, brings things into motion, and brings duration into a materialist discussion as a pattern of difference that unfolds and intra-acts but never runs out. That is inexhaustible, but exhausting. It is the engine of difference and the shape of its mattering. Diffracting time does not make discrete units, of seconds and milliseconds, but generates their expanse, which is the material when all else has left.

And then the work stops.

To breathe again, as the sustained low vibration of a third frame that foregrounds the duration of materiality and the nonmetric rhythms of hearing. This third movement composes a fragile thread of time that breaks material certainty and makes it reappear as the ephemeral co-constitution of things, as all there is, a whistle only, a thin sound of indivisible time.

Philosophy as digging on your hands and knees: A conclusion on gardening

Having heard all three movements the place of listening is different now. The old turbine hall is opened, available to the infinity of meaning, its material and institutional built an invisible configuration, ready to be recomposed. Once we have experienced its resonance we know it in a different way. We have tuned into its wolf tone, which 'in the parlance of performers, "speaks" differently', it speaks to us of its invisible capacity and the indivisible volume that we excite and produce by being with it, intra-acting its expanse.[67]

Listening and sounding fragment the representational preconceptions of matter: that of architecture, music, the cello and the score. They highlight and perform its creative and transformative capacity – the vibration of an amorphous shape within which we recognize the inarticulate, the unthought and the unthinkable – and reperform it through the language of a minor practice: A feminine voice that is symbolic of a general marginality and works through agitation, intra-activity, processes and diffractions of inclusivity.

This intra-action is, according to Barad, not an issue of choice but of a much less predictable necessity, a wild and dangerous causality that makes us part of its tuning and teases out new resonances without harmonic reference or name. It is a plunging into the world of a composition without a score, without grammar, but with the strength of the radical contingency of a collaborative production of music that imagines a collaborative production of the world. This agential reality of co-production and co-constitution articulates through the new materialist elaboration of performativity as 'agential intra-action', and creates an ethics of entanglement that reconfigures interbeing through agential forces rather than through essentialisms and a priori. It informs an ethics of doing as an ethics of doing together, of entanglement and participation in difference. Thus it brings correlationism, and particularly Merleau-Ponty's notion of intersubjectivity as an interobjectivity in action, as intra-objectivity and modest collaborator into the unthinkable doing of matter, to ensure the situatedness of the marginal subject even in a nomadic world.[68]

Sound and listening, as a sensory-motor action fuelled by phenomenological doubt, makes the new materialism of Barad and Braidotti tangible, audible and thinkable and asserts their feminine focus by insisting on diffraction and creativity as an inhabited and reciprocal practice. In comparison, Meillassoux's mathematical fiction of an absolute exteriority found in the ancestral purposefully bars the access to direct experience. It suspends habits of thought and expectation to reach the unthought via an intellectual disappearance. Thus it forces us to rethink how we might grasp and articulate such a world. Since we have to articulate it, or perform it, if it is not simply to be a mute unthought of belief and dogma: a blind faith in numbers, which he set out to critique in the first place.

Meillassoux's focus on calculation rather than experience implodes the philosophical ground as the symbolic and literal baseline of knowledge and reality. In that sense it represents an emancipatory force that equals Braidotti's cartographies that are 'more like a weather map than an atlas', that mutate and change and do not offer a mapped out ground but a practice to stay grounded in mobility, and is not unlike Barad's agential realism of diffraction that explores invisible difference instead of similarities and outlines.[69] However, without an a priori ground, without a visual cartography and an optic structure of sameness, philosophy has to be performed, even if in numbers. We cannot escape being human by plunging into mathematics instead of into the world. It needs to be dug into, digging in 'the field of possibility', of practice and of discourse that according to Barad is not static or singular but plural and moving,[70] and that according to Braidotti encourages 'a sort of intellectual landscape gardening' of an embodied mind.[71] Digging and building on our hands and knees to sense the amorphous shape of the work and the world's complex possibility to grasp them as a consequent and accountable real.

It is not the matter of the human being, her movements or thoughts that undermine the possibility of materiality, but the mute thinking in categories and dualisms. And these we can unperform by writing different scores, not as legible instructions but as a dialogue with things, and by following them differently, not to hear the correct interpretation but to participate in their contingent configuration through a rhythm that does not alternate the sign, but breaks into the infinite possibility of material fragmentation to realize its political possibility in renewal.

> For rhythm is a subject-form(er). The subject-form(er). That it renews the meaning of things, that it is through rhythm that we reach the sense that we have of our being undone [*défaire*], that everything around us happens as it undoes itself [*défaire*], and that, approaching this sensation of the movement of everything, we ourselves are part of this movement.[72]

Meschonnic's nonmetric rhythm presents a strategy of diffraction that brings time into a materialist and speculative realm, and sees things in their duration as configured timespace, rejecting a dualist visuality through the entangled movements of sound that renew the realist frame in the simultaneous plurality of a spatial time.

This renewed possibility of digging in an irregular beat brings phenomenology back to materialism as a modest collaborator. It makes its speculation inhabited, experienced and real in its consequence rather than as probability and calculation, and takes account of the situatedness and the responsibility of the subject, who while matter herself is accountable for her actions. In turn, the materialist project opens phenomenological intersubjectivity to the notion of intermateriality, as intra-materiality, recognizing the independent causality of the non-human, and fostering the notion of interaction as a process 'that blurs all boundaries' between objects and subjects, as well as between disciplines and knowledge institutions.[73]

Through sound realism finds a new relationship with correlationism, not as a visuocentric intersubjectivity 'merely the space of what faces us', but as the invisible in-between of what we do together, as indivisible matter mattering an entangled interbeing of the world that takes care also of its exclusions. This invisible in-between creates a performative rather than a dogmatic doubt that finds in the concept of the ancestral a possible space from which to suspend habits of thought and rethink, reperform and reinvent the present beyond a dualist view. This sonico-feminine materialism, in collaboration with a phenomenology as a modest partner, creates Barad's agential realism in Meschonnic's political rhythm, where agency is not an attribute but a verb and where reality is not 'this' or 'that' but the dynamic irregularity of their mobile in-between.

The collaborative composing of Radique and Curtis, their tuning of the instrument to the wolf tone and the tuning of the performance in to its environment creates this intra-activity where music and performance attain an ethics of entanglement, where they are part of the production of the place and take responsibility for the phenomenon of body and instrument, subject and object, generated in their irregular rhythm, not as dialectical opposites but through an entangled co-production of their differences and possibilities.

Naldjorlak I produces not a score to re-interpret correctly, but the unrepresentable movement of the performance as an architectural score of contingent resonances, their differences and inter-dependencies. As such a contingent and fluid map it does not present a cartographic scheme or firm instructions that exclude what else we might do, but creates the mapping of fleeting things in the movement of sound. It enables participation and the recording of simultaneous and overlapping trajectories through movements that are deliberate and rigorous but are not limited to what we think the instrument, the bow, the body or the breath of the space are capable of, but what their unthought capacity makes possible.

While a masculine new materialism insists on the absence of the human to get to the unthought, and thus ultimately proposes the end of philosophy in its own mathematical probability, a sonico-feminine new materialism brings us to the creative performance of matter and language not in words but on the body and on things: doing, digging, gardening as a revocalization and rephysicalization of theory through its intra-activitiy with things. Through this practical philosophy and the performance of matter I can reach the outside of the discipline not as its disavowal and end, but as the place of its renewal: working on the outside of its conventions, at the nonchronological and noncanonical place of thought, at the margins, to produce a different path for thinking as doing. At the same time, I can, from the edges of its possibility, through the practical act of a sonic thinking as movement and performance of irregular rhythms, reconfigure the notion of historical sonic and musical production and its discourse.

This is a working from the margins to an entirely different centre of philosophy and of music that is shared and sharable, made from differences in an entangled and embodied materiality. The ethics of this music is an ethics of entanglement and embodiment rather than that of categories, good practice virtuosity, and a certain form. It is not the ethics of rules and commandments, but of process, of performing and unperforming place, instrument, body, score, musical materiality and expectations. It is an ethics of digging, plowing into the framework and apparatus that give rules and see a singular actuality, in order to respond with a contingent practise from the voids in its history and the plurality of its time, creating a 'subject-unformer', an 'object-unformer'.

And maybe that is what new materialism has to do, it has to start digging into its own material to perform it, to write a different score on the body of the philosopher and on the body of theory, and to let them be diffracted, plural, different and nomadic, not located but creating a place as an extension, as the elastic and expanded space of its agential reality. Philosophy has to become a digging, a digging down, into language, into canons and authority, to unperform them, to undo them in an affirmative action of recomposition. This is a new materialism of doing and undoing, of uncreating and of unperforming what there is: subjectivity, materiality, relationships, procedures and processes, not to deconstruct but to be affirmative in the non-dialectical practice of making a fresh planet of the unthought through the futurism of ancestrality, creating a place of pure possibility that is not mathematical but inhabited and agentially real.

They go on. They leave Omelas, they walk ahead into the darkness, and they do not come back. The place they go towards is a place even less imaginable to most of us than the city of happiness. I cannot describe it at all. It is possible that is does not exist.[74]

Notes

1 Edith Södergran, 'The Stars', in *Complete Poems*, trans. David McDuff, Newcastle upon Tyne, UK: Bloodaxe, 1992, p. 63. Reprinted with permission.

2 Quentin Meillassoux, *After Finitude*, New York: Continuum, 2009, p. 7.

3 In *After Finitude*, Meillassoux states that: 'the de-absolutization of thought boils down to the mobilisation of a *fideist* argument.' An argument in other words that defends a quasi and generalized religious thought and thus, according to Meillassoux, leads to the obscurantism of correlationism, at the very point where it wants to escape the dogmatism of rationalism (Meillassoux, *After Finitude*, p. 46).

4 Meillassoux, *After Finitude,* pp. 126–7.

5 Ibid., p. 17.

6 The unthinkable is not what is too horrific to be thought but what escapes thought's normative boundaries, what remains outside our imagination of what can be thought conventionally.

7 Karen Barad, 'Posthumanist Performativity: Toward an Understanding of How Matter Comes to Matter', *Signs: Journal of Women in Culture and Society*, vol. 28, no. 3 (2003): 810.

8 Karen Barad, interviewed in *New Materialism: Interviews & Cartographies*, Rick Dolphijn and Iris van der Tuin, Ann Arbor, MI: Open Humanities Press, 2012, p. 68.

9 Luce Irigaray, *To Be Two*, New York: Routledge, 2001, p. 20.

10 Christoph Cox, 'Beyond Representation and Signification: Towards a Sonic Materialism', *Journal of Visual Culture*, vol. 10, no. 2 (2011): 145–6.

11 Ibid., p. 148.

12 Adriana Cavarero, *For More than one Voice, Toward a Philosophy of Vocal Expression*, Stanford: Stanford University Press, 2005, p. 57.

13 Ibid., p. 61.

14 Rick Dolphijn and Iris van der Tuin, *New Materialism: Interviews & Cartographies*, Ann Arbor, MI: Open Humanities Press, 2012, p. 119.

15 Cavarero, *For More than one Voice, Toward a Philosophy of Vocal Expression*, 2005, p. 61.

16 Hélène Cixous, 'The Laugh of the Medusa', trans. Keith Cohen and Paula Cohen, *Signs*, vol. 1, no. 4 (Summer 1976): 875.

17 Ibid.

18 Ibid., pp. 886 and 877.

19 Rosi Braidotti, *Nomadic Theory, the Portable Rosi Braidotti*, New York: Columbia University Press, 2011, pp. 70 and 72.

20 Graham Harman, *Towards Speculative Realism, Essays and Lectures*, Winchester, UK and Washington, DC: Zero Books, 2010, p. 113.

21 Rosi Braidotti, *Patterns of Dissonance*, New York: Routledge, 1991, quoted in Braidotti, *Nomadic Subjects, Embodiment and Sexual Difference in Contemporary Feminist Theory*, 2nd edn, New York: Columbia University Press, 2011, p. 9.

22 Braidotti, *Nomadic Theory*, p. 2.

23 Ibid., p. 60.

24 Braidotti, *Nomadic Subjects*, p. 128.

25 Barad, 'Posthumanist Performativity', p. 803.

26 Barad, interviewed in *New Materialism: Interviews & Cartographies*, p. 49.

27 Ibid., p 50.

28 Ibid., pp. 52–3. Diffraction places an emphasis on open, 'indefinite boundaries' between disciplines, which echoes also Braidotti's sense on the need for a 'transdisciplinary approach that cuts across established methods and conventions of many disciplines', to produce an articulation and being in the globalized labour market (Braidotti, *Nomadic Subjects*, p. 7). The challenge to 'separate academic division' through the creative diffraction of their knowledge base appears an important and central target of feminine new materialist thought: promoting an interdisciplinary mattering, which effectively reimagines 'the entanglements that already exist' (Barad interviewed in *New Materialism: Interviews & Cartographies*, pp. 50–1).

29 Barad, 'Quantum Entanglements and Hauntological Relations of Inheritance: Dis/continuities, SpaceTime Enfoldings, and Justice-to-Come', *Derrida Today*, vol. 3, no. 2 (2010): 253.

30 Braidotti, *Nomadic Theory*, p. 20.

31 Ibid., p. 41.

32 Irigaray, *To Be Two*, p. 27.

33 Barad 'Posthumanist Performativity', p. 802.

34 Braidotti, *Nomadic Subjects,* pp. 29–43.

35 Irigaray, *To Be Two*, p. 17.

36 Barad, 'Posthumanist Performativity', p. 812. While Barad suggests a performative turn to avoid the pitfuls of semantic language, Braidotti suggests the reimagining of figuration as a cartography that resembles weather maps (Braidotti, *Nomadic Subjects*, p. 13), and Irigaray infuses her critical writing with poetry.

37 Irigaray, *To Be Two*, p. 3.

38 'Goofy' is the term used by Manuel DeLanda when describing Irigaray's work in a conversation with Christoph Cox. In answer to a question about Gilles Deleuze and his circle of friends, that is, like-minded philosophers, De Landa suggests that: 'Deleuze was close to Foucault and Lyotard, but not to Derrida, and certainly not to Irigaray and her goofy notion of a "masculinist epistemology"' ('Possibility Spaces: Manuel DeLanda in Conversation with Christoph Cox', in *Realism Materialism Art*, Christoph Cox, Jenny Jaskey and Suhail Malik [eds], Berlin: Sternberg, 2015, p. 87). This statement is not only embarrassing but also paradoxically demonstrative of the masculinist view point, deliciously unaware of the dominance of its logic and the suppression of the other, what is unfamiliar and unknown, while searching for the unthought.

This apparent unawareness of the dominance of a masculine position within new materialism finds a further example in the English translation of Meillassoux's *After Finitude* (2006). In the French original version by

Meillassoux, the correlationist, who stands accused of fanaticism, is identified as masculine: 'Le corrélationiste intervient alors pour disqualifier ces deux positions: Il défend, quant a lui, un strict agnosticisme théorique. Toutes les croyance lui paraissent également licites' (Meillassoux, *Après la Finitude, Essai sur la nécessité de la contingence*, Paris: Éditions du Seuil, 2006, p. 75). In the English translation of these passages, by contrast, the correlationist is identified as failing in 'her' ability to see and think an absolute outside, for being caught, in other words, in the relativity of her own position and prone to the fanaticism of fideist perception, 'all beliefs strike her as equally legitimate' (*After Finitude*, p. 55). In all other passages of the book the impersonal plural of the pronoun 'they' is used, avoiding gender specificity. Thus the sudden choice of the female pronoun produces the sense of a deliberate assignation of fideism and fanaticism to the feminine. Given that phenomenological philosophers and correlationists, on the whole, and those addressed by Meillassoux in the particular are male, this seems a very strange choice of pronoun, even if made in an attempt at gender inclusivity.

It is hard to say whether this decision on the part of Ray Brassier, a fellow new materialist who translated the book, is entirely deliberate or just unthinking of its context. Nevertheless, as I will argue later, there is a most striking difference between what I call a masculine and a feminine interpretation and application of new materialist aims and ideas: the first looks for the bones and stones of this world, the other for our responsibility.

I am not mentioning these incidences to prejudice this enquiry into the possibility of realism and its access to an unthought world, but because it brings the absolute outside into a potentially totalitarian position that is not as neutral in its motivation, starting position and design as claimed, and that needs to be considered since speculative realism has built into its method a guaranteed defence against any form of critique, given that we cannot reach the reality or even discuss it without undoing its claim of absolute outsideness.

39 Braidotti, *Nomadic Theory*, p. 42.

40 Christoph Cox, 'Beyond Representation and Signification: Towards a Sonic Materialism', *Journal of Visual Culture*, vol. 10, no. 2 (2011): 145.

41 Barad, interviewed in *New Materialism: Interviews & Cartographies*, p. 51.

42 Ibid., p. 63.

43 Ibid., p. 53.

44 Ibid., p. 70.

45 Irigaray, *To Be Two*, p. 3.

46 Meillassoux, *After Finitude*, p. 126.

47 Ibid., p. 7.

48 Braidotti, *Nomadic Theory*, p. 42.

49 Cixous, 'The Laugh of the Medusa', p. 877.

50 Erin Manning and Brian Massumi, *Thought in the Act: Passages in the Ecology of Experience*, Minneapolis and London: University of Minnesota Press, 2014, pp. vii and 134.

51 Barad, 'Posthumanist Performativity', p. 824.

52 Braidotti, *Nomadic Theory*, p. 42.

53 Ibid., p. 230.

54 In his text on the experience of working on *Naldjorlak*, Curtis explains how upon his arrival at Radique's apartment in Paris to start the process of co-creation, he was presented with a single white sheet 'with some faint and tentative pencil marks on it' (Charles Curtis, 'Éliane Radigue and *Naldjorlak*', in *Attention Patterns*, Black Pollen Press/Important Records, 2010, p. 3).

55 Since 2007 there are two further parts to the work, forming a trilogy: *Naldjorlak* I, II and III, the second of which is for two basset horns composed for and with Carole Robinson and Bruno Martinez, and the third for cello and two basset horns. My writing here will focus on the first part only, not to show a preference or distinction but to create an engagement with one particular material entanglement.

   The original solo cello piece was premiered at the Tenri Cultural Institute in New York on 5 December 2005. The performance that I experienced was at the Geometry of Now exhibition/concert program at GES-2 in Moscow, on 25 February 2017.

56 Curtis, 'Éliane Radigue and *Naldjorlak*', p. 6.

57 Ibid., p. 6.

58 Barad interviewed in *New Materialism: Interviews & Cartographies*, p. 55.

59 Curtis, 'Éliane Radigue and *Naldjorlak*', p. 5.

60 Ibid.

61 Irigaray, *To Be Two*, p. 28.

62 Barad discusses this co-reading of the apparatus or practice of observation and the material observed in her interview with Rick Dolphijn and Iris van der Tuin in *New Materialism: Interviews & Cartographies*, p. 55.

63 'The linkage between the rhythm and the poetic matter/subject, comes from what I understand through poetic thinking as an invention of the rhythm, in the sense that the rhythm is not anymore a formal, metric alternation, but an organisation of the poetic matter' (Henri Meschonnic, *Politique du Rythme, Politique du sujet*, Paris: Editions Verdier, 1995, p. 9, my translation).

64 The idea of the rhythm permits precisely the rendering infinite of sense; to infinitively fragment its unity, the notion of totality; to show the heart of discourse.

   (Henri Meschonnic, *Critique du Rythme, Anthropologie historique du langage*, Paris: Verdier Poche, 1982, p. 19, my translation.)

65 In *The World of Perception*, trans. Oliver Davis, London and New York: Routledge, 2008, pp. 46–7, Maurice Merleau-Ponty suggests that

   honey is a slow-moving liquid; while it undoubtedly has a certain consistency and allows itself to be grasped, it soon creeps slyly from the fingers and returns to where it started from. It comes apart as soon as it has been given a particular shape, and what is more, it reverses the roles, by grasping the hands of whoever would take hold of it.

Being honeyed expresses the reciprocity of phenomenological intersubjectivity. The honey can only be felt through my stickiness. It cannot be grasped as a remote object but comes to being in my honeyed-hands as the complex phenomenon of the subject and the object. It articulates a phenomenological intra-activity; a correlationist material speculation on the being of being honey as being a mobile and sticky configuration of matter, a phenomenon of honey and hands.

66 Charles Curtis remarking on Radique's move from composing with synthesized sounds and reel to reel tape, as a performance without audience or instrumentalists, to working with an interpreter in a collaborative effort of composition as a sharing of time in 'Éliane Radigue and *Naldjorlak*', pp. 8–9.

67 Ibid., p. 6.

68 Phenomenology is a modest collaborator in this context since the aim is not to find a phenomenological truth about the work, as a work for me, but to understand its entangled performance and materiality: to get to its 'intra-actions', Barad's nondeterministic causality, which is not appreciated via the interactions of entities in an additive fashion, this caused this caused this, but as itself existing as the between of entity and the action that impacts on it, as an invisible force, whose 'diffractive' thinking is motivated by phenomenological doubt, and is afforded a method in its reciprocity and intersubjectivity understood as an intra-objectivity: the action between objects and subjects that enact their being a phenomenon together.

69 Braidotti, *Nomadic Subjects*, p. 13. Braidotti's weather maps elaborate embodiement as the grounding for a nomadic subject. Producing not maps of positions and locations but maps of positionings. I remain sceptical of the term map, but appreciate that her maps represent, in many ways, an unmapping, a cartography of unrepresentable movement, highlighting its unrepresentability by insisting on the authority of the map.

70 Barad, 'Quantum Entanglements and Hauntological Relations of Inheritance', p. 819.

71 Braidotti, *Nomadic Subjects*, p. 46.

72 Henri Meschonnic, *The Rhythm Party Manifesto*, trans. David Nowell Smith, *Thinking Verse*, vol. 1 (2011), p. 165.

73 Braidotti, *Nomadic Theory*, p. 2.

74 Ursula K. Le Guin, *The UNREAL & The REAL*, *Selected Stories Volume 2 Outer Space, Inner Lands*, London: Orion, 2015, p. 7.

References

Barad, Karen, interviewed in *New Materialism: Interviews & Cartographies*, Rick Dolphijn and Iris van der Tuin, Ann Arbor, MI: Open Humanities Press, 2012, pp. 49–70.

Barad, Karen, 'Posthumanist Performativity: Toward an Understanding of How Matter Comes to Matter', *Signs: Journal of Women in Culture and Society*, vol. 28, no. 3 (2003): 801–31.

Barad, Karen, 'Quantum Entanglements and Hauntological Relations of Inheritance: Dis/continuities, SpaceTime Enfoldings, and Justice-to-Come', *Derrida Today*, vol. 3, no. 2 (2010): 240–68.

Braidotti, Rosi, *Nomadic Subject, Embodiment and Sexual Difference in Contemporary Feminist Theory*, 2nd edn, New York: Columbia University Press, 2011.

Braidotti, Rosi, *Nomadic Theory, The Portable Rosi Braidotti*, New York: Columbia University Press, 2011.

Braidotti, Rosi, *Patterns of Dissonance*, New York: Routledge, 1991.

Cavarero, Adriana, *For More than One Voice, Toward a Philosophy of Vocal Expression*, trans. Paul A. Kottman, Stanford: Stanford University Press, 2005.

Cixous, Hélène, 'The Laugh of the Medusa', trans. Keith Cohen and Paula Cohen, *Signs*, vol. 1, no. 4 (Summer 1976): 875–93.

Cox, Christoph, 'Beyond Representation and Signification: Towards a Sonic Materialism', *Journal of Visual Culture*, vol. 10, no. 2 (2011): 145–61.

Cox, Christoph, 'Possibility Spaces: Manuel DeLanda in Conversation with Christoph Cox', in *Realism Materialism Art*, Christoph Cox, Jenny Jaskey and Suhail Malik (eds), Berlin: Sternberg, 2015, pp. 87–94.

Curtis, Charles, 'Éliane Radigue and *Naldjorlak*', *Attention Patterns*, as part of a 48-page booklet that accompanied a double LP, Che Chen (ed.), Black Pollen Press/Important Records, 2010.

Landa, Manuel De, 'Emergence, Causality and Realism', in *The Speculative Turn, Continental Materialism and Realism*, Levi Bryant, Nick Srnicek and Graham Harman (eds), Melbourne, Australia: re.press, 2011, pp. 381–92.

Dolphijn, Rick, and Iris van der Tuin, *New Materialism: Interviews & Cartographies*, Ann Arbor, MI: Open Humanities Press, 2012.

Harman, Graham, *Towards Speculative Realism, Essays and Lectures*, Winchester, UK and Washington, DC: Zero Books, 2010.

Irigaray, Luce, *To Be Two*, New York: Routledge, 2001 [1994].

Le Guin, Ursula K., *The UNREAL & The REAL, Selected Stories Volume 2 Outer Space, Inner Lands*, London: Orion, 2015.

Manning, Erin and Brian Massumi, *Thought in the Act: Passages in the Ecology of Experience*, Minneapolis and London: University of Minnesota Press, 2014.

Meillassoux, Quentin, *After Finitude, An Essay on the Necessity of Contingency*, New York: Continuum, 2009.

Meillassoux, Quentin, *Après la Finitude, Essai sur la nécessité de la contingence*, Paris: Éditions du Seuil, 2006.

Merleau-Ponty, Maurice, *The World of Perception*, trans. Oliver Davis, London and New York: Routledge, 2008 [First published in French as *Causeries 1948*, Paris: Éditions de Seuil, 2002, from a radio series commissioned by the French national radio and broadcast on its National Program at the end of 1948].

Meschonnic, Henri, *Critique du Rythme, Anthropologie historique du langage*, Paris: Verdier Poche, 1982.

Meschonnic, Henri, *Politique du Rythme, Politique du sujet*, Paris: Editions Verdier, 1995.

Meschonnic, Henri, *The Rhythm Party Manifesto*, trans. David Nowell Smith, *Thinking Verse,* vol. 1 (2011): 161–73.

Södergran, Edith, 'The Stars', in *Complete Poems*, trans. David McDuff, Newcastle upon Tyne, UK: Bloodaxe, 1992, p. 63.

Work

Radique, Éliane and Charles Curtis, *Naldjorlak I* (2005) three movements for Cello performed at the Geometry of Now exhibition/concert program at GES-2 in Moscow, on 25 February 2017.

Reading fragments of listening, hearing vertical lines of words

This magnificent trumpet is going to change your life.[1]

In Leonora Carrington's *The Hearing Trumpet* (1974), Marian Leatherby, an old lady, 92 years of age, receives the gift of an ornate hearing trumpet from her friend Carmella. Using this rudimentary amplification device enables her to hear more clearly what is being said and what goes on around her.

The first thing Marian overhears thanks to its amplification is her family plotting to send her to a nursing home out in the suburbs, run by The Well of Light Brotherhood, a Christian organization that houses old ladies in bungalows shaped like toadstools, igloos, a boot or an Egyptian mummy, and makes them endure strange rituals of fortification and self-betterment.

Seemingly unable or unwilling to resist this move to the institute, Marian arrives at the home where she is immediately accommodated in a tower whose walls are painted with furniture, a bookcase, a wardrobe and even a window that are not there but simply present themselves as two-dimensional depictions of what is supposed to be there. Meanwhile, a large oil painting of a winking abbess dominates the dining hall of the institution and comes to preoccupy Marian's imagination in a very three-dimensional and fleshly way. The hearing trumpet and the fantastical story of the abbess's live soon tie her into this peculiar community of ten elderly women, whose past and current secrets are not heard to summarize and conclude their existence but to generate a future that is fantastical and prophetic. Emboldened by the unity of rhythmic dancing and chanting they recognize their singularity and common strength and abandon their obligation to male authority expressed in the domineering language of dead husband's, chivvying sons and now Dr Gambit, who governs the place through strict institutional rules and the Original Teaching of the Master. Instead, they come to articulate their own voice through riddles and the inarticulate calling of wild bees.

The hearing trumpet is at once a metaphor and a portal to see beyond the conventional, the expected and what is presented as complete and coherent in a mute contemplation. Through its concept and sensibility, we come to appreciate invisible connections and mobile complexities that insist on proximity and reciprocity and produce unseen fictions that make the unfamiliar part of actuality and reveal the possibility of a sonic reality. Thus it opens Marian's deaf ears to the acoustic reality of her surroundings and grants her access to the possible slices of a sonic world. Initiating her into the hidden dimension of this community of elderly ladies, the hearing trumpet at once demands and enables her participation and admits her into that which eludes a visual perception but nevertheless determines its consequences. Soon Marian's world opens to the depth of sound and becomes forever more fantastical, illusionary or maybe visionary.

The narrative quickly leaves the path of chronology and spatial coherence. The story of the abbess and the pneuma of Mary Magdalene, a vapour that induces levitation and a different state of mind and body – 'and it hath changed my darkness into light, and it hath rent the chaos which surrounded me'[2] – the death of Maude Somers, who had been Arthur Somers all along; as well as séances, fasting and chanting, tilt the story world's reality and earthquakes start the rotation of the Poles to the Equator. Snow starts to fall and covers the land, which is now roamed by werewolf cubs and honey bees, and Marian enters the sonorous possibility of her own life.

Listening, Marian delves into the depth of the real and comes to see the strange that is a part of the unremarkable, and to accept the inexplicable not as an aberration but as the real fabric of truth. Standing at the top of steep stairs, she is drawn by the warm wind of the earth and descends down its vertical steps, deep into the tower in which she meets herself.

At the farthest end of the gallery a final flight of steps led down into the large round chamber. As I reached the bottom of the steps I could smell sulphur and brimstone. The cavern was as warm as a kitchen.

Beside the flames sat a woman stirring a great iron cauldron. She seemed familiar to me, although I could not see her face. Something in the cloth and the bent head made me think I had often seen her before.

As I drew near the fire the woman stopped stirring the pot and rose to greet me. When we faced each other I felt my heart give a convulsive leap and stop. The woman who stood before me was myself.[3]

The descent is dark. She cannot even see her own hands. She is afraid of falling into the unknown below, to lose ground and a verifiable sense of reality. And yet she follows the pull into the complexity of her life where a sense of smell, warmth and sound enables her to inhabit its depth from which we are barred by a visual perception. The gaze disavows the view upon the self, whose hidden sphere we reach in sound: listening to the reciprocity of our voice as a sort of 'echo location' that affirms our being simultaneous with the environment, with what we see and hear. This same sonic sense of an unseen simultaneity enables the reader to inhabit the complex possibility of the text without denying responsibility for its invisible dimension, which is the location of the reading-self that grasps the semantic line but cannot see behind it, into its depth, into the back of language, where meaning is produced between letters and words, rather than from them, and where the reading self hears herself and her environment as a reverberation of participation, chanting and singing.

Listening thus becomes a mode of diving into a literary reality verified not by the horizontal line of semantics, history and spatial relations, but practised in conversation, chanting, singing and re-citations; moving vertically into the sonorous material of words that crosses time and space and ignores the necessity of reason, the ground of culture and the pull of forward motion by moving into the dark depth of things, whose articulation comes from the future.

Belzi Ra Ha-Ha Hecate Come!
Descend upon us to the sound of my drum
Inkalá Iktum my bird is a mole
Up goes the Equator and down the North Pole.
Eptàlum, Zam Pollum, the power to increase
Here come the North Lights and a flight of wild Bees.
Inkalá Belzi Zam Pollum the Drum
High Queen of Tartarus Hasten to Come.[4]

These lines are spoken by Christabel Burns, one of the inhabitants of the home. They are intoned to the rhythm of her drums, chanted again and again, they rouse the group of elderly women to exclaim in unison, to agitate and move the world through the force of their voices: 'Then it seemed that the cloud formed itself into an enormous bumble bee as big as a sheep. She wore a tall iron crown studded with rock crystals, the stars of the Underworld.'[5]

The shared chant generates a sonic fiction that is not a fiction in the sense of a falsehood or a story world parallel to the world we refer to as our actual reality. Instead it presents the radical reality of sound that breaches referential language and generates as 'world-creating predicate'[6] the environment of its own truth that articulates in excess of representation and semantic sense, and that has the capacity to restage chronological order and expectations and work from the body into the invocation of letters that call another real.

As a visual text, words write a literary fiction, a mute thought of images and significations. Listened to and performed however, they attain their sonic reality, which is an actual possibility of this world, since, unlike literary fictions, sonic fictions are only separate from the actual world when considered visually: when their material is negotiated as a 'shadow' of a visual source, dependent for its meaning on their correspondence and a textual referent; a signifier that rehabilitates its lack of definition on the horizontal line of semantic relations. When listened to in the 'dark', free from a lexical source, and the authority of a (masculine) language, however, its letters and words sound in the actual world its possibilities and invite the invocation of alternative articulations in-between the letters as sound.

Zam Pollum, Ave Ave Queen of all Bees![7]

Reading with a hearing trumpet

This book of essays is written in fragments that can be read out of order for a contingent in-between rather than for a chronological completeness, which might provide a seemingly more comprehensive and intelligible meaning but lacks the inexplicable, where the text loses its solid ground and attains a hidden dimension. It is a collection of texts that are fragments of writing, written from fragments of listening to the world and to works as a cosmos of interactuality, where things are possible in their mobile interbeing, made visible and graspable by sound. Writing fragments of listening I try to write the unseen in-between: ephemeral connections and moments of coincidence that invite Christabel's chanting and my participation rather than a comprehensive sense of things. In response I hope to trigger a reading that 'listens' to words rather than 'sees' them and that approaches the textual image with a sonic attitude: an attitude of doubt towards signification and its structures of communication, and an acceptance of the ephemeral, the inarticulate and the meaningless, as well as an appreciation for reciprocity and the reader's own fragile position in the text, which is constrained in a semantic reading. Thus I try to write with a sonic sensibility, with an awareness to what remains invisible in the world and in language; what remains unseen, outside discourse: the mute logos, its semantic harmony, 'spoken by the silent voice of the soul, and constituted by the pure signifieds that can be contemplated by the mind's eye'.[8] Moreover, I try to entice a reading of the text as a reading with a hearing trumpet to access the possibilities behind and at the back of language where, in our coincidence with its letters and words, meaning attains a visceral and corporeal dimension that questions the silence of the textual frame and opens it towards different noises.

Adriana Cavarero, referring to a platonic conception of language, which according to her establishes the basis of contemporary theoretical writing, states that the sound of semantic speech, the vocal utterances that fulfil the purpose of intelligibility and meaning, is not sonorous. Instead it is determined and limited by the orders and rules of a visual signified. She writes about the devocalization of the logos and of language that stands as a universal, univocal and perfectly transparent expression to serve the Platonic ideal of theory and identifies the logos as the mute seat of language: the horizontal joining of letters and words with 'right' links form the intelligible of a universal (symbolic) order within which the phonetic signifier signifies rather than sounds.[9] 'Freed from the acoustic materiality of speech, this pure semantic – which is the privileged object of *theoria* – occupies the place of origin and rules over the phonetic.'[10] Within the preoccupation with total intelligibility and semantic meaning, language that does not connect words in the right way, and does not follow the universal rules of signification; that does not fulfil the criteria of definitions and a priori references, fails to have a signifier, and thus fails to count and be counted. It sounds unintelligible, a sound only, and becomes marginalized, ignored as inaudible noise.

For these essays about sound to be able to hold the sonority of their own observations within language, the notion of a mute theory needs to be challenged and different interactions need to be practised that do not read to find meaning and the right connection, but practice the sonic texture of its image to generate sense from coincidental overlaps and the failure to connect but the capacity to sound between: between letters, words and sentences, as well as between essays as rhythms and a score for chanting.

The sound of written words constructs Cauleen Smith's 'awkward objects' and 'speculative artefacts' mentioned in the introduction to this book:[11] they 'loosen our assumptions of what we know and encourage us to embrace the instability of knowledge rather than the certainty it broadly offers'.[12] Smith's work is discussed in the introduction to frame my intention of writing as a re-engagement with what we thought we knew through the playful misappropriation of things and a sensibility towards the invisible in order to reach its political possibility. Her sculptural works are made from technology, objects, images and sounds that have their own purpose but whose aim she ignores in an improvised reassembly that restages their function towards unexpected tasks. Through this reconfiguration the assembled objects come to include their own fragility and possibility for failure, and remind us that things could be different, that they could have different names and purposes and that they could be put together differently to construct a different meaning and reality.

In this final essay, I reflect on whether critical writing can carry this speculation and awkwardness: to be as fragments of meaning not a building block of semantic language but a possibility for a different thought. Therefore I ask whether a rigorous criticality can be established that does not use the meaning of language, but plays with its invisible elements, to build new connections, fabulations, fantastical things that appear impossible but which can materialize between fragments of text as unthinkable thought that eventually will generate a new language that expands the possibility of thinking and thus the possibility and heterogeneity of the critical voice.

The writing in fragments of listening, which these essays pursue, aspires such fragmentation. They need an equivalent reading as a hearing of fragments that does not translate the sonic into a visual sign but allows for things to remain invisible: not to make sense according to language but according to listening; to make sonic non-sense, Maurice Merleau-Ponty's sensate sense opened in listening;[13] and to remain fragile, ephemeral and maybe even inarticulate, providing it is sounded in dialogue and in conversation, read aloud, alone or together, to hear the in-between of essays, letters and words give a contingent meaning to the logos of the semantic text.

In this essay, I pursue, through the concept and metaphor of the hearing trumpet, the idea of a sonorous textuality that is able to challenge the devocalization of the logos and of theory, as articulated by Cavarero via Plato, and come to suggest a revocalization of the textual field through the invocations of Leonora Carrington's writing, a performance of real, technological and ventriloquized voices by Andrea Pensado live at the Back Alley Theatre in Washington, and *The Wanderer*, a field recording composition by Jana Winderen.

Winderen's recordings of Zooplankton and Pythoplankton under the surface of the ocean and of lakes juxtapose the horizontal connections of the semantic field with a vertical depth. I invest this underwater world with Maurice Merleau-Ponty's depth: his notion of 'depth and "back" (and "behind") – It is pre-eminently the dimension of the hidden',[14] which is paradoxically the place of my looking, my simultaneity with the thing, which my gaze obstructs and I cannot see, and where I am too close to read signs and signifiers but exist in simultaneity with letters as sound. Here I have to read the text as a phonography, which I hear along vertical lines as the possible slices of writing. This reading as a textual phonography on vertical lines of words meets the rhizomatic networks of Gilles Deleuze and Félix Guattari in their critique of a taxonomical and phallocentric language. The invisible verticality of reading sonic textures joins in the challenge to the arboretic, the image of the tree that starts from one point and fixes an order, which Deleuze and Guattari stage via the rhizome 'that connects any point to any other point'.[15] The rhizome critiques the transcendental and the a priori of writing and thinking on mobile and interconnected plateaus. However, listening into these mobile dimensions, we come to appreciate, via Alexander Kluge, Silicon Valley's takeover of their networks and come to understand that the rhizome has lost the ability to critique the infrastructure of power, which now progresses along horizontal lines. Therefore, a different plane of agency and interaction needs to be found that can counter-poeticize the platforms of a virtual authority beyond the reach of the market, in the depth of an inarticulate sound.[16] Thus at the end of this essay we fall, with Hito Steyerl, 'towards objects without reservation, embracing a world of forces and matters' that needs to be heard to sense its critique of what got us there in the first place.[17]

These suggestions and contextualizations try to entice a sonic engagement with all the essays in this book so that the fragments of writing can entice a reading of fragments, that does not seek completion, comprehension or meaning; that does not pursue the idea that motivated it but finds the one that is proposed in its own material, between rather than through the connection of things. In this sense, this final essay responds to the introduction to these texts and follows its fragments of writing into the deep to try and promote reading according to the hidden image of a material sound.

The fact that this reading attitude is proposed in the last essay is deliberate and should not frustrate or confuse. The text rereads with its own sound after the event. This is when we perform it, in discourse, in dialogue and in our exchanges with others from where it obtains its present sonority and truth, and we our reciprocity in the world. Speaking as Cavarero tells us is speaking to someone, it is a reciprocal exchange of sound making and listening. This listening voice of reading brings the text into a shared sphere that is not the common ground of theory and its a priori understandings and values. Rather, it is the shared practice of reading together, as chanting together, in an unrepeatable performance that generates rather than receives the truth of the text. It is Marian Leatherby and her fellow women from the home for 'senile females', dancing and chanting together that invokes through riddles a future that is not destined but articulated, brought into motion beyond the intelligibility and history of language. Its truth is plural and possible. It does not obey a chronological order or a semantic form; it does not follow the logic of time or the constraints of place, but practices sonic fictions written not through the harmonious linking of syntactical joints but through listening to the in-between, the depths of inarticulation, at the excess and the overflow of language and the narrative where they do not serve theory but the movement of breath. This sonic between is the depth also of memory and the 'dis-illusions' of remembering out of which in dialogue we make the untruths of a present interpretation that are not irrealities, falsehoods or lies but the contingent truths and understandings of a present speaking of it.[18] The rigour of these interpretations and exchanges does not come from the text. It is not what Cavarero via Hannah Arendt calls 'the oral dead [rigor mortis] which is writing', but the vitality of speaking, as a putting into action, breathing and moving.[19] And its legitimacy comes not from established genealogies and taxonomies of the known, but from the need for the unknown to be heard.

As a concluding essay, this text does not conclude, it does not summarize or complete, but suggests how the previous texts, and any writing, could be engaged with by reading as listening with a hearing trumpet and voicing the phonographic field of the text aloud to get to the sonorous of theory. 'The point is not to simply revocalize logos. Rather, the aim is to free logos from its visual substance, and to finally mean it as sonorous speech.'[20]

Andrea Pensado live at the Back Alley Theatre (2014)

Andrea Pensado performs electronics, voice and a ventriloquist dummy live at the Back Alley Theatre in Washington, DC (2014). Seated on a chair facing the audience, to her left is a table of electronic equipment, to her right another chair with a bright red lump of fabric that later turns out to be her ventriloquist dummy that does not speak another's voice but agitates the voice of technology and the distortion of language. The visual scene is rudimentary, technological rather than theatrical, cables around Pensado's shoeless feet and across the floor, a microphone inelegantly attached to her head obscures her face but grants her hands the freedom to perform between the technology and the dummy as a body that does not speak as a function in relation to meaning and sense, neither musical nor linguistic, but that expels meaning as interaction: the forward movements of expression that sound an exchange rather than what it says.

Her voice is amplified as well as erased by technology that increases its volume but severs its relationship to semantic language.[21] The shrieks, screams and on occasion even whispers are entirely unintelligible as words but mobilize as sound the scene staged by the visual. This sonic does not complete the scene however, but puts it in motion and agitates its elements towards the erasure of its composition and semantic function. In this way, it adds the complexities of invisible connections to the disorganization of leads, plugs, chairs and tables, and mobilizes things through their in-between.

According to the programme notes 'the combination of the performance situation, the often abrasive sounds, the irrational use of the voice and the inherent uncertainty of improvization contributes to discoveries of unknown places in her mind'.[22] It contributes also to discoveries of unknown places in electronic music and in semantic language by improvising their possibility without the need to communicate. In this way, her work opens the historical norms of articulation and empties them from their own expectations and values: producing a raw material that reinvests articulation from the between of things rather than from a lexicon or symbolic order, de-historicizing music and challenging the semantic code of language through contingent physical interactions that emphasis the improvisation of expression and of the heard.

The performance of the unknown places in her mind, in music and in language, challenges comprehension and urges an exploration of the condition of intelligibility: the cultural frames and limits that ensure understanding but control what can be heard. In this way Pensado counter-poeticizes meaning, as a phallocentric assertion of sense, historical reference and the 'right' connections of sounds as tones and phone, through impossible utterances. Thus she reinvests both music and language with the exigency of performance, as a temporal and vocal act of exchange from which meaning gleans its currency and the confidence of a contingent sense.

At one moment, a rhythmic Tango interrupts the flow of abrasive inarticulation and tries to reassert the sense of a melodic line, but it gets destroyed, shot at, chased away and utterly demolished through electronic signals and distortions that severe the harmonic sequence. The lungs and cavities of the body and of technology, the dummy and the performance space produce shrieks and screaming, the expulsion of words and sounds that are equivalent rather than hierarchized - ordered in a grammatical or harmonic sense – and sound the disjointed simultaneity of inarticulation. While they might be unable to produce meaning within conventional terms, they engage the basis of sense making and reinvest it with the temporality of a trans-objective sound: a sound that cannot be sourced from one subject or one thing as locus and signifier of its meaning but exists in-between things and from their inter-agitation. Listening to her voice we hear the vibration between technological manipulation, amplification and the utterance of the body, which at times still resembles words, but which have left signification in favour of materiality, breath and expanse. Her inarticulation creates not a solipsistic monologue however, but produces a complex communication between herself, the technology, the audience and the ventriloquist dummy, seated on her lap in a red dress, long blond hair and staring at us with a demonic smile and bright red lips.

Subverting the convention of ventriloquism as the body that speaks for somebody else, her dummy amplifies and extends rather than acts as a funnel for a disembodied voice. Pensado makes no effort to hide the relationship between her actions, the input of technology and her voice and the sounds attributed to the movements of the dummy. This ventriloquism is not about the pretence of an autonomous voice sounding in an inanimate body, which is the curiosity and pull of the ventriloquist stagecraft. Instead, it highlights the manipulation and ventriloquism of Pensado's own voice, and potentially of every voice, and recaptures from this control of speech the speechless by destroying the intelligible with abrasive shrieks, shouts and murmurs to sound the unknown. This recapturing of the unique voice from the organization of language does not destroy comprehension but questions its parameters and authority, and generates other possibilities that do not lack in competence but have no common grammatical or harmonic ground, and have to generate it contingently in order to be heard in their own voice.

Pensado's inarticulate articulations are extremely fluent, displaying a competence of language and music without grammar and harmony, measured instead in its contingent performance, whose rigour lies in its putting into action and into movements the unknown and the unheard to make language lose its rigid frame. Thus it produces a communication that is not measured by what is said but what says, what sounds, what is there. In this sense her work produces a pragmatic object of sound that is awkward and speculative in relation to semantic and musical language but articulate and intelligible in relation to the contingent moment of its performance, and that invites the participation of a listening self that hears the unexpected and the inexplicable not as aberrations but as the fabric of the real.

For Cavarero 'the privileging of *theoria* over speech is ... first of all the erasure of the voice.'[23] The aim is to lose the disruptive power of its sonorous force which endangers the pure semantic that ensures the universal 'I' and ignores the singular existence that is unique and unrepeatable and therefore puts the possibility of communication in doubt. Pensado's work performs this disruptive power of the voice and lends the force of the body, expanded and amplified by technology, to language, so it might step out of linguistic constraints and come to sound the political possibility of speech.

Her performance stages the erasure of an intelligible voice, and disrupts its form and structure, which is its organization as the location of its politics. The inarticulation of the voice intervenes at this location of politics and challenges the management of its structure, which is the infrastructure of its political ideology. This inarticulation requires we hear its excess, its overflow, the voices that remain unheard, and make them count within the political practice and institution of norms and expectations.

In this sense, Pensado's use of technology is comparable to Marian Leatherby's hearing trumpet. It is its sounding counterpart, a 'speaking trumpet' that does not overhear but overflows the limitations of language to sound its excess and generate unknown articulations from the mundane possibility of the voice. However, her devices sound not language but the larynx, the lungs and the breath, and utter their technology through the technology of amplification and electronic manipulation, and with the help of a staring dummy they disrupt what was meant to be said and speak in their own tongue the unfamiliar.

This is where the work counter-poeticizes the horizontal drive of meaning and the semantic plane. Where it dives inwards, into language and into the voice to get a different register: the register of Pensado's unique articulation and the introspection of its tone. What Alexander Kluge speaking to Hans-Ulrich Obrist on *What Art Can Do* calls 'the individual capacities, the eyes, the ears, the soles of their feet' which are the capacities from which we come to work together to form a 'counterworld' that 'permeates the pores of reality, and then counters reality's systemic terror by forming connections of its own'.[24] Kluge's notion of a counter-poetic world is articulated in relation to the language of the digital: the Silicon Valley generated algorithms that increasingly determine our movements, actions, walks and articulations, and that have to be countered by turning inwards to counteract, in alliance with others, the terror of its seemingly inevitable flow and meaning. His suggestion is we collaborate, dig canals and build gardens together to counter act the desert of the microchip in order to counter what we are everyday subjected to: The digital pathways of online networks, and the semantic pathways of authoritative language.

Kluge's counter-poeticizing performs, in relation to digital networks and algorithms, the revocalization that is sought in relation to theoretical language by Cavarero, and that I would promote for the reading of these essays and any writing: to listen into the text to hear the excess and the overflow of the semantic so the sonorous might become part of thinking and reading words and ultimately the world. In this way we could perform with language to determine how we move and dig through the pervasiveness of its code rather than following it.

The safeguarding of mute thought in writing is the refusal to let the unspeakable take part in knowledge. It is a linguistic curbing of the politics of language, of what its practices could be, and its preference demonstrates the logocentricity of politics as an administration of mute thought.[25] In this sense, it recalls Jacques Rancière's distinction between the possible and the impossible and the need on the part of a political authority for a belief in 'the only thing possible', which ascertains the universal but necessitates that 'scholarly authority is required to fill in all the holes in the possible/reality' that might belie its horizon.[26] Therefore knowledge, in order to fulfil this need to represent the only thing possible, has to write comprehensively and completely. It cannot leave gaps and doubts into which the sonorous might flow to disrupt its totality by naming what it sees contingently and out of the bounds of definition; and it has to entice reading as an acceptance and recognition of the totality of words on the page.

By contrast, to produce a knowledge that includes the impossible, reading has to become a chanting and singing of letters and words. It has to become a performance of our capacities to break the seal of mute thought, to let sound agitate the in-between of things that is at once the relationship and the difference that produces not 'this' or 'that' but things together as interbeings.

Belzi Ra Ha-Ha Hecate Come!
Descend upon us to the sound of my drum
Inkalá Iktum my bird is a mole
Up goes the Equator and down the North Pole.[27]

Such chanted words as interbeings do not connect along the 'right' semantic lines, but sound as invocations, as a generative naming, rather than as a reference according to a lexicon. In this chanting the voice meets the other since while the voice is itself 'it is at the same time the invocation of the other'.[28] Speaking is reciprocal and generates listening. It is a collaboration between mouth and ear, between sounding and hearing. Chanting is digging into the mute authority of language. It meets the other not in the paternal voice of platonic meaning and authority, but in the fleshly singing of the body which breaks into a maternal tune: where the voice is as breath and as 'languelait', as an expulsion of first air and as mother tongue and mother milk, nourishing and relational, 'given to the ear and the mouth'.[29]

Thought in my lungs

Referring to R. B. Onians, Cavarero suggests that thought in ancient Greek is linked to the voice and to breath. It is an embodied action, 'whose seat is in the corporal organs that extend from the area of the breast to the mouth'.[30] It is the expulsion of audible air formed into words. It is invisible and centrifugal, presenting as the movement from the lungs into speech and ultimately to the listener's ear. In this scenario, speech does not simply convey thought but produces it. Thought is therefore performative and sonic. It is produced in the expulsion of sound as air and generates what it is contingently. Language does not translate and communicate thought that exists before articulation but is simultaneous with its conception an embodied process of articulated thinking. It is the techno-fleshly body of Pensado that expels thought as shrieks and shouts that generate the unknown places of the real.

In contrast to this noisy breath of non-sense, in Plato's metaphysics, which serves as predecessor to a contemporary scientific point of view, the logos, as seat of knowledge and understanding is visual and mute. It is positioned in the head, in the location of the brain, the encephalon, and eschews the body and corporeality. In this way, thought becomes autonomous, separate from the body, it becomes ideal.[31]

Thus, after Plato, a pure semantic, freed from the vagaries of the acoustic materiality of speech and the viscerality of a corporeal body, directed instead 'by the silent discourse of the soul with itself', dominates the phone, the sonic gesture of language, that does not sound as noisy breath but articulates meaning according to the right joining of signs towards the harmonious idea of totality and intelligibility.[32] This platonic idea of language precedes and enables Immanuel Kant's rationality, his analytical philosophy of language, which according to Richard Rorty builds 'a world inside our minds by tying concepts together so as to package sensations more conveniently'.[33] In his review 'Kripke versus Kant' (1980), Rorty suggests that just as metaphysics had come to be considered as first philosophy of its time, establishing a new appreciation of knowledge and thought, so Kant's analytical philosophy of language too had come to be seen as a first philosophy that defines our thinking still today. Kant's philosophy of language develops a sense of reference and truth relations dependent and enforcing semantic lines of correspondence and attribution that produce taxonomical definitions and enable a categorical organization of thought whose pervasiveness is demonstrated by how 'everything from politics, to literature to religion is, after all, shot through with Kantian assumptions'.[34] Rorty critiques this inescapable influence of the Kantian philosophy of language for focusing on the structure of representation rather than on what is being represented and thus missing, according to Rorty, the pragmatic turn towards 'what is really there'. He complains that we take 'Kant's notion that we structure the world by representing it' for granted, and that we treat the privileging of semantics, the study of the structure of representation, without circumspection as universally applicable and transparent. In this way, he suggests we forego a consideration of content, of what is being represented and how it might be affected by the mechanisms and ideologies of its representation.[35]

While Plato shifts thought from the lungs into the head and reorganizes the relationship between thinking and speaking, thus making speech, its bodily performance, a vehicle rather than a generator of thought and its possibility, Kant makes language the semantic structure of knowledge that presents the universality of its articulation and application, while preventing it from being able to say anything else. In that sense, language's privilege is a poisoned chalice. To attain its status as transparent authority, it has had to cut its throat at the location of the larynx and block the conduit to its lungs. It had to become a form that does not produce or discover but only says what is already there; and it had to make the appearance of intelligibility universal by silencing the plural rasps of breath, the coughs, splutters and other noises that try to speak with another tongue.

Rorty presents Saul Kripke's theory of naming as articulated in *Naming and Necessity* (1980) as the key of how to unlock the closed off frame of analytical language and to confer the status of the philosophical object back to the thing under scrutiny away from the frame of its reference and the structure of its articulation. He explains that by rediscovering Aristotle's 'metaphysical necessity' as opposed to the 'epistemic necessity' of a Kantian world view, Kripke challenges the linguistic frame of truth and introduces the possibility of calling things what they are contingently in their encounter rather than what they are per definition.[36]

Kripke's philosophy of language suggests that language does not describe or structure the world but names, as in baptizes, the objects and subjects in the world. His philosophy is based on the rejection of description theory: the idea that a thing is denoted in a particular way according to the criteria that it fulfils as an account of meaning, and it relativizes prioricity as a possibility rather than a necessity, and thus it reconsiders the process of referencing things and moves away from essentialism and certainties, to the act of naming. Therefore, things are not just there, fulfilling the criteria that defined them, without needing to be mentioned or called, but rather 'everything needs to be decided to make a total description of the world'.[37] Such a designative theory of language does not reference, instead it is a tool to speculate around the existence of the thing, which might well become an awkward object refusing a priori definition and demanding the agency of calling a contingent name. On this point, Kripke's realist philosophy of language stands opposed to and critiques Kant's analytic philosophy, and demands a reconsideration of the relationship between words as names and the object, subject named.

In a Kantian consciousness language precedes experience, the definition is an a priori set against criteria that demonstrate correspondence and justify the name as description. In this categorical thinking we can find the reliable definition of things and establish a sense of certainty from which taxonomies and a taxonomical thinking are achieved. However, it also means some things will remain unnamed, and thus without authority and agency, and other things will have their signifiers revoked, if they no longer hold and the signified breaks down: if the chair loses a leg, or the table collapses, if a human changes gender or revokes her identity. Thus as soon as the thing does not fulfil the criteria it falls out of definition and becomes unspeakable. A language of designation by contrast holds in all counterfactual situations because it does not rely on givens but creates, from an anti-foundationalist position, the contingent possibility of the thing. I keep my name as I am what there is, even if I change what it is I am. Similarly, a sonic sensibility of the text brings the action of naming, with letters and words as sound rather than visual signifiers into consciousness and makes us appreciate the instrumentality of semantic language and hear alternative combinations sound a different sense. This empowers the thing and the subject as thing, and reconnects language to its lungs and ears to articulate its own contingency.[38]

Silent Running

In the half hour before she rises
a submariner cannot drop a comb
for fear of echo. Down there

it all depends on silent running.
In the pitching dark,
nothing but the crying of fish,

throat-murmurs of boats.
They're as deep as can be,
holding a steady trim.

seeing only the blood
in their brains. Air is short,
the darkness wide,

and they cannot blink too fast
for the sound of their eyelids
shudders the North Sea charts.

Miles and miles of night,
pegging for jabber or clack
of passing trawlers.

They might be moles
but the silence gives them back
their eyes, the twitch of their hearts,

and when they sky has bled
all scratch of light,
a man surfaces, opens the hatch,

Enters the lean-to of black
and listens to the ocean
filling up.

Sarah Jackson[39]

As the image of a quantified utterance of sense, visual/textual language is a lexical resource. As such it is the cornerstone of Western thought and decisively influences the organization and possibility of our thinking, speaking and writing in quantifiable epistemologies of meaning and reference. This mute text has taken from the body its ephemeral and fluid expression and reduced its unique sounds and noises into a system carved in the head rather than intoned and chanted. Its phone is 'reduced to an auxiliary role that is basically superfluous or in any case inadequate with respect to the realm of truth'.[40] It cannot contribute its unique and vertical sonority to the production of meaning and truth and is forced to receive 'from the visible order of signifieds the very rules of its sonorous labor'.[41] The horizontal joining of letters, words and sentences, as signifiers and signifieds, dictates the sense of sound to articulate an apparently reliable, harmonious definition of the real. However, this definition does not produce but reflects the idea that precedes it, and it reduces the plural uniqueness of utterance into a universal articulation, whose universality by necessity is limited and exclusive: excluding the sonorous, its body and vibration, and thus the potentially revolutionary action of speaking the unknown and the voice that is not heard.

In this way written language, as a visible language, enables intelligible articulation whilst its own limits, what it can't say or won't hear, disable and exclude what cannot be thought. The visual text defines and delimits the scope and articulation to the thinkable, as the limit of the real, boundaried by its own taxanomical norms that create a consciousness and a sense of truth about what things are and how the world is. In this way written language grants legitimacy. It enables consensus and permanence. But at the same time it carries with it the asymmetries and biases of those taxonomies in terms of gender, race and class, preference and solidarity, that enable and legitimize it. Thus it excludes without acknowledging this exclusion, that which falls outside the remit of its ideological framework; that which appears opaque to the set of its articulation: the sensate materiality of the voice when it speaks between words and letters the invisible and the inaudible, and when it creates formless utterances, whose appearance has no letters to follow a definition and whose shape cannot be recognized in relation to an idea: *it all depends on silent running. In the pitching dark, nothing but the crying of fish.*[42]

The semantic line is the political reality of language. Through definitions and exclusions it acts as a borderline between the speakable and the unspeakable and delineates the linguistic institution of politics: the administration of what can and cannot be articulated, and what can and cannot take part in the definition of the world. The sonorous counter-poeticizes this borderline through the invisible overflow of a noisy breath. It represents the political possibility of language, where from the possibility of sound it questions the actuality of its structures and norms, and where from the potency of the invisible it creates the unknown and articulates its name contingently. In this way, sound revocalizes the logos understood not simply as the locus of a mute knowledge and understanding but also as the location of its political investment, ideology and norms.

To transgress the borderline of semantic articulation and its political institution, this essay promotes reading with a hearing trumpet and proposes we consider text as a phonographic field, engaged with through the sounds of letters and words organized as a contingent notation. It proposes that if we do not read them as an encoding of signs, according to the rules of a semantic order, but as the invisible textures and rhythms of sound, the access to language's impossibilities, its unthinkables, might become possible, and the partiality of the visible text might become apparent. The suggestion is to do a 'textual phonography': to step into the field of words, the textural marks on a page understood not as the description of another world, but as inviting a performance of the variants of this-world; to inhabit their inaudible sound and to take on their rhythms and place ourselves among them in order to, in our simultaneity with each other and the world, hear the invisible of language and sense, and perform its possibility through the thought in our lungs.

Vertiginous sound

This stepping into the field of words performs the verticality of introspection mentioned earlier in relation to Kluge's counter-poeticizing of the language of algorithms and the authority of Silicon Valley and mentioned also in a footnote in relation to Morton Feldman's 'Vertical Thoughts' on composition. It is a diving in, digging in effort that prevents the horizontal line from sublating the individual capacity for articulation through the persuasiveness of its networked rules. The vertical resists the pull of connecting interfaces. It counteracts in alliance with the other in speech the rules of its semantic logic, and revocalizes its horizontal weave. It puts to use the vertiginous: the sense of falling without a ground, to resist the a priori and the necessity of an established reading in favour of what comes towards it from the dark. It is Marian Leatherby walking down the steep steps of the tower to meet herself cooking herself and becoming her invisible other, and it is 'the downfall of linear perspective' and the acceleration towards a vertical view that can see in slices the possibility of interactions: stacked up on top of each other, rather than laid out on the ground; not a certain territory, but enabling an experience of the simultaneity of the unseen.[43]

Hito Steyerl's text *In Free Fall: A Thought Experiment on Vertical Perspecitve* (2012) celebrates, via Theodor Adorno, this new verticality, as a new representational freedom: 'A fall toward objects without reservation, embracing a world of forces and matter, which lacks any original stability and sparks the sudden shock of the open: a freedom that is terrifying, utterly deterritorializing, and always already unknown.'[44] This interpretation of verticality expresses the excitement of a groundless world, often feared and criticized in philosophy, for its ability to give us a new perspective and new insights into social and political dynamics and realities, determined not along horizontal lines, and its a priori meanings and hierarchies, but in the depth of the world's volume, where it is too dark to see but we can make sense through participation. In this sense, this new representational freedom of the vertical recalls also Rancière, when he suggests that 'the collapse of representation of another life does not nullify that life but instead lends it a vertiginous reality.' A reality of falling, without a ground, towards 'the desire to partake of equality', to be defined not on a horizontal plane, whose ground is its prejudice and creates difference, but to partake in the simultaneity of things and subjects as things interbeing along vertical lines.[45]

The vertiginous in this context is a critical verticality that eschews the horizontal line to critique its transcendental hierarchy and exclusive connections. In this sense, it picks up on Gilles Deleuze and Félix Guattari's critique of hierarchical language and arboretic values of knowledge that support and are supported by taxonomies, lexica, the a priori and analytical givens. Their articulation of the rhizome as a weave of flat multiplicities, as connecting plateaus that negate genealogies and build infinite connections made by 'the abstract line, the line of flight of deterritorialization according to which they change in nature and connect with other mutliplicities',[46] counters the arboretic: the system of knowledge rooted in a particular location and rising phallocentrically towards an ideal. Instead, the rhizome proposes a heterogenous and organic connecting in n dimensions, creating a network 'where any point in the rhizome can be connected to anything other, and must be'.[47]

However, since the first publication of their seminal text *Mille Plateaux* in 1980, their weave of n dimensions has been colonized by neo-liberal capitalism that transports its ideology along digital networks that have taken the rhizome hostage for their own ends. Thus the critical possibility of a network of multiplicities, able to connect 'any point to any other point' has been blocked as a route to radical thinking.[48] Instead, the way is down, into the text, into the world and into the self. 'Introspection is the only authority from which you can obtain advice. You can't ask the internet what you love, You can either notice this yourself or not.'[49] I take Kluge's introspection to hold beyond the interests of the individual as a broader gesture, as an 'introspection of the world', a diving into the depth of things into an in-between and interbeing that is not endless alliance, 'the conjunction, "and ... and ... and"',[50] of a digital attention deficit, but is the responsibility to the moment that is not observable but needs to be felt at the back of myself and of things.[51]

The idea that 'the rhizome is an acentred, non-hierarchical, nonsignifying system without a General and without an organizing memory or central automaton, defined solely by a circulation of states'[52] in a contemporary digital context describes the deterritorialization of the self by a virtual power that pretends acentricity and promotes endless circulation as a means to force boundarieless and timeless consumption as the only territory left. In the digital age, the rhizome's short-term memory is not antigeneological but is the ten-second fame of Snapchat, which, erases my memory but not that of my search history that produces the arboretic text for my exploitation.

Deleuze and Guattari's critique was based on the idea that the arboretic preexists the individual who is allotted only a given place, preventing multiplicity and transformation. While I agree with this critique as a critique of a Kantian thinking and its taxonomical consciousness, the infrastructure and metaphor of the rhizome has been taken over by Silicon Valley: 'Silicon Valley-imposed algorithms, the rules of which are now embedded in our neurosystems directed by connecting interfaces'.[53] They control the direction of power along the plateaus on which a radical becoming was meant to happen.

Instead then of a rhizomatic becoming of the text as a writing in endless conjunctions along *n* dimensions, writing has to fall into the depth of its own infrastructure to find a critical voice, and reading has to follow these lines as a falling into the groundless depth of language, where semantics do not reinstate and rehabilitate the formless into the hierarchy of meaning, but where the formless finds sonorous words in the dark.[54]

To follow the vertical, to fall vertiginously into the text, is to discover its invisible textures not to a ground but to the cosmos, the volume, in which they agitate meaning contingently and in which we inter are with things in our individual capacities together.[55] Thus the vertiginous is the sensibility of the sonic. It is sounding and reading, as digging and falling into the depth of the text, as the point where I coincide with its articulation, where I cannot see it but have to perform it in proximity and reciprocity behind and at the back of semantic language.

This back of semantic language is Merleau-Ponty depth. It is the place within which things remain distinct without having to be different and producing a sign, and without existing in relation to a 'synthesis' of (different) 'views', producing a totality. It is the 'dimension of the hidden': within this dimension, according to Merleau-Ponty, things coexist in degrees of proximity and in simultaneity, and 'remain things, while not being what I look at at present'. Thus they are not tethered to my interpretation and look, but have a flesh that is their resistance to my visual inspection, 'a resistance which is precisely their reality, their "openness"'.[56]

For Merleau-Ponty the depth is the point from which I see and in which I remain invisible to myself looking. It is the impossible of vision, the obstacle to its total view. The look cannot overcome its invisibility. It cannot break through its resistance to being seen. Instead, seeing goes around it, tries to make up for it from different points of view synthesized into one total vision, which however lacks this depth. I suggest that it is listening that can take account of this invisible dimension and that can engage in its depth without having to compensate for its ungraspability, or go around it to avoid what it cannot see. In listening I inhabit this depth: I am in the world, which surrounds me. I am simultaneous with it and in its proximity we are our interbeing as the reality of our 'openness'. Such a sonic sense expands the seen from the flesh of this depth. Through its being with my flesh, sound challenges and augments its limits to add sensation to visual interpretation.

The Wanderer (2015)

Jana Winderen's field recording composition *The Wanderer* plays us this impossible of vision from the depth of the sea. The work is a 30-minute composition of underwater recordings made of Zooplankton and Phytoplanktons, two organisms that drift in the sea and in lakes and produce half of the world's oxygen through photosynthesis. Thus what we hear as crackles, hisses, pops and bubbles is the base-rhythm of the world as a liveable volume of air, moving and standing still, retracting and expanding between 0 and 90 metres below the water's surface.

The composition is produced from hydrophone recordings made by Winderen on her travels between the Equator and the North Pole, following the movement of the plankton on their drift north.[57] Listening we follow the long cables of the hydrophones into the deep of the sea, into its textures that remain unseen but that make appreciable the physical and scientific interbeing of the Equator and the North Pole, whose reciprocity performs the environmental condition of the world.

The far reach of the recordings reminds of the ubiquity of the unseen while its depth invites us into the enormity of a shared volume down below, where the simultaneity of sound allows us to understand the correlations of actions and agencies: where 'events, peoples, climates, economic systems and cultural life-worlds in one part of the world have bearing, meaning, and impact on places and people in other parts of the world'.[58] Where, in other words, the world is a cosmos, and where sound shows its connections on a four-dimensional map.

This vertical depth does not enable a synthesis of different viewpoints and opinions, it resists visual inspection, but generates a participatory sense. Through the simultaneity of my audition and its sounding, back to back, it shows us the necessity and consequence of what we are together; and it gives us the imagination of depth as a geographical dimension that can be explored without having to chart and map it on a two-dimensional plane, but through the designation of a blind experience.

The microphone cables plot vertical lines for hearing the text of murmurs, blurbs, shrieks and hisses that do not mean as semantic signs and do not connect on the horizontal line of meaning, but provide the unspeakable complexity of their relationship in invisible slices stacked up under the surface of the sea. The recordings illuminate an ecology of verticality in the same sense that we can grasp a 'politics of verticality'[59] from the consciousness of a sonic in-between: when things are not 'this' or 'that', organized along a series of horizontal events and connections, but when they are understood as simultaneous, on the back of and behind, on top and underneath, and potentially invisible to each other, but nevertheless creating the cosmos of their interaction.

This sonic in-between of a four-dimensional cosmos does not work as a simple montage: the juxtaposition of two sound images that is resolved through an imaginary third that compensates for the gap in representation. Rather, sound creates an ephemeral in-between of opaque intensities that are not hauled to the surface but remain in the deep, that resist visual inspection, and instead need to be grasped through the proximity of listening to hear the reciprocity of their sound.

The recordings of hissing and crackling Zooplankton invoke the other of ecology: the voices and breaths we are dependent on for our own. They set us into vertical reciprocity where just because something is lower down does not mean they cannot impact on how we live and what we are, up here. In this way, they put into question and invite a rethinking of the power lines built invisibly but persuasively on the horizontal lines of a semantic navigation of the world, and reconfigure reciprocity in a multidimensional volume.

The extended microphones and a sonic sensibility allow us to grasp this invisible volume and enable us to comprehend its interconnectedness physically: to understand global warming, pollution, fishing, food and breathing, not as a scientific fact removed from our being, but as the lived experience of interbeing. Where we do not add up different viewpoints or resolve what we thought we saw in a synthesis of different points of view, but where we dive, with Winderen, into the depth, to hear what the air is made of, to hear the rhythms and textures of its formation, and come to appreciate our bond with its processes not through the scientific lexica and history of ecology but through the simultaneity of an unseen sound.

This sonic sense challenges the notion of semantic meaning, the infrastructure of its production and categorization, as well as its value and validity. However, it does not represent its opposite but augments and contributes to its possibility by going into the depth of its articulation: its signs and symbols, to uncover the possibilities of its performance and to attempt the unperformance of its limits and exclusions. Freeing language from the code of the logos, which develops through horizontal connections, and finding connections as slices of possibility in a reading of vertical lines in free fall.

The long cables of Winderen's hydrophone recorder meet the hearing trumpet of Marian Leatherby. The sonic fiction of her composition, that show us the real complexity of an invisible world, meets the fabulations of Leonora Carrington, created 55 years earlier, in the foretelling of the rotation of the poles and the equator, and the coming of an endless winter. Both the Zooplankton and the chanting of elderly women produce co-cantanations of the world that give us insights into its condition that remain otherwise unseen, speculative and ungraspable. These insights are gained from the deep of the sea and the deep of the text. This is not a frivolous or silly comparison but a point to be pondered when texts are taken apart and put together again without the logic of a semantic sense or the 'representation of another life', and a vertiginous reality becomes apparent that connects them both in the dark. Winderen's work invites us to listen to this inter-connectedness, and allows us to hear it in our need to breathe. Through our unique and shared necessity we are brought into the processes of the ecosystem and are faced with the consequences of the possibility of its and our disappearance.

Conclusion: chanting vertiginous songs

To the Peoples of Earth

Proper evaluation of words and letters
In their phonetic and associated sense
Can bring the peoples of earth
Into the clear light of pure Cosmic Wisdom

Sun Ra[60]

To promote the reading of sonic sense, I follow Sun Ra, and propose we hear 'words and letters in their phonetic and [vertically] associated sense' understood as a sonic sense achieved via a sonic literacy that does not read but hears written signs and symbols as textures and rhythms of an invisible language below the surface of the semantic but creating its eco system. Written words are the inscription of sounds, thus they are the possibility of its performance and hold below their mute surface the opportunity to unperform conventional meanings and reperfom their form as a formless sound that undoes the horizontal logic of analytical language and its political ideology, in favour of the experience of its material and the opacity of a vertical drive.

This call to listen to writing is not a deception or a perverted language game. Rather, it is a sincere and critical endeavour to reach a different place vis-à-vis words as signs and their cultural significance and signification from their sound, where the infrastructure and politics of nominal meaning making itself can be discussed and challenged, and that which so far appeared as opaque, awkward and outside of language, and thus outside of political possibility, can be reconsidered, and can start to gain influence and an ear.

The watchers who slept will now be awake
And over their land I will fly once again
Who is my mother? What is my name?[61]

The riddle given by Christabel Burns to Marian Leatherby presents a participatory form of text. It is a question, a score, an invitation and invocation to participate in its writing and reading: to dig into language and sound it together as the dissolution of a mute theory that presents rather than performs knowledge. The riddle is an invitation so speak, to utter and to make a voice; to participate in a sonic writing in the depth of letters and words that reverse the hearing trumpet and write the rhythms of the heard as a visual texture that carries with it the depth of sound and shows us the forensics of language reached by digging into its infrastructure.

The hearing trumpet serves as a conceptual device to reach this practice in writing and reading. It allows us to appreciate the textuality of the text and to perform its contingent inarticulation: to listen into its depth and hear what lies behind and beneath its semantic meaning; to appreciate the invisible textures of its words that construct another possibility, which is equally true but that does not express a normative reality and instead reveals the possibility of the impossible.

Sound is a political concept and sensibility. It is a conduit, a portal into the appreciation of the invisible and the mobile dimension of the world. It does not produce this invisible language but enables its voice, since to provide a voice for that which cannot make itself count in the normative formation of actuality would in any event only amount to a ventriloquism or a subsumption. Therefore, language cannot be given, but space for an unknown and unheard voice can be made, which might not articulate in a recognizable register, but vibrates with what we do not have words for.

As such vibrations of the unknown, sonic words are not even signifying. They cannot perform Julia Kristeva's fourth signifying practice of the sign that does not stop, that does not rest in meaning but moves on and on in 'endless mobility'.[62] The verticality of sound does not move on but resonates, vibrates behind and at the back of language as a language that as yet seems impossible, awkward, time consuming, and not up to it; that fails the register, fails to communicate and yet it sounds, has a depth and an agency. This agency is activated in the move from incomprehension into song: if the text seems to make no sense sing it, riff it, participate in its sound and see what happens, what volume, what subjectivity and what possibilities it might perform. Sing a little louder, let the body sway while you form movements from signs on a piece of paper. Go into public spaces, stand on a step and chant it louder and louder until the context starts to resonate with your voice and meaning starts to emerge from the mobile depth of the words as song.

Now in the precincts of Hampstead Heath there is a certain cavern used by a coven of witches who hold their ceremonies there in secret in order not to be molested by the law. From ancient times the witches had danced in the cavern through wars and persecutions; many a time when I was pursued I would hide with the witches, and was always received with courtesy and kindness. As you are no doubt aware, my mission through the ages has been to carry uncensored news to the people, without consideration of either rank or status. This has made me unpopular with the authorities all over this planet. My object is to help human beings to realize their state of slavery and exploitation by power-seeking beings.[63]

Notes

1 Leonora Carrington, *The Hearing Trumpet*, London: Penguin Books, 2005, p. 5.

2 Ibid., p. 100.

3 Ibid., p. 136.

4 Ibid., p. 117.

5 Ibid.

6 Marie-Laure Ryan, *Possible Worlds, Artificial Intelligence and Narrative Theory,* Bloomington and Indianapolis: Indiana University Press, 1991, p. 22.

7 Carrington, *The Hearing Trumpet*, p. 117.

8 Adriana Cavarero, *For More than Once Voice, Toward a Philosophy of Vocal Expression*, trans. Paul A. Kottman, Stanford: Stanford University Press, 2005, p. 57.

9 This evaluation on the non-sonority of a theoretical voice is echoed by Morton Feldman writing about music composed with the aim of differentiation on a horizontal line: 'When sound is conceived as a horizontal series of events all its properties must be extracted in order to make it pliable to horizontal thinking ... the work resulting from this approach can be said not to have a 'sound'. What we hear is rather a replica of sound, and when successfully done, startling as any of the figures in Mme. Tussaud's celebrated museum.' This articulates a close connection between the horizontal muteness of semantic language and that of music when it is in the service of theory and intelligibility, and attests to the fact that even music can be non-sonorous when it strives towards the theoretical. Feldman counteracts this mute horizontality with 'Vertical Thoughts' (Morton Feldman, 'Vertical Thoughts' in *Give my Regards to Eighth Street*, Cambridge, MA: Exact Change, p. 12).

10 Cavarero, *For More than One Voice*, p. 57.

11 In the introduction to this collection of essays, I discuss Cauleen Smith's lecture at Pacific Northwestern College of Art, PNCA, on 2 November 2016, to introduce the notion of things and subjects, that do not fulfil their purpose, remain irresponsive to expectations and the demand of definition, but make aware of themselves as transgressive and fragile things, that inspire re-engagement to think what they might be.

12 Cauleen Smith, Visiting Lecture at Pacific Northwestern College of Art, PNCA, 2 November 2016, https://www.youtube.com/watch?v=-1mwULFTXRk (accessed 12 December 2017).

13 In a collection of his essays brought together in the book *Sense and Non-Sense* (1964), Merleau-Ponty articulates 'non-sense' not in reference to rational sense, as its nonsensical opposite, but as a sense that comes out of 'sensation'. Here this non-sense of sensation is adapted to the notion of a sonic sense.

14 Maurice Merleau-Ponty, *The Visible and the Invisible*, trans. Alphonso Lingis, ed. Claude Lefort, Evanston, IL: Northwestern University Press, 1968, p. 219.

15 Gilles Deleuze and Félix Guattari, *A Thousand Plateaus: Capitalism and Schizophrenia*, London: The Athlone Press, 1996, p. 21.

16 Ibid., p. 15.

17 Hito Steyerl, 'In Free Fall: A Thought Experiment on Vertical Perspective', in *The Wretched of the Screen*, Berlin: Sternberg Press, 2012, p. 28.

18 These 'dis-illusions of remembering' are Merleau-Ponty's illusions of a first impression set in the past. His dis-illusions name what we think we see, which, as we step closer reveals itself as to what it really is. In relation to a remembered dis-illusion it is the generative nature of dialogue that gets us closer to what there was. However, as with the dis-illusions of distance, the initial/remembered perceptions are not unreal or wrong, and play a part in what it is we finally articulate to have been there or remember to have been there, which equally remains subject to the vagaries of the world and of perception, a possible truth only (*The Visible and the Invisible*, p. 41).

19 Hannah Arendt in Cavarero, *For More than Once Voice, Toward a Philosophy of Vocal Expression*, p. 180.

20 Ibid., pp. 178–9.

21 This erasure of the voice is and at the same time is not Jacques Derrida's erasure, his *sous rature*, his writing under erasure: 'This is to write a word, cross it out, and then print both word and deletion. (Since the word is inaccurate, it is crossed out. Since it is necessary, it remains legible.)' (*Of Grammatology*, Baltimore: Johns Hopkins University Press, 1997, translator's preface, p. xiv).

 The distorted voice does not erase the visual word, the sign that marks the difference between the originary, familiar and lexical definition of the signified and a present experience of it. Performing outside the semantic the voice does not articulate within this play of inadequacy and necessity, but is its own object in sound. Every shriek and scream, amplified here by technology, is its own sound rather than a signifier for something else. Therefore the sound of the voice does not exist within the contortion of its own inadequacy and difference to what it is supposed to be. Sound is not genealogical but present and thus no past can be confirmed and erased. And so while the vocalization is not an erasure but a performance of the contingent in sound, the voice as a signifier of a semantic body, and the notion of technology as a signifier of electronic music, as a genre and category, are under erasure. ~~Woman, electronic music,~~ the originary and historical referents express the inadequacy of their definition and need to be 're-called', as in re-baptized, in order to be able to account for the contingency of their performance without recalling the necessity of their history.

22 Program notes, Back Alley Theatre, http://backalleytheater.tumblr.com/search/pensado#100603204961 (accessed 5 December 2017).

23 Cavarero, *For More than Once Voice, Toward a Philosophy of Vocal Expression*, p. 169.

24 Alexander Kluge and Hans-Ulrich Obrist, 'Alexander Kluge and Hans-Ulrich Obrist -What Art Can Do', *e-flux journal*, no.81 (April 2017).

25 Jacques Rancière, *Disagreement, Politics and Philosophy*, London: University of Minnesota Press, 1999, p. 133.

26 Ibid., p. 132.

27 Ibid., p. 117.

28 Cavarero, *For More than Once Voice, Toward a Philosophy of Vocal Expression*, p. 169.

29 Ibid. In her articulation of the maternal voice, Cavarero refers to Hélène Cixous and Julia Kristeva, who find a non- or pre-semantic place for the voice in infancy and the link to the mother: 'The mother I speak has never been subjected to the gramma-r wolf' (Cixous, *Coming to Writing and other Essays*, Deborah Jensen [ed.], Cambridge, MA: Harvard University Press, 1991, p. 22).
   While I do not want to read this notion of the maternal through the emphasis on an actual biological mother, understanding the term as exclusive and unable to encompass all of the feminine, and thus implicit in reducing women to mothers and marginalizing their voice, the concept and metaphor of the mother tongue, nevertheless serves to articulate the fleshly of a feminine writing that insists on the breath and on a reciprocal voice, on hearing and sounding. As such a concept then the mother tongue presents a critique and revocalization of a disembodied and autarchic expression of paternal authority and its mute voice.
   It is in relation to this emphasis on a maternal voice interesting that despite her ripe old age, Marian Leatherby has a mother who, at 110, lives in England and regularly sends her postcards. Her maternal voice remains and sustains her throughout her life and seems to find particular emphasis during her uprising against the patriarchal order of things.

30 Cavarero, *For More than Once Voice, Toward a Philosophy of Vocal Expression*, p. 63.

31 At this point Cavarero makes a distinction, which will become important later on in relation to the contemporary renewal of metaphysics by Saul Kripke, between Plato's metaphysics and that of Aristotle, to whom Kripke's notion of naming relates. While Plato's metaphysics is based on the notion of a universal and ideal, perfect world from which to derive knowledge, Aristotle believed that the natural world was real and imminently available for contemplation, and should be the context from which to derive understanding.

32 Cavarero, *For More than Once Voice, Toward a Philosophy of Vocal Expression*, p. 60.

33 Richard Rorty, 'Kripke versus Kant', *London Review of Books*, vol. 2, no. 17 (September 1980): 4.

34 Ibid., p. 5.

35 Rorty considers Kripke's critique of Kant's 'marvelous internal coherence', articulated in *Naming and Necessity*, which his essay reviews, as a necessary and exciting break with the Kantian project. He suggests the book implodes a Kantian premise of definition through a 'naïve' realism that calls something X rather than by suggesting we call something X if it meets all the following criteria (Rorty, 'Kripke versus Kant', p. 4).

36 Rorty, 'Kripke versus Kant', p. 5.

37 Saul Kripke, *Naming and Necessity*, Oxford: Blackwell, 1981, p. 44.

38 In this way, agreeing with Rorty, and leaning back on Aristotle, rather than Plato via Kant, a new relationship between thought and its object can be established. Kripke's idea of naming things with 'rigid designators' give a new attention to the 'what is there' and shift the focus away from the mechanism of representation and its epistemology towards the encounter between the thing and its articulation.

39 Sarah Jackson, 'Silent Running', in *Pelt*, Northumberland, UK: Bloodaxe, 2012, p. 39. Reprinted with permission.

40 Cavarero, *For More than Once Voice, Toward a Philosophy of Vocal Expression*, pp. 65–6.

41 Ibid., p. 61.

42 Jackson, 'Silent Running', p. 39.

43 Steyerl, 'In Free Fall: A Thought Experiment on Vertical Perspective', p. 20.

44 Ibid., p. 28.

45 Jacques Rancière, *On The Shores of Politics*, London, New York: Verso, 2007, p. 64.

46 Deleuze and Guattari, *A Thousand Plateaus: Capitalism and Schizophrenia*, p. 9.

47 Ibid., p. 7.

48 Ibid., p. 21.

49 Kluge and Obrist, 'Alexander Kluge and Hans-Ulrich Obrist -What Art Can Do'.

50 Deleuze and Guattari, *A Thousand Plateaus*, p. 25.

51 This depth is the ' "back" (and "behind") – ' that Maurice Merleau-Ponty discusses in the working notes of his book *The Visible and the Invisible* (1968). It is the place where I coincide with my looking and therefore cannot see myself. It is 'the dimension of the hidden' at my simultaneity with the thing, which I am too close to see (*The Visible and the Invisible*, p. 219).

52 Deleuze and Guattari, *A Thousand Plateaus*, p. 21.

53 David Mollin and Salomé Voegelin, 'Overlapping Environments, Made by Moving through Buildings and Paragraphs', in *Aurality and Environment*, Madrid, Spain: Ministry of Education, Culture and Sport, 2017, p. 93.

54 This vertiginous depth that I propose can re-radicalize the multiplicities plateaus/networks, could be seen in parallel with internet communication of blockchain: a growing list of records/blocks that avoids the centralized power of the net by peer-to-peer networking. These alternative systems of one-to-one networking online are created due to a loss of faith in established institutions (Marco Iansiti and Karim R. Lakhani, 'The Truth about Blockchain', *Harvard Business Review*, January–February 2017, https://hbr.org/2017/01/the-truth-about-blockchain). However, just like the rhizomatic pathways of the network, those peer-to-peer systems will no doubt soon be high-jacked by a centralized power, and so I am aware of the inevitable failure of the vertical and how it has to reroute and rethink constantly. The vertiginous is, then, in the longer term not a direction as much as an attitude of groundlessness and vertical slicing that demands of us as users to be participants, to be covert, to play against the trend through constant critical reassessments of the status of reality, actuality, possibility and impossibility through a sonic sensibility: reading the internet with a hearing trumpet.

At the same time, or in return, the plateaus of Deleuze and Guattari can still retain radicality if we can find a way out of the neo-liberal weave and read them backwards through their back and depth.

55 Here the notion of volume is clarified not as a measure in decibels but as an invisible and viscous expanse of the world in sound.

56 Merleau-Ponty, *The Visible and the Invisible*, p. 219.

57 In an email exchange, Winderen explains that she had visited many places to realize this work: rivers in Thailand, Russia, Norway, Sweden, the United States, and from the Barents Sea by the North Pole to Greenland, Iceland and the Carr. She spent some time on research boats and also on the vessel *Dardanella* for TBA21 Academy.

More about some of her fieldtrips can be found here: http://www.janawinderen.com/fieldtrips/.

58 Garrett Wallace Brown and David Held in the introduction to *The Cosmopolitan Reader*, Wallace Brown and Held (eds), Cambridge, UK: Polity, 2010, p. 1.

59 The notion of a 'politics of verticality' is informed by and resonates with Eyal Weizman's definition of the phrase articulated in relation to the Israeli occupation of the Palestine (Weizman, *Hollow Land, Israel's Architecture of Occupation*, London: Verso, 2012). I develop his ideas in relation to sound in the essay 'Geographies of Sound: Performing Impossible Territories', included in this book, where I propose that sound could be a tool and device to explore the vertical necessity of an occupational politics, to unearth its causes and consequences, and attempt to offer an alternative interpretation and course of action.

60 Sun Ra, *Pathways to Unknown Worlds El Saturn and Chicago Afro-Futurist Underground 1954–1968*, Anthony Elms, John Corbett and Terri Kapsalis (eds), Chicago: WhiteWalls, 2006, p. 115.

61 Carrington, *The Hearing Trumpet,* p. 134.

62 Julia Kristeva, *Revolution in Poetic Language*, trans. Margaret Waller, New York: Columbia University Press, 1984, p. 102.

63 Carrington, *The Hearing Trumpet*, p. 145.

References

Brown, Garrett Wallace and David Held (eds), *The Cosmopolitan Reader*, Cambridge, UK: Polity, 2010.

Carrington, Leonora, *The Hearing Trumpet*, London: Penguin Books, 2005, [orig. 1974].

Cavarero, Adriana, *For More than Once Voice, Toward a Philosophy of Vocal Expression*, trans. Paul A. Kottman, Stanford: Stanford University Press, 2005.

Cixous, Hélène, *Coming to Writing and other Essays*, ed. Deborah Jensen, Cambridge, MA: Harvard University Press, 1991.

Cixous, Hélène, 'The Laugh of the Medusa', *Signs*, vol. 1, no. 4 (1976): 875–93.

Derrida, Jacques, *Of Grammatology*, trans. Gayatri Chakravorty Spivak, Baltimore: Johns Hopkins University Press, 1997.

Feldman, Morton, 'Vertical Thoughts', in *Give my Regards to Eighth Street*, ed. B. H. Friedman, Cambridge, MA: Exact Change, 2000.

Guattari, Félix and Gilles Deleuze, *A Thousand Plateaus: Capitalism and Schizophrenia*, London: The Athlone Press, 1996.

Iansiti, Marco and Karim R. Lakhani, 'The Truth about Blockchain', *Harvard Business Review*, January–February 2017, https://hbr.org/2017/01/the-truth-about-blockchain.

Jackson, Sarah, *Pelt*, Northumberland, UK: Bloodaxe, 2012.

Kant, Immanuel, *Critique of Pure Reason*, trans. Friedrich Max Müller and Marcus Weigelt, London: Penguin Classics, 2007 [1781].

Kluge, Alexander and Hans-Ulrich Obrist, 'Alexander Kluge and Hans-Ulrich Obrist – What Art Can Do', *e-flux journal*, no.81, April 2017, http://www.e-flux.com/journal/81/126634/what-art-can-do/.

Kripke, Saul, *Naming and Necessity*, Oxford: Blackwell, 1981 [1980].

Kristeva, Julia, *Revolution in Poetic Language*, trans. Margaret Waller, New York: Columbia University Press, 1984.

Merleau-Ponty, Maurice, *Sense and Non-Sense*, trans. Hubert L. Dreyfus and Patricia Allen Dreyfus, Evanston, IL: Northwestern University Press, 1964.

Merleau-Ponty, Maurice, *The Visible and the Invisible*, trans. Alphonso Lingis, ed. Claude Lefort, Evanston, IL: Northwestern University Press, 1968.

Mollin, David and Salomé Voegelin, 'Overlapping Environments, Made by Moving through Buildings and Paragraphs', in *Aurality and Environment*, Alex Arteaga and Raquel Rivera (eds), Madrid, Spain: Ministry of Education, Culture and Sport, 2017, pp. 84–97.

Rancière, Jacques, *Disagreement, Politics and Philosophy*, London: University of Minnesota Press, 1999.

Rancière, Jacques, *On The Shores of Politics*, London, New York: Verso, 2007.

Rorty, Richard, 'Kripke versus Kant', *London Review of Books*, vol. 2, no. 17 (1980): 4–5.

Ryan, Marie-Laure, *Possible Worlds, Artificial Intelligence and Narrative Theory*, Bloomington and Indianapolis: Indiana University Press, 1991.

Smith, Cauleen, Visiting Lecture at Pacific Northwestern College of Art, PNCA, 2 November 2016, https://www.youtube.com/watch?v=-1mwULFTXRk.

Steyerl, Hito, 'In Free Fall: A Thought Experiment on Vertical Perspective', in *The Wretched of the Screen*, Berlin: Sternberg Press, 2012, pp. 12–30.

Sun Ra, *Pathways to Unknown Worlds El Saturn and Chicago Afro-Futurist Underground 1954–1968*, ed. Anthony Elms, John Corbett and Terri Kapsalis, Chicago: WhiteWalls, 2006.

Weizman, Eyal, *Hollow Land, Israel's Architecture of Occupation*, London: Verso, 2012.

Work

Pensado, Andrea, Performance at Back Alley Theatre in Washington, DC, 24 September 2014.

Winderen, Jana, *The Wanderer*, Album of field recording composition, Ash International, ASH 11.8, 24 September 2015, 40 min.

PUTTING ON LIPSTICK

get a lipstick (any colour)
stand in front of a mirror or another reflective surface
start to paint your lips while singing your favourite pop song.

5 March 2017, 11:03 pm, www.soundwords.tumblr.com.

INDEX

Abu Hamdan, Lawrence 10, 22–3, 28, 38
Adorno, Theodor W.
  and essay 5–6
  and verticality 201
affect; affects 18, 31, 125
  as experiential force 25
  and truth 23
affective 37
  energy 47
  possibility 28
  volume 66
Afrofuturism 85, 98 n.30, 165
Afro-Futurist science fiction 14 n.4
Agamben, Giorgio
  and imagination 31
agential 104, 153 (see also Barad)
  ethics 105–6
  forces 173
  in-between 106, 170
  intra-action 173
  realism 12, 15 n.15, 168, 174, 175
  reality 105, 172, 173, 176
  subjects 110
agentially real 172, 176
agents 26, 48, 88
agonistic
  game 38
  and playful 21, 80
Al-Samman, Ghada 35
Angel, Moss 119
antagonism 18
anthropocentric 47, 156–7 (see also non-
  and post-anthropocentric)
  hierarchy 47
  intentionality 52
  worldview 12, 160
anthropocentrism 131, 156–7
anti-violence 17–18, 21, 29, 35, 116 n.9 (see
  also violence)
Anywhen (Parreno) 10, 48–9, 52, 57,
  64, 73
architecture 10, 45, 50, 52, 168, 170, 173

soft 58–9
static 83
visual 94
as volume 47, 53
Arendt, Hannah, 39–40 n.4, 191
Aristotle 128, 210 n.31, 211 n.38
asymmetrical 82
  production 58, 69 n.15
  reciprocity 90
  world 56
asymmetry 61, 63, 159
  of the world 55
Auden, W. H.
  Secondary Worlds 26, 41 n.24
auditory imagination 17, 24, 37, 94
autonomous 6, 18, 151, 196
  agency 12, 111
  and fiction 26, 28
  identity 57
  imagination 36
  objects (things) and subjects 104, 127–8, 169
  voice 21, 193
  and writing 6, 13
autonomy 63, 135, 153 (see also
  nautonomy)
  and agency 142
  of fictional worlds 26
  and identity; subjectivity 126–7, 129, 134,
  135–6
  of the invisible subject (unknown woman)
  129–30
  and political participation 55–6, 69 n.15
  of things 132
avatar; avatar-I 124, 131–2, 137–8, 142

Baldry, H. C. 71 n.41
Balibar, Étienne 86, 103, 135
  ethic of self care 110–12, 148 n.55
  equaliberty 110–11
  and the political 10, 17–18, 39 n.1, 135
  and violence 12, 17–18, 29, 39 n.2, 122–3,
  141–2, 116 n.9

Barad, Karen 12, 15 n.15, 160, 180 n.62
    agential realism 104, 168, 174–5
    diffraction 160–3, 174, 178 n.28
    entanglement 152–4
    intra-action/-activity 168, 173, 181 n.68
    language 161–2, 178 n.36
    (new) materialism 153–5, 160, 173
    objectivity as responsibility and
        accountability 165
Bergson, Henri
    quantitative divisibility 81
between-of-things, the 12, 48, 56, 67,
    121
    listening to 58–9, 147 n.39
    and reality 163
    and score 107
between-subjects-as-things, the 47
bionic
    appendix 133
    femininity 134
    man 134
blindspots 23–4, 41 n.21
    and echoes 28–9
    and maps; cartography 87–90, 93, 95, 99
        n.38
    and sonic sensibility 38
Boland, Philip 78
Blockchain 212 n.54
Bök, Christian, 115
border(s) 22–5, 62
    and body 133
    fluid 110–11
    and lines 60, 63, 65, 88
    and listening 124
    and maps 60, 79
    Mediterranean as 30
    and politics of territory 93, 96
borderline 82, 200
Braidotti, Rosi 12
    cartographies 174, 178 n. 36,
        181 n.69
    creativity 14 n.5, 163
    gardening 174
    hyperrealism 159
    locationality 154, 162, 174
    margins 165–6
    materialism 152–5, 160, 163, 173
    Nomadic Theory 161–2
    transdisciplinarity 178 n.28
Brassier, Ray 178–9 n.38
Breathing (Pamela Z) 132, 136–7,
    143, 150
Bumsteinas, Arturas 76

capitalism 142
    global 112, 141
    neo-liberal 35, 107, 138, 154, 202
Carrington, Leonora 12, 185, 190, 205
cartography 75–6, 89
    as unmapping 99 n.38, 181 n.69
    visual 174
    and weather maps 178 n.36
Castells, Manuel 148 n.55
Cavarero, Adriana 13
    and Kripke 210 n.31
    and mute philosophy (Plato) 155, 189–91
    and voice (revocalization) 194–5, 196,
        210 n.29
Caygill, Howard 126, 145 n.19
Cixous, Hélène 134, 143
    and Afrofuturism 165
    and Clément 129, 138, 140,
        146 n.34
    dé-penser 147 n.42
    feminine writing 129–30, 158
    maternal voice 210 n.29
    rupture, 12, 122–3, 129–30
    and trans-subjectivity 130
Claudel, Paul 30
Clément, Catherine
    and Cixous 129, 138, 140,
        146 n.34
collaboration 13, 15 n.16, 196
    composition (work) as 12, 87, 153–4,
        167
    contingent 122–3
    and DIY 13, 15 n.16
    modest 164–7, 175
    score as site of 153, 169
collaborative
    composing; composition 168–9, 172, 173,
        175, 181 n.66
    cross-time 1
    frame 69
    sphere 54
    world 7, 107, 173
colonial 56, 122
    and language 141
    rule 92
colonialization; colonialized 66 (*see also*
        decolonialized)
    and the digital-lexicon 141
    of 'her' 130
    and subjectivity 133, 138
composition 4, 25, 50, 76, 79, 110, 192,
    201
    audiovisual 31

collaborative; and collaboration 87,
167–9, 181 n.66
contingent 173
as echography 21
feminist 3
field recording 12, 190, 203–4
as intra-activity 170–1
and sonic fiction 205
and space 47, 86, 87
conflict 104
affirmative 170
deny (reduce) 69 n.19, 80
dialectical 68–9 n.13
and difference 80–1, 88, 112, 131, 163, 168
invisible 50
and participation 110
political 25
and responsibility 131
and territory 55, 87
Connolly, William E. 33–6
Conti, Nina 50, 63
cosmopolitanism 10, 48, 56, 69–70 n.19
contemporary 54
and education 59–60
historical 54–5, 66
and Kant 65–6, 71 n.40
local 56, 57
and morality 55, 66, 68 n. 6
and phenomenology 63–6
sonic 53, 58, 63, 66–7, 68 n.6
cosmos 52, 54, 55, 61, 65, 67, 138, 203, 204
indivisible 106
non-anthropocentric 52 (see
also anthropocentric and
post-anthropocentric)
and possibility 121
shared 58, 65, 68–9 n.13, 14
of the work 57, 60, 188
world as 54, 86, 188, 204
Cox, Christoph 12, 153–7, 162
and DeLanda 178–9 n.38
curating 67 (see also volume)
Curtis, Charles
and Radique, *Naldjorlak I* 12, 154, 166–
71, 175, 180 n.54, 181 n.66

decolonialized; decolonialization 86
and geography 95
DeLanda, Manuel 155
goofy 178–9 n.38
Deleuze, Gilles 155, 178–9 n.38
and Guattari; rhizomatic networks 13,
190, 202, 212 n.54

depth (*see also* depth barrier)
and the digital 202–3
and geography 76, 83, 86, 89, 96, 201–2,
204
invisible 28, 88, 140
Merleau-Ponty 13, 89–91, 93–4, 190, 203,
211 n.51
mobile 29, 87
as political location 93–5
and rhizome 191, 202–3
of sound; sonic; listening 37, 121, 124,
186–7, 191
vertical 12, 91, 190, 204, 212 n.54
watery 30–2, 34, 203–5
and writing 206–7
depth barrier 93–4 (*see also* depth)
Derrida, Jacques 178–9 n.38
erasure 209 n.21
Descartes, René 31
Description d'un combat (*Description of a
Struggle*) (Marker) 8
deterritorialization 202 (*see also*
territorialization)
dialectic; dialectical 17, 55, 155, 155
and conflict 68–9 n.13
and cosmopolitanism 66
and ethics 105
and rhythm 175
and violence 17–18, 35, 39 n.2,
135–6
world view 78
difference; *différence* 27–8, 86, 80, 111,
201, 209 n.21
contingent 131, 152
and cosmopolitanism 65, 69–70 n.19,
70–1 n.35
and the digital 142
and diffraction 154, 160–4, 166, 170–2
and entanglements 15 n.15, 168–9, 173–4,
175, 176
irreducible 69–70 n.19
masculine and feminine 158, 178–9 n.38
and Meillassoux 157
negotiation of 112, 114
performing 92, 160, 175, 195
and possibility 175–6
and self 131, 134, 136, 141
and similarities 56, 120, 156
total 82, 92
diffraction 12, 15 n.15, 163
difference and 154, 160, 163, 166
and inclusivity 173
and transdisciplinarity 178 n.28

and rhythm 174
dimension; dimensionality 11, 49, 79, 81, 83,
    98 n.30, 87, 189
  of the actual 49, 75
  and capacity 46, 82, 94
  and depth 203, 93, 96
  ethical 11, 18, 22, 106
  geographical 90, 91–2, 204
  of the hidden (the unseen) 2–3, 87, 89,
    185–8, 190, 211 n.51
  indivisible 4, 50, 53, 82, 96
  of interbeing 131, 135
  of possibility 75
  and rhizome 202–3
  sound's 91, 124–5, 207
  and volume 89, 96, 205
discipline; disciplinarity 19, 90, 105, 131
  between 175, 178 n.28
  boundaries 105, 160, 163, 170, 175–6
  of geography 77–9, 90–1, 95–6
  interference into 11, 79, 160
  knowledge 4, 77–9, 151, 161, 175
  outside of 166, 176
Disco Breakdown (Ifekoya) 123, 125, 127,
    145, 150
dis-illusions 33, 42 n.37
  of remembering 191, 209 n.18
DIY 3, 4, 7, 13, 15 n.16, 106–7
Doty, Roxanne 10, 19–20, 29
doubt 12, 31, 33, 37, 38, 131–2
  and cosmopolitanism; cosmopolitan
    project 11, 48, 57, 61, 63, 65, 66, 69–7
    n.19
  dogmatic 175
  and education (listening-) 59–60, 64
  and language 161, 188, 194, 195
  and listening (sound) 57, 61, 64, 120–1
  materialism and 159, 161, 164
  Merleau-Ponty 61–3, 164, 173
  phenomenological 61–3, 64, 66, 164, 181
    n.68
  unity of 64, 65
dualism; dualistic (see also nondualistic)
  knowledge 160
  and new materialism 155–6, 158
  thinking 155–6, 174
  and visuocentrism (visuality) 155, 157–9,
    174
Dulac, Germaine 7
duration; durational 8, 62, 76
  composition 12, 169, 172
  as geological timespace 41 n.29
  and new materialism 172, 174

and performance 86
  and space 81
  of volume 89
Dyson, Frances 10 (see also echography)
  echo 20–1, 29
  The Tone of Our Times 20

Eades, Caroline 6–7, 14 n.9, 107
echo; echoing 32, 58, 198
  and acclamation 20–1
  anti-nomic 17, 37
  and breath 20–1, 35
  location 187
  plural 20, 29
  and political imagination 28
  and responsibility 12, 37
  singular 33
  of the unheard 64
echography 21 (see also Dyson)
  and blindspots 28
  of the inaudible (unheard) 21, 35, 38
  and knowledge 37
  political 38
Eco, Umberto
  small worlds 26, 41 n.24
ecological; ecology 7, 20–1, 33
  of belonging 161
  and echo 20–1
  in global context 54–6
  of sound 205
  vertical 204–5
economic; economical; economy 4, 10, 30,
    37, 54, 143
  asymmetries 152
  and echo 20–1
  erotic (libidinal) 137, 144
  and geography 77, 82
  and identity 125
  neo-liberal 110, 142
  in a relational (connected) world 54, 55–6,
    82, 204
  of the visual 33
education
  access to 55
  asymmetries of 55, 69 n.15, 152
  civic 59
  listening (sonic) 59–60, 64
Einhorn (Unicorn) (Horn) 137–8, 142, 150
Elster, Jon 22
  limbo of politics 23
  Logic and Society, Contradictions and
    Possible Worlds 23, 41 n.20
  political possibility 22, 24, 28

entanglement 180 n.55
  and diffraction 154, 178 n.28
  and difference 15 n.15
  ethics of 104–5, 107, 173, 175–6,
    176
  and materialism 160–1, 163, 166–7, 168
  and morality 103
  multisensorial 157
essay 4–6
  audio 22
  audiovisual 24
  and crisis 7, 107
  film 6–7, 8
  as fragment 10, 13, 188, 190, 191
  performative 106
  and possibility 7–8, 17
  as rhythm 189
  score 11, 103, 106, 107, 189
  and sound 9, 189, 200
  vertical 106, 191
  video 10, 22, 28
ethical; ethics 4 (*see also* post-ethical and
    unethical)
  agential 104–6
  and collaboration 164
  and cosmopolitanism 54–5, 61, 66
  of cultivation 36 (*see also* Connolly)
  the dark face of 111–12 (*see also* Balibar)
  of engagement 86, 127
  of entanglement 104, 107, 173,
    175–6
  of the inaudible 11, 103, 114
  of listening (sonic) 104–6, 113
  and morality 68 n.6
  of participation 36, 48, 58, 61, 66
  and possibility 21–2
  of (self-)care 18, 35, 110
exclusion 139, 157, 175
  and inclusion 94, 157
  and language 200, 205
  and modern thought 156
  precarity and 111
  and woman 126, 165

Feldman, Morton
  Vertical Thoughts 201, 209 n.9
Fell, Mark 82–3
feminine
  and precarity 160
  neo-logisms 162
  new materialism (speculation) 12, 160–1,
    162–3, 166, 173, 175, 178 n.28, 178–9
    n.38

realities 158
  song 139
  sonic materialism 162–3, 172
  and sound 139
  subjectivity 130, 138–9
  voice 173, 210 n.29
  writing (*écriture feminine*) 130, 158
feminist 123
  and Afrofuturism 85
  identities 11
  science fiction 166
  sound 3, 7
fiction; fictional 23, 26, 54
  of the body 126
  and essay 6
  future 85–6
  literary 188
  mathematical 156, 157, 165, 173
  and non-fiction 6, 8
  parallel 5, 19, 27, 31
  as possibility 26, 27, 186
  sonic 27, 29, 37, 85–6, 187, 188, 191, 205
  textual 29
  and untruths 78, 187, 188
flesh; fleshly 154
  and body 144 n.2, 152, 160, 196
  and cartography 89
  Cixous 130
  and feminine writing 210 n.29
  Merleau-Ponty 61, 91, 94, 203
  and new materialism 12, 153, 160
  painting 185
  singing 130, 196
  sonic 94, 119
  techno- 196
  and the unicorn 128, 137
  as resistance 203
Foucault, Michel 178–9 n.38
  creativity 14 n.5
  geographical knowledge 77
  geography 80, 87, 99 n.36
  and military logic 80, 87, 92, 99 n.36
  pouvoir and *savoir* (power and
    knowledge) 97 n.8, 99 n.41
  space 76, 97 n.3
future science 85, 87

Gallagher, Michael 78
gaze 9, 62, 64, 134
  authoritative 158
  and depth 187, 190
  and geography 90
  and mirror 124, 131–2

and sound 124
gender; gendered 124, 129
  asymmetries 200
  biological 138–9
  hierarchy 4
  identification 12, 122, 125, 141
  inclusivity 178–9 n. 38
  subjectivity; subject 159, 165
  trans- 122, 141
Gender Song (Ifekoya) 123, 125, 129, 150
geographical 23, 59, 62, 76, 82 (*see also* geography)
  depth 204
  imagination; imaginary 77–8, 79, 90, 94, 204
  knowledge 77 (*see also* Michel Foucault)
  mapping 59
  rhythm 77
  science 11, 79, 85
  and sonic possible worlds 77, 81, 96
  subjectivity; identity 34, 76, 88
  truth 80
  volume 82, 87
geography 11, 32, 33, 59, 83, 92 (*see also* geographical)
  anxious 79, 89
  and imagination 86, 92
  and knowledge 60–1, 78, 94, 95–6
  of migration 80
  military logic of 76, 80, 91–2, 99 n.36
  and (political) possibility 78, 81–2, 94
  of (sonic) possible worlds 11, 78, 84–5, 95
  pouvoir and *savoir* (power and knowledge) 77, 97 n.8 (*see also* Foucault)
  as science 81, 96
  and science fiction 85–6, 96
  social- 78, 88
  socio-material 89, 92, 96
  of sound 75–6, 77, 78, 79, 80, 81–2, 88, 90, 92, 96
  vertical 88, 90, 91, 93
  visual 21, 94–5
geopolitics of sound 88
globalized; globalization
  anti- 18
  and cosmopolitanism 54
  forces of 60
  labour market 178 n.28
  teaching 59–60
  world 11, 48, 60
government; governmental
  choices 19

control of space 93–4
  curbing of politics 80, 137
  regulator 85
  rules 66
Graeber, David
  imagination 31
  possibility 22
Guattari, Félix 155
  and Deleuze; rhizomatic networks 13, 190, 202, 212 n.54
Guyer, Jane I. 10, 18, 39
  possibility as ethical stance 21

Hajjar, Lisa 22–3
Hanh, Thich Nhat
  interbeing 48, 68 n.5, 120, 135, 144 n.4
Haraway, Donna
  diffraction 160
Harman, Graham
  object-oriented ontology 159
Hegel, George Wilhelm Friedrich
  history 68–9 n.13
Held, David
  asymmetry of the world 55–6
  autonomy; nautonomy 69 n.15
  cosmopolitanism 10, 48
  non-state actors 55
hierarchy; hierarchical 4, 34, 103, 113
  angelic; of angels 20–1, 27, 35
  anthropocentric 47, 155
  of humans 27
  and language 202, 203
  and new materialism 156–8
  of things 103, 193
  of thought 6
  vertical critique of 201
  without 25, 31, 140
Holland, Jack 40 n.8
  International Relations 10, 19
honeyed (*see also* Merleau-Ponty)
  being 10, 68 n.3, 46, 181 n.65
  existence 51
  -hands 181 n.65
  water 52, 60
horizon; 39, 89–90
  future 39
  of knowledge 195
  mobile 171
  of politics 17, 39 n.1
  sociopolitical 114
horizontal 50
  compulsion of 10
  connection(s) 189–90, 199, 201, 204

drive (narrative) 6, 194
line(s) 106, 187–8, 191, 201, 204–5
logic 206, 208 n.9
thinking 208 n.9
weave 201
Horn, Rebecca 137–8
humanism; humanist
brotherhood 55, 65
as monotheism 65
philosophy 33, 35
secular 27
humanity 54
common 55
and cosmopolitanism 54–5, 69–70 n.19
and finitude 165
formless 34–5
shared 25
suffering 69–70 n.19
humanitarian 112, 137
hyper-invisibility 89, 95
of conventional reality 11, 78
of masculinity 159–60
of unseen norms 97 n.7, 159
of the visual 77, 89

Ifekoya, Evan 12, 123–6, 127–30, 131–2
online 142
unperforming 139, 143
immigrant 82
impossible worlds 28 (*see also* possible worlds)
impossibility 1, 5, 23, 139
and abjectness 157
blindspots as 87, 93
of the body 137
cartographic 91, 93
of a continent 32
erotics of 144
of the impossible 80, 136
and reality 21, 142
as threat 25
of the unsound 58
and utopia 107
and vertical 212 n.54
improvization; improvised 189, 192–3
and composition 169
construction 1
of doing things 3
resources 7
world 6
inaudible; inaudibility 5, 58, 131
and echo 35
echography of 21

ethics of 11, 103, 114
as impossible 38, 114
and the in-between 64, 158
inclusion of 23, 114
and the invisible 128, 200
and listening education 64
and music 171
as noise 189
and silence 58, 63
subjectivities 132
and violence 132, 136
in-between, the 12, 51, 49, 62, 64, 66, 192, 202
agential; agent of 106, 161, 168, 170, 193, 195
as blindspot 58, 99 n.38
and cosmopolitanism 56
depth of 89, 94, 191, 202
geographies of 79, 82, 88, 89, 90, 92, 95
inhabiting 10, 172
invisible 58, 59, 83, 84, 123, 175, 192
listening to (sound of) 58, 130, 132, 158, 161, 190, 191, 204
mobile 58, 86, 168, 175
morality and ethics of 104, 106
perceptual focus of 48, 120
performing 154, 157, 195
political possibility of 93, 135
practice of 48, 50, 64, 106, 153, 160
and subjectivity 123, 130, 132, 143, 144 n.4
of the text(s); of writing 10, 130, 188, 190
as undefined spaces 130, 132
vertical 204
inclusion
and echographic practice of 37
and ethics 103–4
and exclusion 94, 157
of the invisible 23, 162
pluralized 110
indeterminate 9, 85
semantics 14–15 n.11
and sound 24, 157
index; indexical
actuality 26
inhabiting 27
invisible 57
possibility 26
sonic 122, 143
weave 32, 36, 38
indivisible; indivisibility 81, 87, 89, 120
cosmos 106
dimension 4, 50, 94

and geography 88, 95
and new materialism 157, 163, 175
sphere 59, 60, 63, 156
territory 11, 79, 91–3, 95
and time 172
volume 50, 53, 57, 60, 64, 67, 75, 82, 86,
    88, 94, 96, 99 n.38, 104, 173
world 55, 105, 168
infinite; infinity 6, 10, 81
device 1
material 2
of meaning 173
and plurality 133
reality 36
and rhizome 202
and rhythm 174, 180 n.64
and sound 27, 140–1, 170, 172, 173
and violence 17, 116 n.9
and women 130, 140
Inside You is Me, July/Surface Substance
    (Kiyomi Gordon) 11, 78, 82, 83, 101
instrument; instrumentality 12, 170–2, 176
and consensus 81
idealized 139
performing
as score 160
of semantic language 198
and technology 143, 146 n.34
tuning 167–8, 175
instrumentalized 133
and digital 142
subjectivity 139
intensity; intensities 12, 17, 49, 171
inarticulate 157
mobile 5
sound; sonic 47, 53, 64, 204
inter-activity 81
and interbeing 168
matter as 161
interactuality 50
and anthropocentrism 52
cosmopolitan 61
and interbeing 48
invisible 10
and participation 57
and political possibility 58
and sonic sensibility (sound) 58, 188
and volume 10, 51–2
of the world 57
inter-agency 57, 82
inter-are; inter-be 12, 55, 48, 68 n.5, 82, 92,
    144 n.4, 164
and sound 119, 132

and volume 82, 203
interbeing 10, 95, 126, 135, 142, 144, 195–
    6, 201–2 (*see also* Nhat Hanh)
agential 104
cosmopolitan 60, 64, 66, 92
and doubt 61, 63
and ethics 105
forced 90
indivisible 95–6, 168
invisible 61, 88, 123, 135, 136
in new materialism 157, 158, 160, 168,
    170, 173, 175
phenomenological 57, 64, 66–7
and possibility 62, 93, 120, 139
scientific 204–5
and sound 48, 50, 53, 57, 121, 144 n.4,
    147 n.39, 167, 170, 188, 203
and trans-subjectivity 137–9
and volume 53, 61, 67, 83, 88, 92, 104,
    188
interdisciplinary 1, 178 n.28
inter-invent; inter-invention; inter-inventing
and cosmopolitanism 57, 60
identity; subjectivity 136, 138
and listening; sound making 46–7, 66, 83,
    135, 147 n.39
place 52
volume 60, 82, 84
International Relations 10, 18–19, 40 n.8
and realism 37
interobjectivity 120, 173
intra-objectivity 173, 181 n.68
inter-vention
as inter-invention 47, 147 n.39
as perceptual agency 46–7
intra-activities; intra-activity 12 (*see also*
    Barad)
of the feminine voice 173
and new materialism 15 n.15, 161, 175
and sonic interbeing 168 (*see also*
    interbeing)
and tuning 167, 170, 175
of being honeyed 181 n.65
Irigaray, Luce 12, 153
and caresses and gesture words 154, 160,
    163, 170
goofy 178 n.38
and language 161–2, 178 n.36

Kanngieser, Anja 78
Kant, Immanuel
cosmopolitanism 53, 64–5, 70–1 n.35, 71
    n.38, 71 n.40

in digital acceleration 141–2
and Kripke 128, 211 n.38
morality 70–1 n.35, 71 n.38
philosophy of language 126–8, 145 n.20, 196–8
and Rorty 146 n.23, 197, 211 n.35
taxonomy and lexical thinking 12, 145 n.19, 147 n.42, 152, 202
Kiyomi Gordon, Jacqueline 11, 78, 82–4, 86–7
socio-material volume 88, 92
Kluge, Alexander
counter-poetizing the digital 195, 201–2
and Obrist 194
and Silicon Valley 190, 195
knowledge 1, 3, 4, 20, 59, 85, 162, 189, 210 n.31
abstract 11, 78, 125, 196
disciplinary 91, 151, 161, 175, 178 n.28
and dualism 160, 163
geographical 75, 77–9, 94, 95, 96
and humanism 34–5
and language 126–7, 128, 140–1, 155, 195, 196, 197, 200, 202, 206
material; matter 161, 166, 178 n.28
to perform; performative 124, 164, 206
phenomenological 61–3
plural 38, 80
and political change (transformation) 37
and power (*pouvoir* and *savoir*) 78, 88, 91, 97 n.8
and representation 164, 166, 174
sonic 37, 88
and subjectivity 139, 146 n.23
and truth 89, 142, 152, 146 n.23
knowing 19 (*see also* unknowing)
collective; social 61
and diffraction 163
as doing 11, 106
and its object 62, 148 n.50
phenomenological 62, 97 n.8
sensorial 59, 141
Kodwo, Eshun
Afrofuturism 85
subjectivity engine 105
Kripke, Saul 12
and Kant 211 n.38
and metaphysics 210 n.31
mini-worlds 98 n.21
Naming and Necessity 128–9
realist philosophy of language 122–3, 128–9, 198

and Rorty 146 n.23, 196–7, 211 n.35, 211 n.38
Kristeva, Julia
fourth signifying practice 148 n.58, 207
maternal language 210 n.29

La Barbara, Joan 148 n.59
Language Gulf in the Shouting Valley (Abu Hamdan) 10, 22, 38, 44
Lebovici, Elisabeth 126
Le Guin, Ursula K. 84–5, 86
Levin, Sonya 82
Lewis, David K.
possible world theory 26–7, 41 n.31
life-world(s)
cultural 54, 204
individual 152
negotiation of 57
private 62–3, 64, 66, 98 n.21
literacy
of the in-between 59, 60
sonic 206
logos 155, 190, 205
devocalization of 189, 190
re-vocalization of 156, 192, 200
visual and mute 155, 188, 189, 196
Lu, Catherine
cosmopolitanism 11, 48, 69 n.19
doubt 57, 61

Manning, Erin
generative environment 81
interference 11, 79
and Massumi 11, 79, 81, 166
map; mapping 11, 33–4, 52, 60, 78, 79, 85, 87, 91, 98 n.21, 204 (*see also* unmapping)
aerial 90
and blindspots 95, 99 n.38
echography as 21
fluid 175
and geography 59, 80
and scores 75
and sound 75, 95, 175
totalizing 89
variants 80–1
visual 80–9
weather 174, 178 n.36, 181 n.69
Marker, Chris 8–9
masculine; masculinist
history 159
idealism 68–9 n.13
language 188

logic 130
new materialism 159, 166, 175, 178–9 n.38
realities 158
theorization 158
visuality 160, 178–9 n.38
Massey, Doreen
geographical narratives 11, 81, 87
spaces of possibility 78–81
spatial imaginaries 76, 78
Massumi, Brian
generative environment 81
interference 11, 79
and Manning 11, 79, 81, 166
material sound 8–9, 152, 167
image of 13, 191
materialism; materialist 153, 157, 166 (see also new materialism)
and cosmopolitanism 56
and dualism 155–8, 174
and duration (time) 172, 174
embodied 152, 153
feminine 160, 166
feminine sonic (sonico-feminine) 162–3, 172, 175
phenomenology 152, 174
masculine 166
and realist; realism 155, 157
and rhythm 166
sonic (sound) 12, 151, 154–8, 162–3, 166
of sonic possible worlds 158
of transformation 12
Matles, David 78
Mediterraneo (Raimondo) 10, 30, 34, 38, 44
Meillassoux, Quentin 12, 165
After Finitude 177 n. 3, 178–9 n.38
ancestrality 152–3, 159
critique of correlationism 151–2, 164, 177 n.3, 178–9 n.38
factuality 164
irremediable reality 157
mathematical fiction 156–7, 173–4
memory
and architecture 58
and dis-illusions 191
of Nakba 25
and rhizome 202
Merleau-Ponty, Maurice 12
being honeyed 10, 46, 68 n.3, 181 n.65
and cosmopolitanism 48
depth 13, 89–90, 91, 93–4, 190, 203, 211 n.51

dis-illusions 33, 42 n.37, 209 n.18
doubt 48, 61–2, 164
and materialism 152, 164, 173
non-sense 70 n.21, 190, 2–8 n.13
openness to the world (*ouverture au monde*) 70 n.28, 140, 148 n.50
Meschonnic, Henri
rhythm 171, 174, 175, 180 n.63, 180 n.64
migrant 112, 165
migration 54
and flux 79
forced 56
geography of 80
mass 37
politics of 31
military 11, 19, 32, 90, 91
court system 22
and geography 80, 85–6, 87, 90, 99 n.36
intervention 33
logic 80
and phenomenological depth 93
power 92
and sound technology 139, 143, 147 n.48
as technicians of space 91
thinking 76
Mollin, David 41 n.21
moral; morality 11, 68–9 n.13, 113 (see also post-moral)
agent 55
and cosmopolitanism 54–6, 65–6, 68 n.6, 70–1 n.35, 71 n.38, 71 n.40
duty 54, 68 n.6
and ethics 36, 66, 68 n.6, 104, 107, 110
of the invisible 103, 108
and participation 104, 105
practical 104, 107
principle 68–9 n.13, 112
and utility 112, 148 n.55
multisensory 29, 47
multivocality 20, 31, 36
mute; muted 33, 62, 83, 122, 162, 186
language 189, 195, 196, 200, 206, 208 n.9
logos 155, 188, 198–200
objects and subjects 33, 141
reality 122
text 188, 199
theorization; theory 106, 189, 206
thinking; thought 155, 174, 188, 195
unthought 174
voices 35, 50, 58, 210 n.29

Najibullah, Akrami 112
Naldjorlak I (Radique and Curtis) 12, 153,
    166–9, 175, 180 n.54, 180 n.55, 183
Nancy, Jean-Luc
    listening 46, 120
    the un-sensed 144 n.3, 147 n.41
nautonomy 56, 63 (*see also* Graeber)
network 109, 126
    and blockchains (peer-to-peer) 212 n.54
    digital (online) 141, 142, 148 n. 54, 195,
        202
    global 91
    invisible 59
    rhizomatic 13, 190, 202, 212 n.54
    rules 201
    and social media 148 n.52
    technological 133, 141
new materialism; new materialist 35, 166,
    176 (*see also* materialism; materialist)
    and agential realism 173, 176
    and dualism 155, 157
    feminine 163, 178 n.28, 178–9 n.38
    feminine sonic (sonico-feminine) 12, 172,
        175
    masculine 159, 175, 178–9 n.38
    and phenomenology 174
    and post-philosophy 153
    and realism 153, 155
    sonic (sound) 12, 153, 155–7, 166
    and speculative realism 152, 156, 158
neo-liberalism 111, 128
Night on the Sailship (Bumsteinas) 76, 101
non-anthropocentric 48 (*see
        also* anthropocentric and
        post-anthropocentric)
    cosmos 52
non-dualistic 160 (*see also* dualism)
    knowledge 163
non-hierarchical
    real 6
    and rhizome 202
    world 160
non-human 36, 86, 154–6, 165
    actors 27
    agents 88
    narratives 80
    and new materialism 152, 159–61, 175
    slices (variants) of this world 35, 80
non-sense 58, 64, 70 n.21, 190, 196, 208
    n.13
Nussbaum, Martha 10
    cosmopolitan education 59

cosmopolitanism 48, 54, 65
    and Kant 64–5, 70–1 n.35, 71 n.38, 71
        n.40

Obama, Barack 90
objectivity
    as accountability (and responsibility) 12,
        153, 163, 164, 165, 166
    as (critical) distance 153, 155–6, 165
    ideal 68–9 n.13
    of natural laws 37
    and technology 133
Obrist, Hans-Ulrich
    and Kluge 194
Onians, R. B. 196

Papzian, Elizabeth A. 6–7, 14 n.9, 107
Parreno, Philippe 10, 48, 49, 50, 51, 52, 57,
    60, 64, 73
participation 2, 5, 65, 78, 119, 135, 188
    in anthropology 18
    in difference 173
    equal 56, 69 n.15
    ethical; ethics of 36, 48, 58, 61, 104
    and geography 84
    and the image 121, 124
    meaning through 35, 107, 201
    political 55–6, 58, 69 n.15, 110, 136
    in possibility 67, 112, 114, 120
    and (essay) score 11, 103, 105, 107
    and sound (sonic sensibility) 31, 38, 67,
        103, 124, 126, 129, 186–7, 194
participatory
    capacity 104
    drive 65
    ethics 58, 66, 68 n.6, 103, 204
    practice 105
    listening 172
    text 206
performance 4, 90, 98 n.22, 181 n.66, 170,
    172
    contingent 194, 209 n.21
    of cosmopolitanism 65
    and diffraction 154, 166, 170
    ethical 105–6
    and geography 11, 76, 78, 86, 87, 88
    identities; subjectivities 12, 124, 127, 130,
        132, 134, 136, 158, 160
    of the in-between 130, 166
    of the invisible 134, 136
    of the unknown 89, 192–3
    and *Naldjorlak I* 167–2, 175, 180 n.55

and (new) materialism 154, 160, 165–6, 175–6
of political possibility 54, 106, 205–6
score 103–7, 170, 175
and speech; voice 12–13, 129, 136, 190, 194, 197
of text; writing 190, 191, 195, 200, 205–6, 209 n.21
virtuosity of 133, 143
performative 11, 12, 90, 103, 126, 160, 162
and diffraction 160
doubt 175
essay 106
knowledge 164
and language 178 n.36, 196
morality 105
place 89–90
reality 167
subjectivity 126, 139
phenomenology 65, 143, 151
correlationism 164
and materialism 152, 174, 175, 181 n.68
sonic 152
phenomenological possibilism 26
phonography
textual (text as) 5, 190, 200
pitch 167
-complex 167–8
diffracted 169
unplaceable 171
Plato 190
language 189, 196, 211 n.38
metaphysics 196–7, 210 n.31
mute philosophy 155
plurality 10, 66, 163, 165
of the actual 13
of the audible 34
complex 30, 35, 109
invisible; unseen 133, 134
'of men' (Hannah Arendt) 39–40 n.4
political 81
of possibility 38, 98 n.21
of reality 30, 108
simultaneous 95, 136, 161, 174
of its time 174, 176
vision and 157
without opposites 17–18
of (possible) worlds 27
political possibility of sound 5, 9, 10, 17, 19, 22, 29, 31, 39, 58
popularism 20

populism 13
possible world(s) 3, 25, 27, 39 n.4, 112
(*see also* sonic possible worlds and impossible worlds)
actual 28, 90
geography of 77, 84, 85, 88, 95
and life-worlds 98 n.21
literary 41 n.24
science fiction 84
theory 26–7
post-anthropocentric 153 (*see also* anthropocentric and non-anthropocentric)
postcolonial
subjects 165
post-ethical 112 (*see also* ethical and unethical)
post-human 52
post-moral 112 (*see also* moral)
post-philosophical 153
precarity 23, 159
and exclusion 111
and feminine 160
and flux 79
pre-human world 152, 164
Prior, Jonathan 78
Pundak, Ron 91

racial; race 200
discrimination 9
hierarchy 4
identity 122, 125, 127, 134
subject 165
Radique, Éliane
and Curtis, *Naldjorlak I* 12, 153–4, 166, 167, 168–9, 175, 180 n.54, 183
tape work 170, 181 n.66
Raimondo, Anna 10, 22, 30–3, 38
Rancière, Jacques
community 136, 148 n.53
consensus 80, 97 n.13, 121
governmental curbing 137
possibility 195
'sans-part' 103, 123, 142, 148 n.53
rationality 31–2, 34, 141
of the digital network 142
and Kant (unity of reason) 64–5, 71 n.38, 71 n.40, 196
limitation of 38
of the nation-state 55
and natural law 66, 70–1 n.35, 71 n.38
realism 15 n.15, 40 n.9, 143, 211 n.35

agential 12, 15 n.15, 168, 174, 175
and consensus 80, 121
irremediable 152, 153
modal 26, 39 n.4
and possibility of 40 n.9, 178–9 n.38
radical 153
sonic (and sound) 26, 175
speculative 12, 152, 156–7, 158, 159,
    178–9 n.38
of the unthought 164–5
re-performance
of cartography 99 n.38
representation 8, 50, 64, 121, 122, 125, 132,
    136, 148 n.52, 152, 187, 201, 204–5
cartographic 83, 87, 89
crisis of 7, 106
cultural 3
of geography 11, 76, 78–9, 81, 88
of identity; subjectivity 123–4, 125, 126,
    135, 139, 165
of the inaudible 131
language and 4, 104, 146 n.23, 160, 166,
    187, 197, 211 n.38
and new materialism 152–3, 154, 155,
    156, 159, 160, 163, 165
and sound 28, 134, 138–9, 156
subject (body) 133, 134, 139, 143, 165
visual (and image) 87, 89, 121, 141, 142,
    148 n.54, 163
Retham, Petra 10, 18
revocalization (see also vocalization and
    devocalization)
and the body 175
and the digital 195
of the logos 156
by the mother tongue (maternal language)
    210 n.29
of the textual field 13, 190
rhizome; rhizomatic 13, 190, 191, 202
and digital networks 202
and text 203
and vertical 212 n.54
rhythm(s) 12, 30, 33–4, 85, 119, 123, 180
    n.64, 187, 193, 205
architectural (sculptural) 83–4, 172
and breath 136, 138
of doing 103, 107
and geography 75, 77, 79, 81
irregular (nonmetric) 174, 175–6, 180
    n.63
of language (reading) 189, 200, 206
and light 49, 53, 126, 189, 193

material 172, 174
political 175
and subjectivity 126, 148 n.58
and transformation (difference) 123–4,
    163, 171, 172
and volume 50, 88
Riot Grrrl 14 n.7
Robertson, Lisa 70 n.22
Rodgers, Tara 139, 147 n.48
Roggenbuck, Steve 75, 76
Ronen, Ruth 26
Rorty, Richard 146 n.23, 196–7, 211 n.35,
    211 n.38
Ryan, Marie-Laure 26, 39 n.4

Schmith, Cauleen 1–5, 14 n.96, 189, 208
    n.11
Schulze, Holger 105
Schuppli, Susan 11, 79, 89, 90, 101
science fiction
Afro-Futurist 14 n.4
feminist 166
of geography 84–5
sonic 86, 156–7
score 75, 87, 104, 170, 173–7
architectural 175
and body 154, 176
collaborative 166–7, 169
as echography 21
as emancipatory force 104
essay 11, 103–4, 106–7, 189, 206
as performance; performative 105, 106,
    107, 169, 170, 175, 176
soundwalk 67 n.2
text 13, 45
sexual body 160
sexuality 143
singing 126, 142, 215 (see also unsinging
    and re-singing)
and breathing 132, 143, 196
flesh 130, 196
about gender 124–5
geography 96
text (writing) 187, 195
transformation 129–30
socio-material
consciousness 163
geography 89, 92, 94, 96
simultaneity 94
volume 88–9, 95
Södergran, Edith 151
song 162, 215

and body 122, 129
breath and 133, 135
Carbon Song Cycle 133
feminine 123, 130, 139
Gender Song 123, 125, 129
speech song 123
vertiginous 206, 207
sonico-feminine (new) materialism 12, 175
sonico-phenomenological cosmopolitanism 60
sonic possible world(s) 6, 11, 25, 26, 27, 28, 112
geography of 77–8, 81, 84, 85–6, 95, 96
materialism of 158
and possible subjects 122
and science fiction 84–5
and Sun Ra 98 n.30
and world creating 39
sonic sensibility 5, 9, 11, 12, 48, 111
and cosmopolitanism 56
for the digital 212 n.54
and geography 77, 95
and image 121
in language and text 188, 198
and new materialism 158, 163, 164
and participation 38
and science fiction 156
and trans-subjectivity 122
and volumes 104, 205
soundwalk 45, 60, 67
score 67 n.2
sovereignty
and autonomy 130, 134, 142
false 135
and globalization 54
language and 127
and subject; subjectivity 126–7, 130, 142
speculative 194, 205
artefact 1, 2, 13, 106, 189
and facticity 164
thought 158
materiality 152
possibility 165, 194, 205
project 155
world 6
speculative realism 12, 152, 156, 158, 178–9 n.38
masculine 159
and time 174
Steyerl, Hito
image 12, 121, 123–4, 126, 130, 134, 148 n.54

vertical 94–5, 191, 201
subjectivity 4, 11, 52, 82, 128, 139, 146 n.23, 161, 176
and agency 131
contingent 125
engine (Eshun) 105
feminine 130, 138, 139
gendered 158
geographical 76, 79, 88
historical 130, 165
idealized 139
inaudible 132
performative (performing) 132, 136, 139, 207
sonic (hearing) 119, 121, 122, 123, 130, 136, 138–9, 143–4, 144 n.4
trans- 122, 130, 131, 135, 137, 138, 142
trans-technological 133, 134
unperforming 143
Sun Ra 1–3, 13, 14 n.4, 15 n.14, 85, 98 n.30, 206

technology; technological 1–2, 3, 5, 27, 140, 146 n.34, 147 n.48
and body 132–3, 134, 137, 138–9, 141, 143, 160, 192–3, 194
DIY 7, 106
and fascism 141–2
networked 140
of representation 76–7
trans- 122, 133, 134–5, 143
and voice 190, 192, 193, 194, 209 n.21
territory 79, 86, 90, 97 n.3, 201
black 158, 165
conquered (colonialized) 68–9 n.13, 99 n.36, 130
digital 202
and geography 76, 82, 95
impossible 88, 90
indivisible 11, 79, 91
invisible 76
Israeli 23
mapped (cartography) 52, 76, 79, 80
and nation-state 55
Palestinian 91, 93
politics of 96
performed 86, 95, 107
sociopolitical 4
textual phonography 5, 190, 200
Thrift, Nigel 11, 78, 86, 87, 95, 98 n.24
timespace
geological 28, 41 n.29

and geography 75, 80, 82, 94, 86, 96
place 39, 86, 80, 90
and rhythm 172, 174
slices 28, 82, 83, 87, 89, 90, 95
sonic 109
as volume 32, 88
world 108
Tlalim, Tom 11, 79, 89, 90
tonality 21, 35, 170
transitive 129, 138
'I' 135
truth 7, 14 n.19, 23, 36, 37, 52, 62, 137,
    159, 186, 209 n.18 (see also untruth)
affective 23, 31
contingent 31, 191
and the digital 141–2
and dis-illusions 209 n.18
geographical 80, 81, 88
of the incommensurable 36
and knowledge 77, 88, 89, 142, 146 n.23,
    165
and language 127, 146 n.23, 161, 187,
    197
and new materialism; speculative realism
    152–3, 156–8, 159, 161, 164
phenomenological 62, 181 n.68
plural 36, 37, 161, 191
rational 36, 141
and reality 97 n.13, 121, 127, 137
singular 40 n.9, 62, 80, 89, 97 n.13
of the text 191, 199–200

Uneasy Listening (Tlalim and Schuppli) 11,
    79, 89, 91, 101
untruth 36, 37, 52, 78 (see also truth)
and dis-illusions 191
unactualised 26, 27, 29, 41 n.31
unethical 105 (see also ethical and
    post-ethical)
unknowable 89
unknowing 7 (see also knowing)
unknown 7, 57, 63, 96, 166, 179, 187, 192,
    193, 201
geography 11, 78, 96
lands 11, 84, 85, 86, 98 n.24
matter 159
performance of the 89
places 7, 192–3, 196
subjectivity 132
and (unheard) voices 194, 200, 207 ·
worlds 13, 15 n.16
women 130

unmapping 181 n.69
and cartography 99 n.38
of territory 80
unperform; unperformance
geography 11, 78, 82, 87, 94–5
identity; subjectivity 139, 143, 170
knowledge 139
language (lexical) 12, 176, 205–6
music 171, 176
and new materialism 174, 176
representation 87, 104, 139, 142
and (essay) score 104, 107
through the breath 136
violence 143–4
unthought
fiction 165
masculinist 175, 178–9 n.38
and new materialism; speculative realism
    151–3, 156, 157, 158, 162, 164, 165,
    173–4, 175, 176, 178–9 n.38
phenomenological 152–3
sonic (sound) 156–7, 166
and unthinkable 152, 153, 158, 162, 165,
    166, 173
and writing 13
unsinging 143
utopia; utopian 6, 85
cosmopolitanism as 67
and the essay form 107
and geography
world 8

ventriloquism; ventriloquist 50, 63–4, 192–3,
    207
vertical; verticality 6
composition 201, 208 n.9
depth 12, 91, 94, 95, 190, 204
geography 11, 88, 90, 91, 93
invisible 13, 190, 212 n.54
lines of words (writing, text) 9, 12, 13,
    106, 185, 190, 201, 203, 204, 205, 206
politics of 79, 91, 204, 212 n.59
and representational freedom 201
separation; partitioning 91, 92, 94, 95
sonic (sound) 89, 90, 92, 95, 171, 187,
    190, 199, 207
visual 91–2, 95, 201
vertiginous
depth 212 n.54
reality 201, 205
song 206
sonic (sound) 201, 203

violence 12, 24, 31, 147 n.41 (*see also* anti-violence)
and anti-violence 18, 21, 29, 35, 39 n.2
circular 18, 21, 29, 32, 68–8 n.13, 107, 116 n.9
emancipatory 136
of identity 123, 134–5
of the lexicon 12, 144
political imagination and 17, 116 n.9
and reality 36
ultraobjective 12, 122, 135, 141, 142–3, 148 n.52
ultrasubjective 12, 122, 135, 141, 142–3, 148 n.52
virtuosity 7, 124, 139, 176
and DIY 4
of listening 58
in performance 133
visuocentrism; visuocentric
anthropocentric 157
and new materialism 175
philosophy 153, 155, 156
vocalization; vocalized (*see also* revocalization and devocalization)
and erasure 209 n.21
theorization 157
volume 24, 32, 45, 46, 75
affective 66
of *Anywhen* 49, 51–2, 64
architectural 10, 46, 47, 49, 60
as crucible 47
discontinuous 92
gallery as 46–7, 60, 67
geographical 82, 87, 84–5, 99
indivisible; indivisibility of 50, 53, 60, 64, 82, 86, 94, 99 n.38, 104, 173
invisible 11, 48, 49, 50, 66, 78, 96, 168, 203, 205
socio-material 88–9, 95

sonic 10, 45, 47–8, 50, 53, 57, 88, 94, 96
shared 90, 203, 204
of space and place 50–1, 83, 88
viscous 51, 168, 212 n.55
world as 61, 67, 85–6, 119, 201, 204, 205

The Wanderer (Winderen) 12, 190, 203, 214
Weizman, Eyal 11, 79, 91, 92–4, 212 n.59
Winderen, Jana 12, 190, 203–4, 205, 212 n.57, 214
wolf tone 167, 168, 169, 173, 175
woman 34, 126, 127, 129, 137, 138, 186, 209 n.21
depropriated (Cixous) 138, 140, 146 n.34
false 132
whole 132, 133
write 130, 158
writing 8, 189
feminine (*écriture feminine*) 130, 158, 210 n.29
fragments 1, 9, 106, 188, 190, 191
and listening 5, 167, 206
the margins 158
mute 191, 199
phallocentric 143
and possibility 7, 106, 190
and the rhizome 190, 203
as science of the world 81
under erasure 209 n.21
vertical 6, 207, 208 n.9
and woman 140

Z, Pamela 12, 123, 135–6, 142, 143
Breathing 132, 137
and Horn 138, 139
(trans-)technological 133–4, 138, 139, 146 n.34
Zakim, Eric 8, 14–15 n.11